STORMIN' BACK

Missouri Basketball Coach
Norm Stewart's
Battles On and Off the Court

Norm Stewart with John Dewey

Foreword by Bob Costas

SAGAMORE PUBLISHING INC.
Champaign, Illinois 61824-0673

Book design: Brian J. Moore
Cover and photo insert design: Michelle R. Dressen
Developmental editor: Dan Heaton
Copyeditor: Adrian S. Hoch
Proofreader: Phyllis L. Bannon

Printed by Walsworth Publishing Company

10   9   8   7   6   5   4   3   2   1

ISBN: 0-915611-47-3
Library of Congress Catalog Card Number: 91-61670

*To my wife Virginia for 35 years of love, support
and understanding, and for coming up with one of the key
answers to the investigation; and to our immediate family, Jeffrey,
Lindsey and Laura. In many instances you thought the ballplayers
were more important than you were. In the final
analysis, you knew the ballplayers were just part of our family.*

Contents

Foreword

It was the 1979-80 season, I was broadcasting the Missouri basketball games on radio. These were the early days of Sundvold, Stipanovich, and Frazier. The senior season of Larry Drew. Often, the games were close and exciting. Sometimes, they were not. When the latter circumstance prevailed, my mind would wander in search of items of interest.

One such item was the curious case of Al Hightower. Affable Al was a baseball player of some note, and a basketball player whose skills were so subtle that many observers could not discern them at all. Hightower was a 5′ 11″ walk-on added to the roster by Norm Stewart for the sole purpose of giving the squad enough bodies to scrimmage. This was a role Al took to with great zeal. During the actual games, however, Hightower spent more time on the bench than Thurgood Marshall.

Still, I saw in Hightower noble qualities befitting his name. Scarcely a broadcast went by without at least a segment spent extolling his virtues as an athlete, student, and son of Missou.

Soon a considerable portion of the student body took up his cause. Fans pined to see his name in the box score. Fanciful banners appeared in his honor. Cub reporters solicited his deepest thoughts. What might the lad accomplish if given a chance? Speculation raged.

Most vocal in support of Hightower were the Antlers, a renowned collection of scholars with a changing membership but a consistent objective . . . mischief. Apparently, one can become an Antler only if one fails to meet the exacting admissions standards at Animal House. The Antlers elite rooting section is located diagonally across the floor from the Tiger bench and about halfway up the lower section of the stands. For nearly two decades their genteel behavior has helped make the atmosphere at the Hearnes Center, shall we say, distinctive.

So where was I? Oh yeah. During the Hightower era (as Missouri historians invariably refer to it) the Antlers led the charge. As soon as the Tigers established anything approaching a comfortable lead, the Antlers chanted Hightower's name, beseeching Stewart to send him in. Night after night, the coach remained unmoved.

Then came the evening when Missouri jumped out to a huge lead over mighty Northern Arizona. "We want Al," the Antlers began. Hightower didn't budge. The lead grew to twenty-three. "We want Al." Hightower glanced at Stewart. Stewart glanced back. "We want Al." The lead was twenty-nine. Fans moved forward in anticipation. "We want Al."

Stewart stared across the floor and upward toward the Antlers — now delirious in anticipation of the golden moment. Stewart beckoned toward Hightower. Al bolted from the bench, removing his warmups quicker than Clark Kent discarded a business suit. By now, Hearnes was a madhouse.

When Hightower reached the scorer's table, Stewart draped an arm over his shoulder. The coach pointed and gestured elaborately, imparting an apparent combination of instruction and inspiration. What excitement. What theater. What . . . is this? Hightower, nodding gravely, leaves Stewart, and walks the entire distance around the edge of the court to the opposite side. (The game continues but no one notices.) Next, he ascends the grandstand steps and heads toward the Antlers. Upon arrival, a sheepish looking Hightower addresses his idolators: "You were yelling 'We want Al' so Coach Stewart sent me over to see exactly what it was you wanted." For once, the Antlers were flabbergasted.

Across the way, the Tiger bench was in hysterics. Stewart beamed. Hightower, a genuinely good guy, got a kick out of it as well. Later Stewart found a few spots ideally suited for Hightower, and Al, by this time revelling in his cult hero status, actually played in some games. Hit a few baskets too.

When I think of Norm Stewart, I think of things like that. I also think of Wednesday nights in Stillwater, Oklahoma. Or Lawrence or Manhattan, Kansas, in the days before Missouri became a consistent national power. I've always thought the quintessential Stewart could be captured on those nights. An old arena steeped in Big Eight history. No national TV. Few outside the Big Eight paying much attention. The competition so pure. The passion for the task so evident. Stewart was energized by the chess matches with a Ted Owens or a Jack Hartman. He seemed to relish his role as the object of the fans' antagonism. Competitive to the point of belligerence. His vision of himself, and his team as an extension of him, clarified by the preparation, toughness, and sense of purpose required to prevail. Stormin' Norman.

Characteristically, years later, Stewart would be as likely to savor a well-played game on those terms as to reminisce about a win over North Carolina or Louisville on network TV.

I spent five years as the voice of the Tigers, and I still rank it among my most enjoyable assignments. Norm Stewart had a lot to do with that. (So did the regular 1:00 a. m. stops for banana cream pie at Gaspers truck stop in Kingdom City on the ride back to St. Louis, but that's another story.) I've spent a considerable amount of time with Norm and Virginia through the years, and the Norm Stewart I know is great company. Norm's dry wit and ability to have fun with his work, despite his intensely competitive nature, are appealing qualities. Knocking around the golf course or hosting late night pizza feasts for friends after a game at his house — the laughter comes easily. The warmth and shared history can be felt.

Not everyone has seen this side of Norm Stewart. Not that I would contend that my view of him is the only valid one. Stewart, it can be safely said, is a complex man. Some reasonable people I know do not feel as favorably toward him as I do. Some of them have had their say. Now it's Stewart's turn. This is his story. Of his childhood and early athletic career. Of the forces that shaped his character. Of the tremendous triumphs and considerable adversities he and his family have experienced.

Here's Norm's perspective on the Big Eight titles. The Number One rankings. The All Americans he's coached, as well as the hard-nosed over-achievers he prizes so highly. On the flip side, here are his thoughts on the bitter NCAA Tournament defeats that derailed some highly regarded Missouri squads. And of course, here is Norm's detailed response to the recent NCAA sanctions against his program. None of us who know him are surprised that Norm demands, and gets, his say.

It is said that success attracts friendship but adversity proves it. While I would hesitate to agree with Norm Stewart one hundred percent of the time, I would not hesitate to call him a very fine coach whose tenure at Missouri has been, all things considered, overwhelmingly positive. I would not hesitate to predict future dramatic successes for the Tigers under Stewart's leadership. More importantly, I would never hesitate to call him a friend.

—Bob Costas
August 12, 1991

Preface

The 1991-92 season will be my 25th year as head coach of the Missouri Tigers, my 36th year overall in coaching. I know of only a handful of active coaches who have been in this business longer. In all my years of coaching, I never would have believed an NCAA investigation would be part of my legacy, but it is.

It's the same way I felt about my health. I never thought about getting cancer. You think, "This won't happen to me."

We built the Missouri basketball program, with tremendous help and assistance, to a level of national prominence. At the same time, I enjoyed a reputation of running clean programs for 33 years. But today, the things that have put me in the forefront of national publicity are my bouts with cancer and the NCAA.

I'm writing this book to tell others about some of the changes that have taken place in college basketball, changes I have observed as a player in the '40s and '50s, and as a coach during the '60s until the present day.

I think I can take the knowledge I've received from the NCAA investigation, go to my coaching colleagues and almost guarantee they would never be put on probation. But I want coaches to understand you can run the cleanest program in the United States — we thought we were — and you can still be in violation of the rules. Don't think you aren't susceptible to an NCAA investigation. I can observe anyone's program and find violations.

This book could be a thousand pages long. Every time I travel someplace, I'm reminded of some story. One of the problems in writing this book was deciding what to include and what to leave out. What will people find interesting about your life?

Hopefully, after 35 years in the profession, I have something to say that people want to hear.

I also want people to know more about my background. My legacy is not just about NCAA probation. I want people to read the complete legacy and where I plan to go from here.

—Norm Stewart

When I told people I was working on writing a book with Norm Stewart, the reaction was almost always, "How did *you* get that job?" Others, who have known Coach Stewart much longer than I ever will, said, "Great idea. But who are you?"

The question "Why me?" has popped into my mind on a number of occasions. Coach Stewart could have chosen from a number of outstanding writers. Instead, he allowed me to enter the picture, without a book published to date.

I guess timing had something to do with it. I first wrote Coach Stewart with the book idea in August, 1990, toward the tail end of the NCAA investigation. It appeared to me that Coach Stewart was being stifled from saying much about the investigation or the nature of the allegations. In the meantime, both of the major newspapers in Missouri conducted their own investigations into the program, and were allowed to speculate about the future of the program, and Coach Stewart's career.

I was familiar with the program, having graduated from Missouri in 1983, and having covered Missouri sports for about a year at KOMU-TV in Columbia, the university-owned station. But after graduation, I moved to another state, and did not follow the program very closely. I worked in television news, and found less time to follow every turn of the Missouri sports program.

In 1988, I suffered a big personal loss. My father died. He had suffered from cancer of the colon, and it had spread to his liver.

When it was reported that Coach Stewart had colon cancer, I found my thoughts at times sharply fixed on Norm's situation. I'm sure many who had suffered from cancer, or had a friend or relative with cancer, felt the same way.

In 1989, I accepted a job as a news reporter for a television station in St. Louis. Norm's cancer recovery and the NCAA investigation were being reported simultaneously, almost on a daily basis.

Because I did not cover sports, I only knew what everyone else read in the newspaper, or heard on television. I couldn't help but feel something was missing from the media coverage. No one was hearing much from Norm's viewpoint.

In August of 1990, I wrote Coach Stewart a letter, outlining an idea for a book. It would be his book, in his words. I called him back about a week later, and to my surprise, he said he would like to meet to discuss the idea further.

From that first meeting came many more meetings and interviews. The result of all this, you have before you.

I still can't help but wonder every now and then why he decided to allow me to work with him on this project. Perhaps his good friend Don Walsworth gave me part of the answer while we were discussing the book. Don said, "One thing about Norm, he likes to support the underdog."

I think if you were to look at the universe of sports writers and columnists who have followed Coach Stewart and Missouri sports over the years, I would certainly qualify as an underdog.

My work with Coach Stewart, over the course of about a year, has been very memorable and rewarding. He is certainly one of the more fascinating individuals I have come across. My only regret is that I am not a novelist. His character could be the center of a great novel, as Norm's wife Virginia has suggested.

—John Dewey

Acknowledgments

The authors wish to thank everyone who has provided assistance in getting this book published. We are extremely thankful for the encouragement given by friends and loved ones, and the support supplied by members of the University of Missouri Athletics Department.

Here are just a few of those to whom we owe a debt of gratitude: close friends Don Walsworth, Dick Savage, and Carolyn Hawks; attorneys Steve Owens and John Miller; Missouri Sports Information Director Bob Brendel; Assistant Sports Information Director Jack Watkins; secretary Dawn McGhee; *Shelby County Herald* editor Roger Hewitt; *Des Moines Register* sports writer Maury White; *St. Louis Post Dispatch* sports writer Bob Broeg; Peter Bannon and the wonderful people at Sagamore Publishing; sports writer and author Skip Myslenski; coaches Bob Sundvold and Rich Daly; assistant Dwight Evans; trainer Ron Dubuque; equipment manager Kit Lisauskas; and pilot Joe Hecker.

Coach Stewart wants to thank all of his former players, assistants, trainers, and student assistants who have made life interesting and exciting. His association with these people has been personally very gratifying and in many cases mutually beneficial.

Please accept our apologies if you've helped us in some way and your name has not been included above.

Introduction

In my years of broadcasting in the NFL, NBA, and major college football and basketball, I have never been around a more compelling individual than Norm Stewart.

His life is predicated on the excellence, high standards, and integrity of his nationally renowned basketball program, the players, those within his program, and above all, his deep devotion to family.

The best years in my career were spent with Norm Stewart and the University of Missouri basketball program.

As a University of Kansas graduate, it's ironic that I ended up broadcasting the Missouri Tigers. The rivalry between the schools is intense — very intense, especially in basketball. With that in mind, I was nervous about meeting Norm Stewart. What would Norm think of a Jayhawk broadcasting his games?

I met him at a preseason practice at the Hearnes Center. As I sat watching him in the empty building, I couldn't help but be mesmerized by his stature, his command, his intensity. All eyes were on him, no movement from anyone, except as he crowded in a defensive stance then shuffled, then back-peddled as he was explaining a drill. He stepped aside and watched as the players fell in and drilled in front of him.

I felt privileged to get this rare view during a closed Stewart practice. You know how you build up something — then are let down by the actual event. Well, the chance to watch Norm with his team behind the scenes was a great career moment for me. Some people never get the opportunity during their lives to be associated with great individuals or a great program, and sitting there that October afternoon in Columbia, Missouri, I realized that my opportunity had just arrived.

During that practice, Norm spotted me in the stands and made a special jog up the steps to say hello. We talked for almost ten minutes before he returned to practice. And our relationship began after that.

A few weeks later I came down to watch workouts and afterward he and his wife Virginia took me out to dinner. We would begin each season that way. It was a favorite time for me.

I hosted Norm's state-wide radio call-in program. He was funny and direct — a master at handling the caller. His wit came through on virtually every answer or comment. But what always impressed me most was the way he would thank people on the air for their help. Regardless of what was done or who had done it, Norm had a kind word. He was always appreciative, thanking the band for making a long road trip, a group of fans for support, the students for always being there. He didn't miss anyone. He went out of his way to say thank you. Few coaches have that sensitivity. Norm Stewart cared so much for their help and support. He made sure that all involved knew how he felt.

Most coaches take help from the support staff or fans for granted — thinking it's owed them. Coach Stewart isn't like most coaches. That's why he's been at the top of his profession for several decades.

One of the most revealing moments regarding how Coach Stewart is perceived came in February, 1989. The Tigers were to play Oklahoma in Norman on national television. [The team flew down that afternoon. There were two planes. Coach Stewart collapsed on one of them.] An emergency landing, an ambulance to the hospital, and a lot of uncertainty followed. When first told, my broadcast partner, Rod Kelly, and I were stunned, along with everyone else. The mood of the Noble Center changed dramatically. What was billed as a major game between two top ten teams was now viewed differently. Reporters, fans and people from Oklahoma University wandered over throughout the night to see if we had an update. Banners and signs were quickly made by Sooner fans and displayed for Norm to show their concern. Players from both sides seemed a bit rattled, but in the end played one of the most unbelievable college games I've seen. The night was unforgettable.

The people in Norman that night showed the kind of thoughtfulness for Stewart that I believe would normally be reserved for one of their own. Stewart was supposed to be the target of the fans that night because he represented Missouri, the enemy. Instead, their respect for him surfaced through the drama of the afternoon. He was no longer the opposing coach, but now a member of their family, so to speak.

Norm had been around as long as the Big Eight, it seemed. Norm Stewart meant something to these people, to people around the Big Eight and throughout the country. Everywhere the Tigers played, the same outpouring of concern was there. Banners and signs and prayers. People genuinely cared. Stewart was the Big Eight and represented what college basketball was all about. Fans, school staff members and the media revealed a great deal of their true feelings for Norm during this time.

Few coaches warrant this kind of treatment. Norm Stewart is one of them. As time passed and more was known about Norm's condition, people grew more anxious. But in typical Stewart style, he was very self-assured, thanked the thousands of people for their prayers and get-well wishes, and talked more about his concern for his wife Virginia, who was hospitalized at the same time.

You don't know Norm if you don't know that Virginia is everything to him. Norm Stewart is a very selfless individual. The least of his concern, at least publicly, was his own condition.

The Stewart's recovered, both serving as inspiration.

I won't forget that time — for its drama, for Stewart's resiliency, for the boundless support he garnered from fans everywhere, and for the courage of his family.

—Kevin Harlan
Former Voice of the Tigers

"Nothing in the world can take the place of persistence. Talent will not. Nothing is more common than unsuccessful men with talent. Genius will not. Unrewarded genius is almost a proverb. Education will not. The world is full of educated derelicts. Persistence and determination alone are omnipotent."

—Calvin Coolidge

1

The Fateful Flight

Our third-ranked Missouri Tigers basketball team stepped aboard two Beechcraft Kingair 200 turboprop planes on a brisk blue February morning at Columbia Regional Airport. Our destination was that city in Oklahoma bearing my given name. My thoughts centered on how we would beat a team ranked No. 1 a week earlier. Thoughts of Stacey King and Mookie Blaylock . . . a national television audience . . . .

And I thought about my wife, Virginia. She was recovering from a major surgery that nearly scared us to death. And I thought about my senior assistant Bob Sundvold. He had just been suspended by the school after it was discovered he may have violated an NCAA rule, an incident he had self-reported. I had plenty to think about. But I never thought my main concern that day was going to be dying in an ambulance with no one else around but a guy from Oklahoma.

It was Thursday, February 9, 1989. In a few hours, our team would enter the Lloyd Noble Center to face the Sooners in a game to be televised nationally by ESPN. Little did I know I would not be courtside to see it.

As a coach, you try to prepare your players for any situation that might come up during the course of the basketball season.

Well, nothing I did could prepare my players for what they would witness that afternoon.

We were coming off our 11th win in a row, 73-68 over Kansas State. Our record stood at 20-3, 6-0 in the Big Eight Conference. Norman was never a welcome sight for our club: My record there was 3-19. At the same time, we dominated the series in Columbia, where we were 16-5 against the Sooners.

We walked on to our charter planes around 11 a.m. Each plane seats up to ten people — eight passengers and two pilots. We sat in nice, comfortable leather seats.

Let me explain a little bit about why we travel the way we do. We had begun the practice of taking charter flights a number of years ago. Before charters, it was a tradition for teams to travel the day before a game, work out the day before and spend an evening in the town we visited.

This could create all sorts of problems. You can't always control what an 18- or 19-year-old kid does on the road. He's not going to get much schoolwork done. This was too much time on the road and it took away from the team's concentration, so we began leaving later and later.

We have had some very good road records since we started using the charters. They travel up to 340 miles an hour, enabling us to get to all conference road games but Colorado within an hour and a half. We can travel closer to game time, eliminating many distractions players run into on the road, and helping them with their studies.

Tip-off time for the Oklahoma game was 6:30 p.m. We'd leave Columbia around 11 in the morning and arrive shortly after noon, plenty of time for a practice before the game. The players would familiarize themselves with the building and get in some extra shooting. At 5 o'clock, we'd suit up and get taped, which would take about 40 minutes. Then we'd wait to take our warm-ups. This was the plan, anyhow. This time, it didn't work out that way.

The planes took off as scheduled. To keep my players and myself relaxed, I oversaw the seating arrangements. We try not to get into that "Big Game Syndrome" because really every game is a big one. After you win against a good team, there is always another one to follow. There's really no time to reach a comfort zone. But because this was obviously a big game, I had no problem motivating the players. My main job was to see to it that they could go out and play their best.

This is why I normally put the starters and the people who will play the most on one plane. I will sit on the other plane with some of the younger players and those who don't get to play that much. I always felt that my presence around the starters during travel time kept them from relaxing; at the same time, it could be a distraction for me. This seating arrangement would also give me a chance to spend some time with some of the players who weren't going to get as many minutes.

Our top players — Doug Smith, Lee Coward, Byron Irvin, Mike Sandbothe, Greg Church, Gary Leonard — sat on one plane with our trainer Ron Dubuque. While Anthony Peeler was another of our top players, he was just a freshman and I thought he should take this trip in my plane along with other freshmen and reserves.

Once in the air, some of the players on my plane started playing cards. My high school coach used to play cards with us, and this is something I picked up with my players. On one hand, you never want to be "one of the boys." You have to draw a line somewhere to maintain discipline. But I would allow myself to play cards with them. On this occasion it was spades, and I was losing.

I wanted to quit and get some sleep. The others probably thought I quit because I was losing. Actually, I didn't feel well.

The nap did not last very long. I woke up feeling lightheaded and dizzy; I felt I was about to pass out. The coaches and players noticed this and everyone became concerned. Someone got out of the seat facing me so I could elevate my feet.

One of the coaches told the pilot, Joe Hecker, sitting about 10 feet away. Joe turned around and saw how pale I looked. He notified air traffic control that he had a passenger who appeared real sick. They gave our plane priority landing.

Hecker told the coaches how to get some oxygen from under my seat because I was having trouble breathing. Assistant coach Rich Daly said it looked as though I was having a heart attack. My eyes apparently started to roll back into my head. Graduate assistant Sam Moore, who administered first aid, would later tell me I almost went into shock.

My memory isn't very good at this point, but I recall that I passed out. When I came to, I felt we were descending into Norman, so I thought. But Hecker radioed for an emergency landing at Will Rogers Airport in Oklahoma City. The other plane was also diverted because Joe wanted Ron Dubuque with me. I really have to say Hecker did a heck of a job. We taxied right up to where the ambulance was parked. The paramedics rushed onto the plane and immediately checked my vital signs.

I was alert enough now to realize the effect all of this was having on the players aboard my plane. I had been sitting near the back, so when the paramedics entered, only one person could exit immediately. The others were forced to wait and stare.

I particularly remember the reaction of one of them, our freshman center Jim Horton. It occurred to me that here was this young man along with the others who didn't know my condition. For all they knew, they could be watching a man die before their very eyes. A frightful thought.

So I asked the paramedics, "Do the players have to stay on the plane? Can't you get them off?" They started moving the players off, all of them filing past me.

It's always been my philosophy that you have to find some humor, even in the worst situations. Some people appreciate this humor, others don't. I saw Horton walk by, his face ashen. I thought it was the right time to say something to ease his fear. Jimmy hadn't been playing much, so I said, "Jimmy, quit laughing. Hell, if I die, Daly won't play you any more than I did."

I walked off the plane, but I needed assistance. You reach a point where you don't deny assistance, and I had reached that point. I knew I wasn't okay.

They escorted me into the ambulance and suddenly I felt all alone. All alone in a place where I wouldn't exactly choose to spend my last dying moments.

I asked the paramedic if there was anyone else inside the ambulance besides him and me. He told me someone else was getting in front.

"What about back here?" I said.

"No, just you."

"Oh, good deal." I replied. "You mean if I die, I'm just going to die with a guy from Oklahoma?"

He said I wasn't in any immediate danger. It was the first time I felt I was going to be alright, and we would soon find out what had happened on the plane.

Lying down in the ambulance, alone, I had the chance to think about more important things than a basketball game. I thought about Virginia, my family, my friends. And I thought about what was probably the most significant period of my life. My mind drifted back to Shelbyville, Missouri, shortly after World War II.

2

The Hammond Hoosier

In the late summer of 1945, Japan surrendered, ending World War II. A new era began in the United States. A new era began in Shelbyville, Missouri, as well. At about the same time General Douglas MacArthur was appointed Supreme Commander for the Allied Powers, a new leader was appointed in Shelbyville. Chester "C.J." Kessler became the superintendent of the Shelbyville School District, and he was soon a local hero. He would become a hero to me, too.

Shelbyville had grown into a thriving community of about 750 people. I say thriving, because now it's under 600. It once reached a population of more than 1,200. The decline of small family farms, and a lack of things to attract young people, led to the drop in population. Those who chose to stay in Shelbyville rather than move away are survivors, third and fourth generation families, many with a farm background.

Shelbyville is the county seat of Shelby County and sits about 35 miles west of Hannibal in Northeast Missouri. When you drive into town on Highway 15, the main architectural structure is the courthouse, built in 1910, and the town square. Government is now the primary employer. Shelbyville was, and still is, your typical small town. During a recent visit, I ran into many familiar faces. I am fond of the nicknames given to many residents. There's "Pooh," not to be confused with "Poo-Poo," "The Governor" and "Duke." Some jokingly referred to me as "Rule," because they said I made up my own rules in the pool hall.

For someone who is unfamiliar with small towns, a visit to Shelbyville may be a bit of a culture shock. The town has one social event, The Old Settler's Reunion, in late summer. Other than that, the simple life dominates this sleepy town. My wife tells me she'll never forget a trip we took to visit my mother and father when we were in college. My wife was an only child who grew up in Kansas City. She found the humor in Shelbyville to have a few rough edges. My uncles would argue over things like, what was better, a Chevy or a Ford. They liked to call me an educated idiot. My wife didn't think it was funny. To me, this was just the normal give-and-take of a rural family. Virginia and I see Shelbyville from a different point of view, but that's just the difference between big and small towns, and being an only child as opposed to coming from a big family.

I was the fourth child, the baby in the family. For that reason, I'm sure my parents were very relaxed and gave me special treatment. I always thought they gave me a little more credit than I deserved.

My parents were hard-working people. My father, Kenneth, worked for Standard Oil. He got to know the farmers of Shelby County really well. He supplied the gas, oil and many other products needed to help the farmer harvest his crops. Fuel oil and kerosene were his staples in the winter time. We weren't poor, but we certainly weren't rich.

My mother, Leona, was very religious. She attended church regularly and gave me an early upbringing in the church. There was no drinking allowed in our house, although my dad smoked.

My mother passed away about twelve years ago. Something she told me long ago had a profound impact on my life. I was just a young boy when she said, "Your life is going to be different than anybody else's in the family. You're going to be living a different life from what our family has known. It will take you away from us in certain respects, but I just want you to know, we will understand."

Her premonition taught me not to be afraid or timid, gave me the confidence to just go ahead and do what I wanted to do.

Sometimes I say similar things to a player if I find he needs encouragement.

If I go back a little farther in time, I can remember when our family lived about 15 miles away from Shelbyville in a town called Leonard. The population was about 100. I recall we had one bedroom with two double beds. Obviously, I had to share a bed with someone. Recently I read a story on an airplane about Jack Buck that mentioned he grew up having to share a bed. I think he slept with his brother. So I wrote him a card saying, "I'm glad somebody else was in that particular situation. I've never told anyone else that I had to sleep with someone else in my family."

There was no indoor plumbing, but we had water — a water pump in the kitchen.

My uncles worked and owned farms in Shelby County, so I spent a lot of time in the field. I wasn't big enough to bale hay, but I could ride the back of a corn planter for 50 cents a day. A guy would drive a team of horses while I sat in back. My job was to make sure the corn was planted right. You would watch these shoes, as they called them, as they dropped corn. If the corn was planted too deep or too shallow, I had to make an adjustment. It was a very dirty job, especially if the wind blew back at you. Many days I would come home just layered in dirt.

Eventually, I worked my way up to five dollars a day, outstanding money then. I never wanted to back down from a challenge, even if I was at a disadvantage physically. My uncles still kid me about driving a tractor through a fence and into some trees. I was too small to handle it. I couldn't hold the hand brake and push a foot clutch at the same time. Sometimes the clutch would fly out and the tractor would jump forward. So one time I drove the tractor with a rake through a fence. I didn't drive that tractor anymore.

Sometimes I just ran around. I shot a lot of pool, and did a lot of swimming. Complete freedom. It was wonderful. I swam in the North River and the Salt River. We would just strip down to nothing and skinny dip. If I were to see that water now, I doubt I'd put my foot into it.

There was another place called Wiggin's Hole, where a bunch of us had a rope tied to a tree. One group would form a circle in the water, and the idea was to swing out over the circle and try to land in it. That was how I learned how to swim. You never would swing back to the bank because another group of kids would stand by the shore and beat you with a branch.

When I was only five years old, a bunch of us liked to smoke. I smoked coffee, catalpa, tobacco, anything we thought would work. It was just something for us to do. Nobody knew about pot at the time. We'd wait for one of these weeds — we called it sourdough — to brown and ripen, then we'd strip it down. We'd get these Phillips 66 cans from the service station. I vividly remember the cans: orange and white, with rings around them. We would take a full can of this ripened weed and we'd start rolling these huge cigarettes. We would take newspapers and spread them out, lay the sourdough in there, roll it up and hold it. Another person would light the other end, and you would smoke this two-foot cigarette. You'd only get about three draws on it because the fire would come right up on you. If you didn't watch it, you'd burn your lungs.

I remember, at five years of age, going to a shivaree and smoking a cigar. A shivaree was a serenade for people who just got married. There would be this big party at the home of the newlyweds. Sometimes you'd surprise them when they came home from their honeymoon.

I had freedom. With freedom, of course, I had to make judgments. I must have made some good judgments because I stayed out of jail. The closest I got was when I shot the street light out in front of the house of my brother's girlfriend. I had a Red Ryder BB gun and became a good shot. My brother Jerry would give me a dime if I could shoot the street light out. He wanted to neck in the dark with his girlfriend. Mr. Parish of Missouri Power and Light would try to catch me. It was like cops and robbers. I think he knew I was responsible, but he never caught me.

I remember a guy named Mr. Green bought me a baseball for a dollar. It really meant something to me at the time. I would throw the ball around with my dad. He would come home from work — and it was hard labor — and he would play catch with me. I was about thirteen or fourteen years old and my dad was in his mid-forties. He walked with a limp because of a leg that had started to atrophy from a crushed disk in his back. I was young and strong and would try to throw it to him as hard as I could. I began to realize my father, limp or no limp, was quite an athlete.

He also managed ballclubs in the summertime. He would get mad if someone didn't show up for a game. One time, just eight players came, so he had to take the field. I remember him playing, this older guy with a limp. He got four base hits. Four frozen ropes. The vision of that accomplishment still stays with me.

One Sunday morning, I was hanging around the service station, not living up to a promise I had made to play a baseball game. My father called me aside and said, "I've never told you to play or not to play. But if you promise a man something, you do it. If you don't ever want to play, that's fine. But if you want to play again, you better play."

I was furious when I picked up my uniform and went to Shelbina for the game. I wanted to be somewhere else. But I got four hits in the game, and I really enjoyed playing. No one ever had to tell me to play again. But the thing I remember most is, if you tell someone you are going to do something, you do it.

I first was aware that I had some basketball talent in the seventh or eighth grade. I played a guy named Orville Stevens, a good ballplayer. I knew I was good when I beat him in HORSE.

You had the two-handed set shot in those days. To be a good player in those days, you needed the two-handed set shot, the layup and the hook shot. Then kids started shooting one-handed when I was in junior high, though it made the coaches unhappy. Eventually, the jump shot came along. It wasn't too difficult for me because I had strong legs. I became intensely interested in playing basketball.

At first, I wasn't your model student. There's not a lot to do in Shelbyville, so you have to use your imagination to have fun. My sister still kids me about the quirky things I would do. I'd make animal noises and imitate things; I'd do it anyplace, unabashedly. I fancied myself quite the entertainer.

Roughhousing was a ritual in school, and like I said, I've always been competitive. Some other kids would pick someone out and challenge me to fight him. I wasn't vicious by any means. These were more impromptu wrestling matches than fistfights, but they could turn into fistfights. You would start with kids your own size and work your way up. Because of my competitiveness, when I was a freshman I would pick fights with kids in the sophomore and junior class and let them have it.

It was just a matter of time before I wound up in the office of C.J. Kessler, the superintendent.

Kessler is a legend in Shelbyville. He met a lady named Gladys McCully (her maiden name) from Shelbyville while attending college at Ball State and married her a short time later. The story goes that they came to Shelbyville one summer to visit her parents. Everyone in town knew Kessler was an outstanding basketball coach in a very competitive setting in Hammond, Indiana. He was a very good-looking, likable guy with many talents. During this visit, the Shelbyville school officials plotted a way to bring him into the fold. If Kessler would become the head basketball coach at Shelbyville High School, the people were willing to give him the responsibility of superintendent.

I've been told that three Shelbyville citizens, Donley Fox, Lewis Meisner and Brag Pickett, people with a great flair for life, invited Kessler out for a few drinks when he was in town to visit his in-laws. All of them over-imbibed, and Fox, Meisner and Pickett used their talents of persuasion on Kessler. When he woke up the next morning, he was indeed the superintendent and the basketball coach.

I guess the idea of being in charge of the whole school system appealed to Kessler, though there were only about 200 students in grade school and high school. After 19 years of slugging it out in a highly competitive Indiana school system, he was ready for a change of pace. I imagine his wife also was happy to be at home with her parents.

I found myself being led to Kessler's office one afternoon. I had made a show of getting my foot stuck in a wastepaper basket and clonking around the room with it. I made the mistake of doing this in Mrs. Kessler's class. She had a great ability to teach English and speech, and when she wanted to, she also had a great ability to grab you by the ear and drag your butt out of the classroom.

I owe a lot to Mrs. Kessler. She motivated me to learn the correct use of the English language, to become more articulate. During my young days, my speech was unsophisticated, full of improper contractions and lousy syntax. I don't think I would have the courage today to go before a microphone, or do my own coach's show, if I wasn't confident that I had a command of the English language. She wanted me to become more than just a basketball player.

Mr. Kessler's office displayed some standard methods of discipline used in those days. There was a board with holes in it, and a paddle. In this instance, he hit me with the board. I didn't think there would be much more to my visit to Kessler's office, but I soon discovered he wasn't going to let me off that easy.

Kessler made a long speech, really reading the riot act to me. I'm sure there was some B.S. involved, but a lot of what he told me I still remember.

"You have an opportunity to be an outstanding athlete," he said. "And you are good in school. But all you do is stuff that disrupts class. You've really become a pain in the ass, and nobody likes to see you around.

"If you want to become an outstanding athlete, if you want to make something out of your life, this is what you have to do: stop fighting and stop being disruptive."

Then he paused and said, "I'm done."

Kessler's words really had an impact on me. I guess I wanted to be something bad enough — and believed in Kessler bad enough — that I stopped, just like that. I never fought from that time on, and never disrupted class again. I began to do all of the things he asked.

I remember sneaking out to play basketball at night. You'd go home around bedtime to make sure your parents knew you were home, then you'd jump out of a window. I'd get out onto the roof and shinny down one of the pillars then meet up with the others at school.

Everyone knew you could get into the building by jumping down the coal chute. You'd go from the furnace area right into the school. We'd pull the shades that were up high in the gym. Anyone could still see that the lights were on, but we thought by pulling the shades, we'd be a bit safer from being caught. The office was always open, so we could enter it and grab the basketballs out of a safe. I remember when we finished playing we'd mop the floor and put everything back in place, because in our minds, no one knew we were there.

Kessler knew we were there, but he stayed silent because he knew it kept some of us out of bigger trouble. He also would have a hard time explaining to citizens how a bunch of kids could sneak in and keep the gym open until 10 or 11 at night.

As far as I know, my parents never found out. Anyway, they never caught me leaving home or returning late in the evening.

Another thing that struck a chord with me was Kessler's competitiveness. He coached boys' and girls' basketball while being the superintendent, and you knew he wanted to win every game. He darn near did, losing just three or four games a season. In the meantime, he took over a school system that had financial problems and turned it around.

Coaching came quite easily to him, and he hit a good crop of country kids in Shelbyville. He had an interesting style. During practice he would never put on a pair of shorts or dress in basketball gear. He would come from his superintendent's office in dress shoes, a coat and tie.

As the superintendent, Kessler barely had time to coach. He'd conduct practice for about 50 minutes, and that was it. Today, if someone did that, he'd be accused of not being very interested in his job. But Kessler knew how to control that 50 minutes; he got more done in that time than some coaches do in a two-hour session.

I started playing guard as a freshman when I was 5 feet, 6 inches tall. Then I started to grow: 5-8 as a sophomore, 6-2 as a junior, 6-3 as a senior, but I remained a guard. I didn't get a chance to play much my freshman year, but during the three other years, I played in 104 games, quite a lot of basketball. I loved to play.

I thought I had a chance to play my freshman year because there weren't that many people in high school, maybe about 90. My brother was playing as a senior, and my father also thought I should be playing beside him. One time my dad told Kessler what he thought and Kessler gave my father what we now refer to as Speech 108.

Speech 108 covers all facets of people interfering with your business. I'm sure Kessler said, among other things, "Look, Mr. Stewart, you run the gasoline business, and I'll be the coach."

My father really took it to heart because he never interfered again. He went to all of the ball games, but he never questioned Kessler. This had an effect on my father into my college playing days. When I played in college, I was one of the first guys 6-4, 6-5, who could handle the ball. We didn't call it point guard at the time, but I brought the ball up. Coach Sparky Stalcup asked if my parents ever came to the games. I told him they came to every one.

"Well, how come I never see them?" Sparky asked.

"You never will," I said, "because Kessler gave my father Speech 108 when I was in high school."

Stalcup really got a kick out of that.

Shelbyville had a tough time advancing in the state tournament because we'd have to beat the larger schools to get there. Hannibal would usually knock us out of the picture. We would play a good game against them, but they would win.

The state made a change my sophomore year to the benefit of schools like Shelbyville, creating a separate division for smaller schools. Finally, we felt we had a chance to go a long way in the state tournament. The entire town would become wrapped up in it, and Kessler loved it because he knew the excitement of tournament competition from his days at Hammond Tech.

Excitement reached a fever pitch in my junior year when Shelbyville went to the state tournament, traveling to Cape Girardeau. It was a long trip on two-lane roads, but we felt right at home, half of Shelbyville was in a line of cars behind us. It was a big event, but we lost the first game.

Basketball fever picked up even more my senior season. Kessler instituted a seating policy that had people fighting to get courtside. He put 118 fold-down chairs near the baskets. You had to pay 10 dollars — keep in mind this was 1950 — to sit in one of those chairs. Those 10-dollar seats were always sold out, and with the money they raised, Kessler purchased three sets of uniforms for us. When we went to an away game in Columbia against University High School, we could afford two nights in a nice hotel. We were first-class. To me, this was an early lesson in how to market a good program, and I had a front-row seat.

When we traveled to the tournament, somebody could have picked up the Shelby County courthouse and walked away with it and no one would have noticed. Everyone was at the tournament.

We played Branson in the semifinals in a game that went down to the wire. Branson was up something like 48-47 with a little more than a minute to play. We were trying to inbound the ball, but each time we would throw it in, a Branson player would foul. A new rule gave the fouled team a choice of shooting one free throw or taking the ball out of bounds. Down by one point, we kept trying to inbound the ball so we could shoot for two points, but each time we did, a Branson player would grab one of us.

15

This continued until there were five seconds left, when they fouled me. "You've got to make this free throw," Kessler said, "and then we will beat them in overtime."

As I stepped to the line, I remembered what had happened in a similar situation the year before. We were playing in Ewing, down 50-49, and I missed two free throws with less than five seconds left and we lost the game. It was one of the most disheartening experiences in my high school career, and I'd made up my mind to never let that happen again.

So now it's a year later, and it's the semifinals of the state tournament. I step to the line and miss the free throw. Before I can really react, my teammate George Chase jumps up and slaps the ball off the backboard. No one blocks me out, and the ball comes right back to me. I shoot it right back in the basket and we win the game.

It's a message I pass on to players today, how quickly you can go from goat to hero. I recounted my Ewing experience to Jon Sundvold after he missed a free throw that could have won a game for Missouri in the early '80s. I told him there would be many opportunities to redeem himself. And I said even though I missed a big free throw in Ewing years back, I hardly ever think about it anymore.

We lost badly in the state championship game to Puxico. I think the score was 85-38. They had three kids who became All-Americans in college.

My high school career ended with me earning All-State recognition and going on to the University of Missouri. I still run into many of the players I played against in high school. I built some good relationships. And it was just the beginning of my relationship with Kessler.

3
General Hospital

The words of the ambulance driver calmed me a bit: I wasn't under any immediate threat. As the ambulance sped toward the Hillcrest Center in Oklahoma City, I tried to figure out what had just happened.

My first reaction was that maybe I'd had a heart attack. Then again, I figured maybe I was just tired. I was worn out, that was for sure.

The rest of the ballclub was back in the air, flying the remaining 25 miles to Norman, when I entered the hospital.

I was surprised to see members of the media there. Somehow they got word that I had become ill. The people at Hillcrest were outstanding, both in attending to my needs and in handling the media professionally.

The doctors told me I had stabilized, and there were no problems with my vital signs. But they found my hemoglobin, normally 14 or 15, was down below eight. They said this was probably what caused my reaction on the plane, and it meant there was some bleeding somewhere. I needed a blood transfusion.

I asked our trainer Ron Dubuque to stay with me rather than go with the team. I still didn't feel confident that there wasn't something seriously wrong; I needed a familiar face to reassure me. Ron was very gracious. He stayed all night and was a real comfort to me.

Don Walsworth showed up a little later. Don's a lifelong friend — we entered the University of Missouri together in 1952. I believe he was in Dallas at the time I was hospitalized. He came to Oklahoma City as soon as he heard about my situation. Another familiar face. It meant a lot to me.

Within a few hours, I was strong enough to make some phone calls. First I called Virginia, who was recuperating from her operation in Columbia. Then I called the team in Norman. I talked with each player for a few minutes while they were getting taped. I wanted them to put the whole experience behind them and just relax.

Suddenly, I was thinking about the game again and wondering whether I could watch it on television from my hospital room. Some Hillcrest people rigged up a television set in time for the opening tip-off.

I'll never forget the emotional performance my players put on. What an effort. At the opening of the game, they threw a salvo at Oklahoma and had them down 21-5. Oklahoma coach Billy Tubbs wouldn't let his players take this thrashing very long, though. He got them back into the game by riling up his players and the home crowd.

The fans were booing a traveling call and began throwing things on the floor. At the request of the officials, Tubbs took the public address microphone. Maybe it was inadvertent, maybe premeditated, but Tubbs said something to the effect, "No matter how bad the officiating is, don't throw stuff on the floor."

Now it's a Big Eight rule not to comment on the officiating, and this remark certainly fell under the category of commentary. There was a whistle and a technical, but the fans loved it.

The Sooners were soon back in the game, and they tied the score at 99 with a few minutes to go.

Mookie Blaylock made a free throw to put them up for good with about two minutes to play. We kept it close until the very end. They scored four points in a matter of seconds and won 112-105, but the game was a lot closer than the score indicated. I was proud of the way the team played and the way Rich Daly took over the coaching duties under the circumstances. It was a great game, later voted the best game on ESPN that season.

On February 10, after spending about 24 hours at the Hillcrest Center, I once again boarded a plane. This time I wasn't heading toward a basketball game. It was a much different game ahead, the game of life.

I was admitted to Columbia Regional Hospital under an assumed name, Nate Reed. I don't know why they selected that name, but later someone asked me if I knew anyone named Nate Reed. Amazingly enough, Nate Reed was a barber in Cedar Falls that I knew when I coached at Northern Iowa.

A more important coincidence was that my wife was still at Columbia Regional. Virginia was recovering from major surgery to remove a tumor. It turned out to be benign, but it was a cause for concern for a long period of time.

The hospital officials went to her and asked her if she wanted to share a room with me. She declined the offer. She and I are both convinced that when you stay in a hospital, it's not a social occasion. You're there to get well. All of the company you get can work against you.

My doctor, Jay Ward, said I'd had an episode of ulcer disease, complicated by internal bleeding. This explained my low hemoglobin count and why I passed out on the plane.

As a matter of routine, the doctors did a series of tests. Don Walsworth and his wife Audry visited me and Virginia while we were in the hospital.

"I've got one more test to take," I told Don.

He said, "I know you're going to be okay. Don't worry about it."

But when they did a colonoscopy, they discovered I had a growth in my colon. It was cancer.

It's all really vague now how they told me. I was still feeling ill from the blood transfusions. I know it was difficult news to swallow, but I didn't go through the feeling, "Why me?" I didn't cry, although I think I would be capable of crying under those circumstances. My feeling was more or less, "I don't know what this means yet, so I'm not going to react."

Once again, my sense of humor helped me to cope. I remember telling Virginia, "Don't spend the insurance money yet."

I called Don on the phone. "I have cancer," I told him.

"You gotta be kidding me," he said.

"No, I'm scheduled for surgery."

The doctors removed a section of my colon along with the cancerous tumor. They also found my gall bladder in terrible condition. And to top it off, I had eight ulcers, seven in my stomach, one in my esophagus.

The doctors removed a two-and-a-half to three-inch tumor from my right side. The cancer was contained within the colon wall and hadn't spread, so my chances for a complete recovery, they told me, were very good. Had the cancer developed more and spread through the colon wall, my chances for survival would have been slim. My collapse on the plane had been a blessing in disguise, because it forced me to get medical attention I might not have otherwise sought.

My family really came together during this trying time, our kids lending support to Virginia and me. I was overwhelmed by their ability to comfort me. Our oldest boy, Jeffrey, asserted himself. While some people had doubts, Jeffrey remained strong, and his strength was very helpful. Lindsey and Laura, too, took time out from their lives and jobs to help out.

My daughter Laura and I have a very special relationship. I remember the first night after surgery, I asked her to stay a little longer. She stayed all night and slept on the chair or on the floor of my hospital room.

Although no one really commented on it at the time, I didn't look very well after surgery. My son Jeff says before surgery, I looked fine, I had plenty of color, and was my normal weight. Afterwards, I looked very pale, and looked considerably lighter. I'm sure this didn't make my family feel at ease.

The first two or three days after the surgery went fine. I thought I'd be out of there in no time. But then I had a reaction. Many people have trouble with their bowels after surgery on their stomach. They can't get their bowels to work on their own. I had this difficulty, and if not for this complication, I would have been out of the hospital within ten days.

I had to do this process with a bag of mercury. It was a very small amount in a container the size of your thumbnail. The bag of mercury would be at the end of a tube. The mercury was inserted through my nostrils and it went down the back of my throat, into my intestines.

The idea was to have the sack of mercury go through your system and open your intestinal tract. They put me on a platform where I could see, with the help of a special scope, the mercury and tube go through my body. Sometimes the mercury sack would only go so far, and I would have to allow the weight of the mercury to do the rest. I had markings on this tube showing the progress.

While I struggled to get my bowels working again, I lost a lot of weight because I couldn't eat. It got to the point where they considered feeding me intravenously. I started a fever. More concern. If I didn't get my bowels going, we knew the situation would become serious.

Finally, after about six days of watching a tube go through my system, the bowels began to work on their own. I was out of danger for the moment.

During this tense period, my wife was allowed to go home. She wanted to visit me at the hospital once or twice a day, but I kept telling her not to come so often. She was still recovering and could hardly take care of herself, let alone me. But she kept returning.

When the hospital finally sent me home, I would try to help her while she tried to help me; we were both very limited as to what we could do. That's when some special people started to respond.

Maybe you've heard that if you break your arm, you suddenly feel a link with everyone else who has ever broken an arm. With cancer that bond runs far deeper, deeper than I could have imagined.

I would hear from people with cancer or with loved ones who had cancer. These calls made me feel very good. Some people called to assure me that they had the same thing happen to them maybe 10 or 15 years ago. So many took the time to write or call, and I still hear from these people. Some of them call me and ask for advice. I have to be careful about what I say because I am not a doctor.

There was great affection from the fans. We received so many cards and letters of support, from around the state, the country, and other universities. We counted over three thousand personal notes and five to six thousand cards. Schools sent cards signed by the cheerleaders and members of the student body. A radio and television station in St. Joseph put together a letter for us. People would come by the station and sign it. It was 66 feet long and had 1,200 names on it.

Missouri Governor John Ashcroft did something I will never forget. I knew the governor because of his interest in the basketball program. He came to a lot of our games and appeared on our television show. Sometimes I would play one-on-one with him, and he would always beat me. I would try to kid myself into thinking I was letting him win, but the fact was I couldn't out-perform him.

Governor Ashcroft was in St. Louis, in a meeting with President George Bush, who was making an appearance. With all of the things Governor Ashcroft must have been trying to cram into the President's short visit, he made sure President Bush sent me a personal note and autographed picture. What a thoughtful gesture.

Aware of the trouble my wife and I would have doing normal chores at home, people brought food over to the house on a regular basis. When it was meal time, someone would make sure food was on the table. Then when we were through eating, someone else would come clear the table and put away the dishes. It was tremendous.

These were special people, and Virginia and I feel a great debt of gratitude towards them.

But as we recovered, the turmoil was far from over. The basketball program soon faced allegations of NCAA rules violations. Some of the things being said about our program were scandalous and threatened my job. Missouri had never been the subject of an NCAA inquiry before.

Now I had two big obstacles to overcome: cancer and the NCAA.

Well, I knew this much: I knew the game of life was more important than the game of basketball. If I've learned anything in life, it's that people count the most.

4

Me and the Show-Me Queen

It was quite an ordeal for Virginia and me to endure, both of us recuperating from major operations at the same time. Some wonderful people came out of nowhere to help, and the situation brought us closer. But we had already been through some tough times. We had come a long way from when I first noticed her outside the jock house on the corner of Rollins and Hitt at the University of Missouri.

It was the beginning of my junior year at Mizzou. I sat on the steps of the jock house, the athletic dining hall, with my friend Dick Jensen, a teammate on the baseball and basketball teams. Dick turned to me and pointed out this girl he knew at Southwest High School in Kansas City, a beautiful young woman named Virginia Zimmerley. She walked by Johnson Hall, where many freshmen girls lived.

Virginia joined the Kappa Kappa Gamma sorority. Her mother had been a Kappa. She became a Kappa. Later, our daughter would become a Kappa. Every now and then we all raise our hands and do a Kappa routine at our house. I'm impressed with the fraternities and sororities at Mizzou. I recommend them to people who want to make them a part of their life. They know how to recognize people for their outstanding talents.

The girls of Johnson Hall nominated Virginia to be their representative in the Show-Me Queen contest, a big deal on campus in those days. A lot of hype surrounded the candidates. The *Show-Me Magazine*, a contemporary, popular student publication, highlighted Virginia and the other candidates.

To promote Virginia, Johnson Hall visited all of the fraternities and dormitories and did a little song-and-dance routine. One day they came by the jock house. Most of us were just relaxing in the dining room when suddenly we heard a big commotion. The girls had begun to sing, and the guys started scrambling for a better view.

All these girls lined up outside the jock house. I remember the song: "It's Up To You." The girls of Johnson Hall were very entertaining, particularly Virginia, whose Show-Me Queen candidacy turned out to be successful.

By now I had drummed up enough courage to ask her out. I was just waiting for an opportunity. Seeing her standing in the student union one day, I walked up behind her and in my off-tone voice sang, "It's Up To You." It was probably not a good way to create a first impression. I'm sure she was thinking, here's this jock, or jerk if you will, trying to impress me in his tone-deaf voice.

Valentino I'm not, but something I did worked. She agreed to go out on a date. The first date was a disaster — for a while it didn't seem like there would be a second. Looking back, I remember myself as somewhat over aggressive; Virginia jokes that it was nearly the end of our relationship. We can agree on one thing: I just came on too strong.

But instead of giving up, I tried to do some patching up. A few phone calls later, she agreed to go out with me again — after setting some ground rules. Soon we were dating regularly.

Of course, there were other bumps to smooth out. I wouldn't go to the Kappa Christmas Formal because it was the night before a basketball game.

"I know other players go," Virginia complained.

"Well, those are other players," I said. "If we're going to have a serious relationship, you want to be associated with someone who wants to make a commitment. If he breaks that commitment, he's not going very far. I've made a commitment to basketball."

Virginia to this day will say she didn't like this particular commitment, but I think she'll agree that commitment has been a big part of my success. Keeping a commitment to my job requires a lot of hours, sure; I look back and think I might have done more for my family. But I knew Virginia would take care of raising the children.

In college, my social life was before the basketball season, and after. I dated in September and October, and then basketball began. I omitted social activities from my calendar from November to March. A basketball scholarship was paying my tuition, and anyway, I loved to play.

We started seeing more of each other in the spring. Then I started to play semipro baseball in South Dakota, which the NCAA allowed then. I wrote to Virginia throughout that summer on the road. I can't really remember what was in those letters, but Virginia says they made a strong impact on her. She now thought of me as more than just a jock, I guess.

The relationship became more serious my senior year. She was elected homecoming queen as a sophomore. It was a glamorous thing: I was the so-called "big man on campus," and I was dating the homecoming queen. How many times do you see that happen? And how many times do you see it last very long?

Virginia met Joe Garagiola and Eddie Fisher that year during the homecoming activities. It was really a fun year for both of us.

I remember being in the stands when they brought her out to the football field during the homecoming celebration. She entered with an escort and was presented to the governor. As she began a little speech, the football team came back from the locker room, halting the ceremony and sending everybody else off the field. It was an unfortunate interruption, but it didn't take away from the glamour of the occasion.

The year became even more special for Virginia and me. After I received my degree, we married.

I laugh now at the lofty aspirations I had as a young man. I told Virginia I was going to play professional basketball and baseball and retire at age 30 with several million dollars.

By the time I reached 30, I realized I was going to fall short by, oh, several million dollars. I reset my goal: I would become a millionaire by age 40.

At 31, I got a little wiser. I did some new calculations and figured if I live to be 643 years old, I might die debt-free.

I still marvel, with her background, at the age of 20, what Virginia was able to put up with while I began my career. By the time she was 25, we had three children.

At one point, with two children, we lived in faculty housing, on a net income of $300 a month, $55 of which went for rent. I was gone all the time — coaching varsity basketball, coaching freshman basketball, coaching baseball, recruiting, scouting, teaching school, going to school. On top of all that, I officiated high school games to help make ends meet.

A woman needs strong character and a solid background to withstand such a situation. Yet I would hope she would tell you that, even under those circumstances, I would go out every now and then and buy something for her which we could absolutely not afford. I remember buying a dress that cost about a hundred dollars. It was my way of saying, "The dream is still there, honey."

We always wanted to have a nice home because we both grew up in nice homes. That was important. Faculty housing was not what we had in mind. It was clean, but boy, you talk about Spartan living, that was it. We had no social life. We weren't invited anywhere. It took some imagination to entertain ourselves.

On our way home from football games in Columbia, we would make our way down a dirt road that led to the faculty housing, the crowds covering us with dust as we walked. Just before we got home, we'd play a game. I would transform us: we would be some anonymous couple going to visit Norm and Virginia Stewart.

"You know, we haven't seen them for a while. Let's see if Norm and Virginia are home," I would say. "You stay here, and I will see whether Norm and Virginia are inside."

I walked up to our place, acting the part of a visitor. I knocked on the door and pretended someone was greeting me. I would turn to Virginia and say, "Yes, they're home. Come on in."

Virginia played along.

"Oh, Norm, hi! Hi, Virginia!"

Then we closed the door and that would be the end of our entertainment. There was just no time, no money and no social invitations.

I think part of our secret was finding things that we enjoyed doing on our own. I could always find pleasant and satisfying things to do. As for Virginia, I don't know what sustained her. I'm sure it took an incredible effort.

Virginia had the foresight to see that she would have some time on her hands after the children grew up. She guided them spiritually and physically, preparing for the day when this would come to an end. Before they left home, she went back to college.

Virginia graduated with a degree in travel administration, an education she used to help the Missouri basketball program. Later, she would turn to a career in television, which also helped the program.

Virginia showed me how to do things off the court to generate support, the kind of support all successful programs need. When we moved to Cedar Falls for the job at Northern Iowa, the first thing she did was see how many University of Missouri people lived in Cedar Falls and nearby Waterloo. She found out how many Kappas lived there. We discovered some Missouri graduates taught there. The base of support for the basketball program steadily grew.

I wanted to know the different groups that showed an interest in basketball. Virginia helped me define these groups. We used social and educational bonds to bring these people together. It turned out to be a successful and meaningful period.

We maintained this philosophy when we came to Missouri. With her travel business background, Virginia motivated people to travel with the team. Some critics became concerned that she used the basketball program to make money, as if there was some sin in that. Well, she made no money beyond paying for her trips. Some people still claim that was a conflict of interest.

The upsetting thing about all this was that no one pushed the idea of traveling with the team except Virginia. Her ideas generated more support. More black and gold filled the seats in places like Manhattan, Kansas, and Stillwater, Oklahoma. She really helped the program out. But the faultfinders were upset that she might make some money doing it.

I owe Virginia so much for all she's done, and I hope I have given her proper credit.

A couple of years ago, to observe a special birthday, I threw a surprise party for her. If nothing else, I think the manner in which it was carried out surprised her. That's one quality I learned from Virginia: If you're going to do something at all, do it properly.

All of the children attended the party, the grandchildren, the whole family. A friend named Ken Dubinsky, a guy with an artistic touch, produced a musical videotape. Some of the tape included footage of Virginia when she was just 4 or 5 years old that her father had taken. We combined this with some videotape I took.

At the time, Virginia and I loved the song "That's What Friends Are For," by Dionne Warwick. The song was the soundtrack for parts of the videotape. We also used the song "Memories." We showed the piece on a big screen at the Country Club of Missouri. I wanted to make Virginia happy and at the same time not bore anybody. Parts of it were funny, because it had a "This Is Your Life" feeling to it.

The night before the party, I broke some of the surprise to her by showing her the videotape. I wanted to make sure it was right and wouldn't offend her. She still didn't know about the party or all the people who would attend.

Her mother, father and entire family were there. I brought in a good friend who was a composer and he wrote a special song for the occasion. It was a memorable event.

I think everyone reaches an age when they feel life has raced by, but Virginia and I have been able to do so many things. Sometimes we stop and wonder how we could have done all of it. An even bigger question is how we did it financially. But somehow we managed.

We took our children to South America in 1972. The kids were 7, 10 and 13 years old. We stayed about a month, and what an experience! There was another month-long trip to Japan, Hong Kong, Singapore, Australia and New Zealand. I was working, doing basketball camps, while they were sightseeing. Toward the end of the trip I arranged for some personal rest. We stopped in Tahiti for the last three days. It was a fabulous trip.

Today, Virginia and I have incredibly busy schedules.

There's not a whole lot of time for romance. But to keep things alive, after 35 years of marriage, we work on communicating. We can have the most engaging conversations in a car, a plane or whatever. Sometimes, she carries the entire conversation. Sometimes I do all the talking.

And we still love to travel, just the two of us. Some of the best times are when we just goof around on a trip.

We like spontaneity. One summer she asked me, "What are you doing the next two weeks?"

"Nothing," I said.

"Let's go to Paris."

So we jumped on an airbus and flew to Paris. We made an arrangement to stay in one place the first night, then we got a car and just took off. We visited parts of Germany and Switzerland, stopping along the countryside whenever the mood hit us.

I think you must make your life an adventure. It has got to be something that doesn't get stale. I remember taking dancing lessons a few years ago, ballroom dancing. I am a terrible dancer, still am to this day. But Virginia's a very good dancer and the experience was great for both of us.

Virginia has been there when I needed help with anything, including the team. I can remember coming home trying to figure out how to capture more people's attention. I remember telling Virginia very early in my career that I thought I wasn't getting enough support from the administration.

Virginia just said, "Can they prevent you from having a good team?"

"No, they can just make it difficult," I said. But the question made me realize an important truth: No one really can prevent me from having a good team.

I've been involved in the sport for a long time, and I've found a lot of success along the way. Virginia is part of that success.

5

Learning from the Best

A coach can know the X's and O's in every book, but without close relationships with good people in the field, he may still find it hard to be successful. I've been fortunate to know some very important people in the world of college basketball.

As I've mentioned, C.J. Kessler made an enormous impact on my life, and not only through the force of his own personality. His close friendship with Branch McCracken helped me find another mentor. McCracken coached Indiana to two national championships, in 1940 and in 1953.

Indiana has a big basketball tradition today, and that tradition had already begun when I was growing up in Missouri. I saw it in the way Kessler, who came from Hammond, Indiana, coached. Kessler coached some 19 years of very competitive high school level basketball before coming to Shelbyville from Hammond Tech. Hammond is not far from Chicago, so I'm sure Kessler saw some great high school talent there.

Because of his years at Hammond Tech, Kessler knew McCracken on a personal basis. I had just earned All-State recognition under Kessler when he had the opportunity to discuss my ability with McCracken one day.

"I've got a good ballplayer down here in Missouri," Kessler told him.

Branch thanked him, but said, "Chet, if that small-town kid came here, he might just get lost."

McCracken told Kessler to send me down to Sparky Stalcup, the head coach at the University of Missouri.

"You send him to Sparky. Because if he can play here, he can play there, also. And if he can't play, Spark's got to take care of him."

McCracken was telling him the way it was — he did Kessler a favor, he did me a favor. But it was a favor McCracken would regret a few years later.

Missouri played at Indiana during my junior year. This was two years after the Hoosiers won the national championship with great players like Don Schlundt and Bobby Leonard.

The Missouri-Indiana game came down to the final seconds. We had the ball and a one-point lead. They were really putting the pressure on us. The ball was passed to me and I was fouled.

I made two free throws to cinch the victory.

When the game was over, McCracken congratulated Stalcup. Then he grabbed me and put his arm around me.

"You know, I'm the dumbest guy in this building," he said.

"Coach," I said, "you know that's not true."

"No. I'm a dumb coach. I lost this game two years ago when I didn't recruit you."

We laughed as we left the court. I always had a great relationship with McCracken after that. When I coached at Missouri as an assistant, we would play against him.

Kessler would come down for those games. On game day, we would go to the hotel room to visit Coach McCracken, and I'd listen to the older coaches' stories. It was always a great trip.

My association with Stalcup opened a lot of doors. If you met Sparky, it would have been an unforgettable experience, because he was an unforgettable man. Sparky was well-known for his quick wit and official-baiting on the sidelines. Maury White, a writer for the *Des Moines Register*, told a great story about Sparky getting invited to speak at an annual clinic for Big Seven officials. He began his speech saying, "Officials are whistle-happy blind men who spend their time standing in front of the bench trying to hear what they think I'm saying about them instead of doing the job they're supposed to be doing." Later, after a little reflection, Sparky paused and said, "Before I go any further, I want to apologize. I don't want to have any retroactive technicals called on me this winter." As White reported, Sparky liked to live dangerously.

I had been a decent player for Stalcup. I helped him coach, or at least I tried. I'm sure I probably didn't have a clue about what I was doing. But I was loyal. I captained his teams in my junior and senior years. It was fun to be a part of those teams. He introduced me to all the big names in coaching, and one of the biggest was "Mr. Iba."

Coach Henry Iba had coached Sparky Stalcup at Maryville, now known as Northeast Missouri State. To appreciate Mr. Iba, you have to know about the Iba Coaching Tree. A long list of college coaches played under him, and those coaches passed along his ideas to another coaching generation.

Iba was born in the small Missouri town of Easton in 1904, not long after basketball was introduced by Dr. James Naismith. Iba played college basketball at Westminster from 1924-28. This was not Michael Jordan's game: There was no jump shot, no one-handed shot.

Beginning even before he graduated from Westminster, Iba coached at Classen High School in Missouri from 1927-29. Then he coached the Maryville Bearcats from 1929-33. He coached some outstanding players. Stalcup was one, Jumpin' Jack McCracken—no relation to Coach McCracken—another.

Iba coached at Colorado from 1933-34. Then he began a long association with Oklahoma State that continues to this day. He coached there from 1934-1970. He had many outstanding seasons and is one of the few to win back to back national championships. He accomplished this in 1945 and 1946 with the help of another great player, Bob Kurland. The arena in Stillwater bears Iba's name. When I went on to coach Missouri, I faced Iba several times.

Iba also coached three Olympic teams and chalked up a total of 767 career victories, the third-highest victory total of any coach.

Iba passed certain things along to me through Stalcup. There was the coaching part of it, sure, but there was a lot more to Mr. Iba than X's and O's. That "Mr. Iba" is a measure of the respect he has earned from everyone who knows him. He's on a higher plain than most of us because of the way he conducts himself. I'm not saying he's some holier-than-thou saint who won't have a good stiff drink every now and then. The point is, he's a class person, a man's man.

I'll never forget a trip I took to Kansas City to talk basketball with Mr. Iba, Sparky and Maryland coach Bud Millikan. Iba had been coaching at what was then called Oklahoma A&M before they came into the Big Eight Conference. We were still the Big Seven. Sparky was coaching at Missouri, and I was his assistant.

Sparky told me to get a projector and some film. We got a car and I drove to Kansas City to meet the others. I remember the trip because the first place we stopped, Spark bought some Spanish peanuts and a few beers. He was a great junk food man. He'd drink root beer and milk shakes, eat peanuts.

"Doesn't that bother you?" I asked him.

"Just a little gas, that's all," Spark said.

We arrived in Kansas City around 3 in the afternoon and met at the Muehlbach Hotel. Coach Stalcup introduced me to Coach Millikan and Mr. Iba. I think it was my first meeting with both coaches; they called me Freddy.

"Now Freddy, you run over to the grocery store and get us something to drink," Mr. Iba would say.

"What would you like?"

"Get a bottle of everything. That way no one will be disappointed."

I got the groceries and went to the hotel room where they began talking basketball. They had a blackboard. One would talk for a while, then another would say, "That won't work. We tried that thirty years ago."

Another coach would step up, only to hear, "That won't work. We tried that last year."

But they kept motivating one another to think deeper about the subject matter, to figure it out. Every once in a while, they'd turn to me.

"Freddy, what do you think?"

At 11:30 p.m., we were all getting a little foggy, so we left to get a bite to eat. We ate at the Italian Gardens, a great restaurant. Carl DiCapo, the owner, is still there today.

After a drink or two, I felt queasy and needed to go back to the hotel room. The others returned in an hour and talked basketball until 3 or 4 in the morning. Finally they said, "It's too late. Let's go to bed and resume this tomorrow."

It seemed like I had just closed my eyes when the phone rang. It was Mr. Iba.

"Freddy, what are you doing?"

"Well, I was just resting my eyes."

"I'll tell you something. You can't learn basketball while you're sleeping. Order breakfast, and we'll meet you there in five minutes."

I looked at the clock and it was 6 o'clock. They were all there by 6:30. Then they talked basketball straight through noon.

Mr. Iba's plane was to leave early that afternoon. He called the airport and changed reservations so he could leave at 4 o'clock. They had a little lunch and kept on talking. They talked until 3:30.

Finally, Mr. Iba got up and said, "Nice talking to all of you. Good to see you, Freddy." And he left.

We had been there about 24 hours. We had talked basketball for about 21 hours.

It was exhilarating and it was a great lesson for me as an aspiring coach. These were three great coaches.

There would be more meetings with Mr. Iba. The late former Nebraska coach Joe Cipriano and I laughed about some of these gatherings. Whenever we would have a session, Iba would put us all to bed. When we woke up a few hours later, the race was on to see if you could beat Iba down to breakfast. He was always waiting when you got off the elevator.

"Where have you been, Freddy?"

Iba helped me get my first head coaching job at Northern Iowa — Iba and Sparky and a fellow named Wayne Lichty whom I'll discuss later.

Before Sparky died in 1972, he had introduced me to many people in the coaching profession. It was quite an illustrious group.

Iba took me under his wing because I was a coach and had played under Sparky. I'm certainly no closer to Iba than the people who played for him, but he allowed me to become one of those kids. At least he made me feel that way.

That says something about what kind of a person Mr. Iba is. He's fun to be around. He knows how to cut through a lot of bull and get right to the subject. Virginia and I still get a chance to take him out every now and then. We really enjoy these moments.

He'll be at every game at Oklahoma State. I wish he could be helping our ballclub. He's getting up there in age, but I'll tell you, he's at someone's practice now, helping to straighten out their ballclub. His influence on the game is immeasurable and will last long after he's gone.

6
The Summer Game

My personal and professional relationships helped propel me to my current stature in college basketball. But coaching was not the ultimate goal as I enrolled at the University of Missouri in 1952. I thought I was good enough to make my fortune playing professional basketball and baseball.

As a sophomore, I played on Missouri's 1954 NCAA national championship baseball team. My getting into baseball at the college level was a bit of a fluke in the first place. It all really boiled down to a one-dollar bet.

One afternoon I headed toward the athletic department to pick up some basketball gear from the equipment manager, a guy named Dusty Rhodes — no relationship to the baseball player.

"Dusty," I said. "I need to get my basketball gear."

Just then a brash young guy out of the St. Louis area, Emil Kammer, walked up to me and said, "What the hell are you doing?"

I knew of Kammer because he was an outstanding player out of Normandy High School. He was to become a leading pitcher on the Missouri staff, and a good third baseman as well.

I thought I would pull his leg a little, so I said, "I'm going out for baseball."

Kammer went crazy.

"Why?"

"I'm a hell of a baseball player."

"If you make the team, we won't win a game," Emil said.

Here's this small-town kid being confronted by a wise-cracker from St. Louis. I had to come back with some sort of response. I took his remark as a challenge.

"I will bet you a dollar I'll make the team."

Emil said, "I'll take that bet."

So I turned to Dusty and said, "Give me some baseball gear." And that's how I got into baseball at Mizzou.

I almost got out of baseball at Mizzou before ever pitching in a game, though, all because of a fashion misunderstanding.

I had made the traveling squad, and we were about to leave on one of the first trips of the season, but I didn't show up for the bus. When I came to school, I had three pair of jeans, a couple of shirts and a suit. All of my dress clothes were winter clothes. In basketball, all I needed was a coat and tie. I assumed you needed the same in baseball, but I wasn't going to wear my winter suit on the trip, so I just didn't go.

When the team returned to Columbia, I saw the coach, John Simmons, coming down the hall, and I thought I was through with baseball. He asked me why I missed the trip and I told him. To my surprise, he said they didn't require guys to wear suits. I was a baseball player again.

We traveled to Oklahoma A&M for a two-game road trip. They beat us the first day, but the second day we had them beat 10-2 and Simmons put me in the ball game, my college baseball debut. I was a flop.

I walked four batters. Two ground balls were hit to me. I threw one of them over the shortstop's head, and the other I managed to get over the center-fielder's head. Three runs had scored and two men were on base when Simmons called on another pitcher.

I felt terrible after the game because I had never suffered a setback like that in sports. Seeing mud on my spikes, I took them off and slammed them on the side of the bus to clean them. That made the bus driver mad as hell. I was not a popular guy that day.

When I got back to Columbia, I told Coach Simmons, "I'm going to quit baseball. I don't think I can help the team any."

"Well, let's do this," he said. "Your performance against A&M was the worst I had ever seen. You were horrible. But we're going to play Fort Leonard Wood soon. I'm going to start you. If you don't do any better than your last outing, you won't have to turn in your gear. I'll pick it up for you."

I pitched against Fort Leonard Wood. With my first-game jitters behind me, I did okay, well enough to keep my gear anyway. I still wasn't good enough to be a regular, but I had a spot on the team. And I'd won my bet with Kammer.

I didn't pitch again until the end of the season against Iowa State. Missouri had already won the Big Seven, so Coach Simmons let me pitch. I had them shut out through eight innings and we were up 12-0. I went out to pitch the ninth, and I got the first guy out. I was feeling pretty good.

I threw two balls to the next hitter. No big deal, right? Coach Simmons came out, and, in the damnedest oratory I ever heard, began to chew me out. Now I had heard people swear. I knew every swear word, so there weren't any new ones. It was just the way Simmons delivered it. He told me if I threw one more ball, my ass was coming out. And he walked back into the dugout.

I was amused, but he'd made his point. So I threw it right down the groove and the guy promptly jacked it over the left field fence. The next voice I hear is Coach Simmons.

"By golly, that's the way to go. If they hit four or five more like that, then I'll take you out. Just keep throwing them strikes and make them hit it."

I got them out and we beat them 12-1. Point proven: Do what your coach says, and everything will be all right.

I was a thrower on a team that had a great pitching staff. My record during our championship year was 2-0, and my earned run average was 3-point-something. The Tigers went 22-4 that year, and we just demolished some teams by scores of 24-1, 18-2.

Our team won the Big Seven and went on to the College World Series, a double-elimination tournament for the national championship.

We were beaten during our second game in the tournament. I pitched relief in that game, and I was so excited I couldn't even see. I just threw as hard as I could, striking out four guys in two innings.

We couldn't afford another loss or we'd be eliminated. After winning our next game, we were scheduled to play Oklahoma A&M, the same team I had the nightmarish debut against earlier in the year.

Coach Simmons looked at the lineup and saw we didn't have any front-line pitchers left. Oklahoma A&M apparently saw that, too. Looking ahead, figuring they would beat us, A&M wanted to save a great left-handed pitcher named Tom Borland for their next game.

John "Hi" Simmons called us together. We were sitting in a meeting room against a wall, guys like me not paying attention because our names never came up. Sitting with Bert Beckman, another pitcher, I just hear bits and pieces.

"They think we're out of pitchers," Simmons says, "but we've got a guy who's been working hard and he's ready to pitch."

Then he announced who's going to be our starter.

I thought I heard my name, but I didn't think that could be right. Beckman says, "Oh, shit."

"Bert, what did he say?" I asked.

"He said you're going to pitch."

I said, "Well, you're not really giving me a lot of confidence with that statement. That's not very supportive."

I was half-joking; I think Bert was, too.

I went to the mound and we beat them 7-3. I pitched a 13-hitter, not exactly a gem, but a big highlight for me nonetheless.

Then, before about 8,000 fans in Omaha, we beat little Rollins College of Florida 4-1 to become the NCAA champions. I was part of a national championship team and I owed it all to Emil Kammer and that one dollar bet before the season began.

The funny thing about all this was, I never told my parents what I decided to do that summer. I went through the whole baseball season, then took final exams. I stayed in Columbia and prepared for the national tournament for four or five days. The team went to Omaha, and the World Series took a week. Then I traveled to South Dakota to play for Yankton, a semipro team. Emil Kammer lined up the South Dakota job following the College World Series and even got me my bus ticket. After being there a week, which had to be about the middle of June, I finally wrote my parents a letter and told them where I was. I said in the letter that I had come from Omaha, where we had won the College World Series.

I got a letter back from my mother, Leona, a dear sweet woman. I could tell you stories that would bring tears to your eyes about how hard she and my dad worked. She said in that letter, "You know, I thought it was about time school would be out. I was wondering where you were, why you hadn't come home. Then we were listening to a Cardinal game on the radio, your dad and I. And when the World Series was on, we knew Missouri was in it. One night, Harry Caray said that Missouri had beaten Oklahoma A&M. And he said the battery for Missouri consisted of Gleason and Stewart. When Caray said that, I turned to your dad and said, 'I bet Norm went out for baseball.'"

Here I had pitched in the College World Series, played in South Dakota for a week, and I hadn't come home or even told my parents what I was doing. Maybe it was because I was the fourth child; I guess I thought they wouldn't get too concerned. I was just playing baseball, no big deal. It didn't bother me that they didn't know where I was. But I realize now it might have worried them a little.

I played about 50 semipro games that summer with Yankton. You could be paid in those days and still be eligible for college athletics. My final year in the semipros I made $600 a month, fantastic money at that time. My rent was five dollars a week, and I could eat on three dollars a day, so I would have more than $400 left. I could buy a good suit of clothes for $40.

After that championship season, scouts started talking to me. The Boston Red Sox offered me a bonus. Players like Robin Roberts were signing for the then considerable salary of $25,000. There was a rule in those days that if you signed a bonus for more than $4,000, you had to stay in the majors for two years. After the Sox offered me a signing bonus, other teams followed, including St. Louis.

The problem was, I came from a family where no one had a degree. I felt strongly about staying in school. I figured if I was worth some money now, I would be worth more later, and I would have my degree. It's an experience I pass along to some of my players today when they are faced with a similar decision.

We had a great basketball season my junior year, but in baseball we lost several of our big senior leaders and didn't meet our expectations.

I had a good season, though, with an earned run average under 1.00. That was a record that held up for a long time — I think Keith Weber might have broken it. I pitched a no-hitter, but I only had a 4-2 record.

I also experienced some humiliation that year, thanks to a Fort Leonard Wood player named Dorrel Herzog, better known as "Whitey."

A few years ago we had a banquet for Jon Sundvold, retiring his number. Whitey had helped me recruit Jon from Blue Springs High School, and he came to the banquet as a guest speaker.

After his speech, I said, "Whitey, you're not going to remember this, but you and I played against one another."

"The hell I don't," he said. "We beat you 2-1."

"How in the hell would you remember?" I said. "You've been a player in the minors and majors, you've coached, you've managed. How in the hell would you remember that game?"

He said, "How many times do you triple twice and steal home twice in one game?"

Those were details I wanted to forget. In those days, pitchers always used the full windup when a man was on third base. Whitey said with my long legs and full windup, it took a long time for me to deliver the ball. Once it left my hand, it didn't take long to get to the plate, but Whitey saw a window of opportunity there, and exploited it twice in one game. Because of people like Whitey, most pitchers today pitch off the stretch when a runner is on third.

Whitey Herzog also knew a thing or two about basketball. Before we signed Steve Stipanovich and Sundvold, Whitey spoke to me at another banquet. Herzog, who had officiated high school and college basketball, thought I was too scientific about coaching. He told me a story about his high school basketball coach. The man took the simple approach to coaching: At halftime he would tell players, "Remember, this half, we're going the other way. Now let's go out and play hard."

Whitey's high school team finished 37-2.

After we won a number of Big Eight championships in a row with Stipanovich and Sundvold, I ran into Whitey again, and he commented on how great the team was playing.

"Well," I told him, "I just remind the players at halftime that, this time, we're going the other way."

We both got a kick out of that.

7

Going for the Dream

With my college career winding down, the plan was to finish my senior year playing basketball in the winter and baseball in the summer. Pro scouts would see my talent, and I would play both sports on the professional level.

My potential for pro basketball looked promising going into my senior season. We completed a 16-5 year under Sparky the previous year, and I was a returning co-captain and all-conference performer.

This is probably the hardest subject to write about because I don't like recounting personal accomplishments. But that season is worth documenting in part because certain events would shape my destiny.

As a senior, I tried to help Sparky coach, even though I didn't know much about coaching. Something I did must have got his attention, however, because Sparky was instrumental in getting me to return to Missouri after graduation.

The traveling squad consisted of myself, Chuck Denny, Lionel Smith, Redford Reichert, Bill Ross, Eddie Richards, Kent Henson, John Stephens, Rodger Egelhoff, Jon Paden, Edward Ronsick, Arnold Kaestner, Paul Stehr, Jim Cotter and Jim Prewitt.

I hear from all of the guys every now and then. Some of these friendships will last my entire life.

We played in Brewer Fieldhouse in those days. When you see pictures of Brewer, they always appear dark. That's not because of bad photography. The place wasn't well lit, but it sure got noisy.

We breezed through our opener against South Dakota.

We traveled to West Lafayette, Indiana, for the next game against Purdue. The Boilermakers had a 6-6 forward named Lamar Lundy, who really controlled the inside. Lundy was a muscular guy who starred on the Purdue football team and later played for the Los Angeles Rams. He grabbed 17 rebounds that night, and also stepped on my chest. We gave up a lot of easy baskets and lost 62-58.

A side attraction to the game was the basketball debut of a player named Lenny Dawson. Lenny, of course, turned out to be one of the all-time great quarterbacks at Purdue. A year earlier he helped blank the Tiger football team 31-0.

We took our 1-1 record back to Columbia to play Texas Tech. The Red Raiders, one of the top-scoring teams in the country, were favored. They had averaged more than 80 points a game the year before, two of their guys stood 6-8, taller than any of our players, and they had an All-American candidate in Jim Reed.

Right from the opening tip, something clicked for us, and we shot about 60 percent from the floor. We broke some school records, including 51 first-half points, and upset Texas Tech.

Next Illinois came into Brewer Fieldhouse, ranked No. 7 in the country. More than 5,000 people packed the Fieldhouse, a good-sized crowd for Brewer. The Illini raced to a big halftime lead thanks to our cold shooting. At intermission, Sparky told us to calm down, not to take so many outside shots.

Lionel Smith and Chuck Denny helped us rally at the start of the second half, hitting a flurry of shots. It was probably one of the best halves of my career. I scored about 25 points in the second half. We upset Illinois 74-73.

Indiana was next on the schedule. Branch McCracken had a great team with veterans Wally Choice and Hallie Bryant and some sophomores named Charley Brown, Archie Dees and Pete Obremsky. Another big crowd at Brewer Fieldhouse had to wait an extra 45 minutes for the game to start because of a power failure. This may have short-circuited some of their enthusiasm.

Indiana's star players rose to the occasion. Choice and

Brown played superbly and they beat us by about three points.

We had the opportunity to become the first Missouri team to win back-to-back pre-season Big Seven Tournaments that year. The experts picked us to win. This was a tournament that was played around Christmas for a number of years until it was moved to the end of the season in the late 70s.

We captured third place, a bit of a let down. I did not have a very good tournament. I remember one time I stepped to the free throw line and asked the referee if I could have a practice shot.

Our game against Arkansas that year was one of the more memorable games of my career. Bill Ross was fouled at the buzzer with the Tigers down by a point. As he prepared to shoot his free throws, I went over to him and said, "Bill, if you miss the first one, go ahead and miss the second one because I don't want to play a damned overtime." I just wanted him to relax. Whether my amateur psychology worked or not, he made them both to give us a 51-50 win.

Bill Ross still sends me copies of that newspaper article, with his name in the headline. I think he must have 500 copies. I write back reminding him to read the article carefully, especially the part that says the only reason he got a chance to make the winning free throws was because I hit two shots to bring us closer.

We nicknamed Ross "Rube" because, we said, "for a guy from the city, you're the biggest country-acting guy we've ever seen."

We liked to see Ross mix it up with opposing players. He had a strong personal rivalry with Gene Elston, who played with the Jayhawks. They had played against one another in high school. When we played Kansas, it was always a nice side-show to watch Bill and Gene fight like little kids. Every now and then we'd see them talking to one another and swatting each other.

Mid-point in the season, things appeared to be going smoothly, though I'd had a few rough outings. I had been bitten by the flu and jammed my finger during the season, the kinds of things you can shake off. But in a game against Colorado, I would hurt my back and shoulder, an injury that would have an effect on my future.

We arrived in Boulder on a brutally cold January evening, it must have been about zero. We shared first place in the Big

Seven race, and we wanted to keep up with the others at the top. Colorado was undefeated.

It was a rough style of basketball during those years. If a guy went to the basket, you ran under him. That was accepted. I played through that in high school and college. It was dangerous, but it never bothered me. I could live with it because it applied on both ends of the court. If you went up for a basket, you knew you were going to get dumped. Getting banged around was just part of the game.

I suffered the injury early in the game. I always figured Colorado's Jim Ranglos or Mel Coffman banged into me. We were under the board when I got hit in the back, not what you'd call in the normal realm of play. I returned to the lineup quickly because I didn't think there was anything wrong, but I had lost my shooting touch. On one occasion, I lost my cool, too, drawing a technical foul for arguing with an official.

Funny, I remember getting a technical only one other time in my playing career, when I kicked a ball. I tell my players today, when you're at the university and on the basketball team, you are very visible. Your actions create an impression: You are building a house. You can build a good house, you can do a lot of positive things, by being a good representative on campus. At the same time, you can tear off a few shingles by your actions, especially if you are frequently seen in the pubs, or if you get into a fracas. If you sit in front of a crowd and moon them, you can pull your roof off. I tore off some shingles with my technicals. I know what I'm talking about: Some people today (though I'd rather have them remember the time I scored 30 points against Illinois) still remember the time I kicked the ball.

I finished the Colorado game with just 11 points, and we lost 79-72.

After the game, I was stiff as a board. They sent me to the hospital in Boulder, where I was examined by an orthopedic surgeon. They said there was no evidence of a bone injury, but the pain persisted. For the first time in two years, I was looking at the possibility of sitting out a game.

At first, Coach Stalcup did not want me to play the next game against Nebraska. But after some hours under a heat lamp, the pain wasn't as bad, and I felt I could play. Stalcup left it up to me.

Maybe I should have decided to sit out a while longer. I

missed my first eight shots against the Cornhuskers and finished the game hitting a miserable percentage from the field. We lost to a team we had easily defeated in the preseason tournament.

That game convinced me we'd be better off as a team with someone else playing. I was put in traction at the Student Health Center in Columbia. I listened to the next game against Kansas State on the radio from a bed.

The team sounded like it was going to upset Kansas State until the final minutes, when the Wildcats scored 10 straight points to win it.

Fortunately, we had a two-week lay-off before our next game against Oklahoma in Norman. It gave me more time to recuperate. In the meantime, others players began to assert themselves.

One that comes to mind is Chuck Denny. In Lawrence, Kansas, Denny led the team in scoring. The amazing thing about Denny is, he had a tremendous senior year, and he did it all while in law school.

I can still remember playing against Denny in high school when he was at Fayette. Shelbyville played Fayette in the quarter-finals of the state tournament and we beat them in a wild finish. We came to the University of Missouri the same year. I don't recall ever seeing anyone play as strong. He was rugged. A hard body. I saw Jim Loscutoff play in the pros with the Celtics. Loscutoff was strong, but no stronger than Denny.

Here's another sidelight to the Kansas game. About 9,000 fans came early to watch the freshman game. Someone called Wilt "The Stilt" Chamberlain played in that game. I'm glad freshmen weren't eligible to play varsity.

After losing to Iowa State, we turned the corner against Colorado. After blowing them out, we beat Iowa State in a rematch, then we beat Oklahoma, and first-place Kansas State in Manhattan.

The Kansas State win was one of the biggest wins of the year for us, to beat the leaders in the conference on their home court. While we didn't have the best record, we were playing the best ball in the league.

We won our regular season finale over Nebraska to finish 15-7 for the year and 8-4 in the conference. Our hopes of sharing the title hinged on the outcome of the Kansas State-Kansas game. If Kansas won, we would share the conference lead and a draw would determine if we went to the NCAA Tournament. A bid to the NCAA would be a great way to finish my career under Sparky. As good a coach as he was, his teams never made it to the NCAA. You had to win your conference.

It didn't happen this time, either. Kansas State won its finale, and with it the NCAA berth. Winning the conference and going to the NCAA were big unfulfilled goals that year. We had been 16-5 the year before, and it had been years since the Tigers had won the conference. This drought would make it all the sweeter years later, when I would coach the Tigers to the conference title.

I earned several postseason honors that helped take some of the pain away from not winning the conference. I led the Big Seven in scoring and was named a Helms Foundation All-American. I still held onto my dream of playing two pro sports, but that injury in Colorado would not go away.

I had a disappointing senior baseball season. I re-injured my back, hurt my arm, and maybe just wasn't as good as I thought. Another stint in the semipros in Watertown was my last chance to prove to the scouts that I was still a good player, still deserving of the $50,000 bonus they had offered me the year before. The money would sure come in handy: Virginia and I were getting married.

At Watertown, I was 12-2 in a 42-game season. That's a pretty good year — good enough, I figured, to impress the scouts. Behind me in the rotation was Ron Perranowski. I still tease Ron, who had a great major league career and is a great pitching coach with the Dodgers, about the fact that he was the second pitcher.

The shortstop for Watertown was Dick Howser. Dick had an outstanding baseball career. He was third base coach for the Yankees for a period of time before managing the team. Then in 1985 Howser managed the Kansas City Royals to a World Championship.

We kept in touch, but we stayed pretty much apart over the years. For instance, he didn't try to interfere and ask for tickets. I would do the same.

After Howser won the 1985 World Series, it was discovered he had brain cancer.

He died a short time later during the 1986 season.

Dick was one of three people who were teammates or

coaching friends whom I had an association with during their last moments.

There was Bob Reiter, a Missouri basketball teammate, whom I had the chance to visit. Nebraska coach Joe Cipriano was another.

It really leaves an impression on you when people want to talk with you when they are dying. In all of these cases, I felt it was amazing they wanted to see me, and that they could somehow talk with me.

I didn't get the baseball contract I thought I deserved after my 12-2 season at Watertown, so I waited to see which way my basketball career would bounce.

The St. Louis Hawks selected a very talented crop of athletes during the territorial draft in 1956. This was before the National Basketball Association went to its current system of drafting by rounds. The Hawks selected UCLA's Willie Nauls, Furman's Darrell Floyd, Wally Choice of Indiana and a guy named Norm Stewart of Missouri.

The Hawks had a losing season the year before, but made the playoffs anyway. There were only eight teams in the league back then, and it wasn't unusual for a team with a losing record to qualify for the playoffs.

St. Louis had the rights to a man who would revolutionize the game of basketball, one Bill Russell, a 6-10 center from the University of San Francisco. But Russell, the future Hall of Famer, one of the all-time greats, would never play with the Hawks. Owner Ben Kerner traded him to Boston for two other great players, "Easy" Ed Macauley, who had played at St. Louis University, and Cliff Hagan. The addition of these two solid players was going to make it tougher for a rookie like me to make the team.

As the *Official National Basketball Encyclopedia* will prove, I did make the squad. My name appears in the *Encyclopedia* right before a player named Steve Stipanovich, whom I would later recruit for Missouri.

The Hawks had a great team that season, however, it took a while for them to jell. Red Holzman was the coach at the beginning of the year. The top player was Bob Pettit, the league's leading scorer the previous season. Other Hawks that year were Jack Coleman, Jack McMahon, Chuck Share and another former Missouri player, Med Park.

Holzman was under a great deal of pressure to produce or be fired. We could sense the pressure on Red because he would only play six or seven men during the exhibition season.

I'll never forget my first look at a confrontation between a coach and a player in the professional ranks. Jack Coleman knew Sparky Stalcup from the service, so I got to know Coleman real well. Although Jack was about 34 or 35 years old, playing against guys 10 years younger, he held his own. One night in Kansas City, Jack stole the ball, which he did pretty frequently. But as he raced for the other basket, his legs gave out, and he just sprawled onto the court. The other team picked up the loose ball, then called a timeout.

As Jack walked over to the bench, Red was waiting for him. "Jack, what's the matter with you?"

Jack looked at him matter of factly and said, "Red, I'm 35 years old and I'm f------ tired."

It was not the kind of language I was accustomed to hearing players use to their coaches. But Red shrugged it off and went on with his pep talk.

According to the record book, I played in about 10 games for the Hawks, five of them in the regular season. The most I scored in any one game was about five points, but then I only averaged seven minutes a game. Some of the players joked that I was one of those guys who shot when I stepped off the bus. Well, you don't get many chances to make an impression in professional basketball as a rookie, especially back then. There were just eight teams and 10 players on each squad. Holzman was in a situation where he needed to rely heavily on his regulars, so I didn't get much playing time. Hell, I wish I'd shot more.

Red was looking for another guy to bring the ball up the court. He was playing Hagan there, but Cliff was not a guard. I remember sitting on the bench in Madison Square Garden one night and watching Hagan run over another guard—his own teammate—at half court.

I have to admit I kind of enjoyed watching that play. My chances of getting in the game had improved just a little bit. Red didn't want to bench Hagan, but he was coming to realize it was best to put Cliff up front.

The team acquired guard Slater Martin in a trade, giving them a backcourt of Martin and Jack McMahon. Ed Macauley and Bob Pettit played forward, and big Chuck Share, 7 feet tall, was the center. Jack Coleman and Hagan gave the team great depth and were occasional starters.

Unfortunately, the acquisition of Martin cost a rookie guard from Missouri a spot on the team. Getting released really bothered me; I wasn't used to losing a job. But in retrospect, it was probably the best thing that happened to me.

Red also lost his job around then. Slater Martin became a player-coach for a few games, and then Kerner hired Alex Hannum to coach the rest of the season. What followed became a part of basketball folklore.

The Hawks really came together late in the season. Pettit was having another great year, finishing second in the league in scoring, despite a broken wrist he suffered during the middle of the season.

St. Louis finished in a three-way tie for first place in the Western Division, with Fort Wayne and Minneapolis. Their record was just 34-38. That should give you an idea how badly the Eastern Division had outplayed the West.

The Hawks beat Fort Wayne and Minneapolis in the play-offs to face the Eastern Division champion Boston Celtics in the championship series.

With Bill Russell changing the way the game was played, the Celts were about to start a dynasty. Russell was known for his incredible shot-blocking and rebounding skills, and Boston had another great rookie that year, high-scoring forward Tom Heinsohn.

In 1981, Heinsohn and I were selected by the National Association of Basketball Coaches to a Silver Anniversary Team, honoring five players who made a strong contribution to college basketball over 25 years. It was quite an honor for me to be named to this team.

Boston's guards were all-stars Bob Cousy and Bill Sharman. With their incredible talent, they finished the regular season with the best record in the league and breezed by Syracuse in the playoffs.

Nobody gave the Hawks much chance in the championship, but they would surprise a lot of people. Large crowds filled the arenas in Boston and St. Louis, and the series, played on national television, would catapult the league into a new era.

Right off the bat, the Hawks amazed everyone with a 125-

123 double over-time win in Boston. The series would go to seven games.

The seventh game was a classic. It was played in Boston on a Saturday afternoon with much of the country watching it on television. Before the season began, there had been some doubts about how long the league would last. This ball game would attract a whole new group of fans and secure the league's future.

The score see-sawed all game long. Boston would pull away, only to have the Hawks catch up. Pettit tied the game for St. Louis with two free throws near the end of regulation, sending it into overtime.

Coleman made a basket for St. Louis with a few seconds left in overtime to force another extra period.

Russell's defense really stood out in the second overtime, forcing some big turnovers. Heinsohn had also played a heck of a game, scoring 37 points. The Celtics went up 125-123 with just a few seconds left in the second overtime on a free throw by Jim Loscutoff.

This set the scene for a dramatic last-ditch effort. With several players having fouled out, Hawks coach Hannum was forced to put himself into the game. During a timeout after the Loscutoff free throw, Hannum diagramed what appeared to be an impossible play. The Hawks had to inbound the ball from the Celtics' end of the court, with no time to bring the ball up. Hannum said he would throw the ball the length of the court off the backboard. Pettit was supposed to wait for the ball to bounce off, then put up a shot before the buzzer.

Hannum was not known for his shooting accuracy. Some joked that he couldn't throw the ball into the ocean, so the players had their doubts about this plan.

It almost worked. Hannum threw it off the backboard just as it was diagramed. Pettit leaped to catch the ball and managed to throw it back toward the basket. The shot bounced off the rim, the buzzer went off, and the Celtics were the champs.

As people swarmed onto the court, a new era had dawned on the National Basketball Association. But I was merely a spectator. Had the sun begun to set on my short-lived professional basketball career?

I wasn't going to give up that easily. I had been able to bounce back from setbacks in my college career; I could do it again. Some dreams die hard.

8

20,000 Leagues Beneath the Majors

After my release by the Hawks, Don Faurot and Sparky Stalcup called me immediately, and I helped Sparky with the Missouri basketball program during the 1956-57 season. I had considered coaching as a possible career, but I still had other options.

About this time, an old baseball player and scout named Del Wilber came through Columbia and said, "Norm, what are you doing?"

"I think I'm going to play for the Minneapolis Lakers," I said. "They've contacted me and I think I have a chance to play basketball there."

Wilber said, "Why don't you play baseball?"

I had turned down some chances to sign out of college because I didn't think I was being offered enough. But with my basketball prospects looking dim now, this offer was tempting.

"You've got your degree," Wilber said. "Go places. Maybe you'll make it."

He said if I didn't make it as a ballplayer, my degree might help me get into the business side of professional baseball as a manager or a scout. It sounded good, and I signed with the Baltimore Orioles.

When the basketball season was nearly over, I went to spring training in the Phoenix area, assigned to the Orioles' Double-A team in San Antonio. We practiced near the Orioles' camp, so the big league coaching staff could watch us practice from time to time.

The competition was stiff in Phoenix. When spring training was over, they sent me to Thomasville, Georgia. The camp in Thomasville included the Orioles' Class A, B and C teams.

With all due respect to Thomasville, it was not high on the players' list of favorite places. There were those of us, in fact, who decided if you had to give the earth an enema, you'd stick the tube in Thomasville, Georgia. But I love small towns, and had I stayed there longer, I'm sure I would have loved Thomasville.

Making the transition to Thomasville was a bit of a shock for most of the players. We had a nice setup in Arizona, with air-conditioned hotel rooms and good meal money. At Thomasville, that all changed.

I thought of what it might be like living in an Army barracks. You slept in a cot in the blazing summer heat. Lying in the cot, you had no desire to move because you were already perspiring and you didn't want to make it worse. I'm sure a lot of career changes were inspired by staring hopelessly at the ceiling on a sticky Georgia summer night.

Occasionally, somebody would lighten things up. A young minor league coach named Earl Weaver would run into the barracks to quiet the troops. I think he was only 25 or 26 years old at the time, but he'd already learned how to issue threats and warnings. Definitely major league material. Of course, Weaver went on to manage the Orioles to half a dozen American League East titles and a World Series championship.

Thomasville's plumbing was minor league, too. Now roughing it wasn't new to me; I grew up in Shelbyville, where we had no plumbing until my junior year in high school. But after being exposed to the nicer side of things in college and in Arizona, I didn't like taking a step backwards.

I recall a few wonderful moments in Thomasville. "Glory days," I guess you'd call them. If you had a sense of humor, anyway.

Steve Barber, who became an outstanding major league pitcher, was assigned to Thomasville the same time I played there. Boy, Barber could really bring it. The ball got to the plate real quick when he was on the mound, but he was also very wild. One time, pitching against my team in a practice game, Barber hit three of our guys in a row with that powerful fastball of his.

After the third guy was hit, no one would step up to the plate. I don't know what got into me, but I decided to grab a bat. Hell, I was your typical weak-hitting pitcher, probably couldn't hit a ball if I threw it to myself, but here I was, stepping up to the plate against a blazing fastball that wasn't going anywhere near the strike zone.

Barber wound up and threw the ball as hard as he could. As I watched that ball come in, I don't think I left any footprints in the batter's box; I didn't want to put any more weight on the ground than I had to. I was terrified. So terrified, in fact, I think I was already running when I hit the ball. A dying dove to right field, it fell in for a base hit.

Chalk one up for Stewart.

Unfortunately there weren't many highlights for me in Thomasville. While pitching against a Class A team, I sidearmed an older guy and he jerked it for a triple. This episode was memorable for two reasons: It taught me not to sidearm someone on the inside part of the plate, and it led to my demotion to Class C in Aberdeen, South Dakota.

When you played at this level in professional baseball, it was jokingly referred to as 20,000 Leagues Beneath the Majors.

I remember the long drive from Thomasville to Aberdeen with a couple of other players in a station wagon. We experienced some trouble traveling through the South because of racism. Several establishments wouldn't allow the black players on our team to eat or stay in their hotels. We stayed together as a team, so if they refused one of us, they refused all of us.

Once we reached Aberdeen, we were introduced to life in the Northern League. We traveled to places no one had ever heard of. The running joke was to run to the outfield just before a game, jump out from behind a player and ask, "Quick, what town are you in?"

The guy's eyes would be glazed over from traveling all night, and he'd grab at a name or two. Half the time, he didn't have a clue.

On one road trip, the local police stopped us for speeding. The officer ordered us to pay up or surrender a driver's license. One of the guys asked if the officer would accept a check. The officer said he would.

After he wrote the check and we started to drive off, this ballplayer began laughing.

"Hurry," he said. "We gotta get across the state line as quick as we can. I just signed the check 'Joe Palooka.'"

When we finished the road trip, the owner of the ballclub called us together.

"Gentlemen," he said, "I have a ticket here for sixty dollars. I'm going to leave the room for five minutes, and when I come back I want to see sixty dollars in the middle of the floor."

Just before he walked out the door, he turned and said over his shoulder, "Joe Palooka, my ass."

So everyone put in two or three dollars, and we paid off the ticket.

During another road trip I had an encounter with Bob Uecker, a good minor league player and a better major leaguer than he lets on. Of course, he's even a better baseball comedian.

Uecker was catching for the Braves' minor league team in Eau Claire, Wisconsin. It was the fifth or sixth inning of a seven-inning game, and I was on the mound facing Uecker.

Well, he hit one, and I mean it was a titanic shot over the left field fence. When the ball left his bat, it felt as if someone had pinned my pantlegs. Uecker's home run put them up 2-1.

When the inning was over, I went into the dugout and one of the players said, "Norm, that ball was foul."

"What do you mean it was foul?" I said. "He hit it so high and so far, how could you tell?"

He pointed out that our side of the dugout looked right down the line, so I thought maybe he knew what he was talking about. Of course, I was grasping for straws, too.

When I went to take my warm-ups the next inning, I barbed the umpire a bit. We began to have a little discussion. I got so absorbed in my argument that we ended up on the outfield grass.

At that point, he turned to me and said, "Now get your ass out of here, and every step is going to cost you."

Well, the umpire couldn't fine me, but my coach did. That home run — or that foul ball, whatever — turned out to be quite educational for me. And I always have to laugh when Uecker jokes about what a lousy player he was.

My wife Virginia was pregnant at this time and was getting a little tired of our moving around from city to city. When I tried out for the Hawks in the NBA, we moved to St. Louis. After the Hawks released me, we moved to Columbia. When I signed the baseball contract, I moved her to Kansas City to be with her parents, while I went to spring training. Later, we both moved to Aberdeen.

The team was on the road in Canada when Sparky called my wife and asked, "Are you tired of moving?"

She had no trouble answering that one.

Sparky said he'd like for me to come back and consider coaching some more at Missouri. Virginia liked the idea; she called me in Canada and left a message.

At that point in my baseball career, I realized I probably wasn't going to make it to the majors. My arm was giving me trouble, and I knew I wasn't good enough. The opportunity to coach now seemed very practical.

I returned to the University of Missouri, coached freshman baseball and basketball, went to school and taught class. I did this all for the tidy sum of $5,000.

Virginia and I moved back to Columbia. There our standard of living in the stucco housing provided for faculty was not much of a step up from Aberdeen. During the summer the air-conditioning would go right through the walls. To make it more comfortable, we would run a water hose on top of the house to cool off the building. Of course, that meant having a yard of mud. In the winter we would have the heat on all day, and the temperature in the house would get up to 70 degrees if we were lucky.

It was a sacrifice, but the benefit was the relationship I continued to build with Sparky Stalcup.

9

Starting Out

Sparky Stalcup's connections and my association with Mr. Iba would be key factors in getting my first head coaching job. And then there was also Wayne Lichty.

Lichty had been a basketball official and was a prominent farmer and businessman in Waterloo, Iowa. When a head coaching job at Iowa State Teacher's College opened up, Lichty arranged an interview for me. The former basketball coach, Jim Witham, was being promoted to athletic director. With Sparky and Iba's help, I was offered the job. I was 26 years old and a head coach. Iowa State Teacher's College later became the State College of Iowa and finally The University of Northern Iowa.

I had a heck of a ballclub my first season. We won our first six non-conference games and passed a couple of good road tests. Here I was just a young coach. I thought I knew something, but I really knew nothing. We won because those players were just tremendous.

Then we started our league play. Our first game was at home against the team that had won the league the year before, South Dakota State, co-favorites with us to win the league. They soon showed us why, beating us on our home floor.

Next we went on the road and played South Dakota and Morningside. We lost to both of them. I was getting quite an indoctrination into the league. In a 12-game race, we were 0-3 to start the season. From that point on, a lot of things stick in my memory.

When we returned home, we came on strong. The guys started doing what they were supposed to in order to succeed. The team won eight games in a row to arrive at 8-3, and wound up in a tie for the conference championship. We played Augustana and beat them in a playoff to go to the NCAA College Division Regionals.

We won our opening-round game, then proceeded to play Nebraska Wesleyan at Nebraska. Our team was up by 10 points with four minutes to go when Nebraska Wesleyan fired back. Our defensive man fell down and a kid shot the ball at the buzzer to win it. Our final record in my inaugural season was 19-5.

The amazing thing about that team was, they were all just five years younger than me. I keep in touch with many of them, and they are good friends.

The next year we came back without one of the school's great players, because Pete Spoden had been suspended. We finished 15-8 that year and second in the conference.

The following year I had a ballclub that put together an incredible record. They went 23-4, two of the losses coming in the last two games. We won our regional in the national tournament and then were defeated by the eventual champion Evansville with Jerry Sloan. They beat us 81-69 in the semifinals, and North Carolina A&T beat us in a game for third place.

At the beginning of the next season, I was approached by Oliver "Hon" Nordly, who had been an outstanding coach at Iowa State Teacher's College.

"I haven't been around very much the first three years of your career," he said, "but I want to come over and watch you this year. I think this will be an important year for you."

"Why do you say that?" I wondered. He had caught my interest because he had coached for thirty years, and I was really curious about what he had to say.

"Well," he said, "I think this year you'll find out whether you want to coach, and whether you can coach. You really don't know if you can coach yet. You have won most of your games. If you lose a few, you'll find out whether you can coach and if you want to coach."

"Man, I really like that," I said. "Why don't you come over here and help me."

He was also the supervisor of officials for the league, so I had to be careful with this relationship, but he liked the idea of helping out, and he and I became great friends.

Nordly was right: The next season was a very important one. I found out that I still loved the game, and that I really loved to coach. We came back and won 16 and lost 7, finishing second in the conference.

The next season wasn't a great one — 13-7 — but I learned an important part of the college game. It was all different back then in Iowa. There were no scholarships, and I learned I had to go recruit.

I started four sophomores my sixth year and they finished 11-11, but that ballclub would later win the championship after I left the team. So I inherited the head coaching job in good shape and I left it in good shape.

After the 1966-67 year, the Missouri head coaching job was up for grabs. They called me, more or less saying, "Just come down and look at it and give us some sort of idea what you think."

I remember driving down to Columbia with Virginia. She was going to meet her former college roommate, Aileen Faurot, while I went in for my interview. Aileen's father, Don Faurot, had a legendary career with the Missouri football program and then became athletic director. But at this time, Dan Devine was coming in as the new athletic director.

After my interview, I remember picking up Virginia and Aileen. "What do you think?" they asked. I told them I had mixed feelings.

"It's almost awful to refuse your alma mater. I have what I think is a good job. But I guess, in the future, this would be a lot better. Plus, it's my old school."

Everything worked out. Spark's influence came into play because he was the assistant athletic director for Faurot and Devine. And, of course, I had coached for 11 years by then, five as an assistant, six as a head coach. I had served my apprenticeship.

The Missouri basketball program had just seen its roughest days when I inherited it in 1967, going 6-43 the two seasons before my arrival. Coach Bob Vanatta won just a handful of games, but he left behind a good crop of freshmen, as well as a player named Gene Jones. Jones would one day become one of my assistants, the first black assistant coach at Mizzou.

I tend to categorize a team three ways. A poor team can't win half of its games. An average team wins half. A good team wins more than half. I always tried to eliminate the possibility of having a poor team.

A combination of factors can give you a poor team. There's illness, injury, ineligibility. You can have an overloaded schedule, or you can fall victim to a rash of bad breaks.

The nucleus of that first team of mine consisted of Jones, who would later be drafted by the Milwaukee Bucks, Dave Bennett, Tom Johnson, Gene Pinkney, Pete Helmbock and Don Tomlinson, another great player. I felt these kids would do all right, maybe win half of their games. For part of the season, it looked like they might.

My coaching debut was a sweet one. We beat Arkansas in Fayetteville 74-58. While Arkansas wasn't a power house that year, it is always difficult to win on their court.

We returned to Columbia for our second game against Indiana. Indiana had its usual good team that year, so I was very pleased when we played respectably against them. We lost 78-69.

We played .500 ball for the first half of the season. We split our conference games and picked up non-league victories against Detroit and Hardin-Simmons.

A big win came in Lawrence, Kansas. The University of Kansas had a excellent team and we were the underdogs. Tom Johnson made two free throws for us at the end of the game for a great 67-66 upset win. Then came victories over Iowa State and Tulane.

There's a great story behind the Tulane game. The players had become accustomed to my pre-game ritual. I don't stay in the dressing room very long, and often leave the players alone a couple of minutes before the opening tip. This particular team assigned Gene Jones as the player to look out the door to see when I was returning. Jones told me this story years later when he was on the coaching staff.

Don Tomlinson had told the players they were not getting in the proper mind set for the game. Some players were clowning around, one in particular, Tom Johnson.

Tomlinson told the players, "Look, the coach doesn't ask us to do very many things. But one of them is, when we get in the dressing room, we get ready to play the game."

Apparently, Johnson didn't heed this warning from Tomlinson, and continued to carry on. Tomlinson said, "Look, I told you to be quiet, so you better be quiet." Johnson continued to mouth off, so Tomlinson hit him, almost knocking him unconscious. The players realized they had to react quickly, because I would be heading back to the dressing room at any time.

As Gene Jones alerted the players I was coming, they sat Tom Johnson up on a bench and put a shoe in his lap and his hands on the shoe. I noticed all the players were very quiet when I walked in and I saw Johnson staring at his shoe. I didn't really think much about it, so I turned around and left.

Jones told me they put Johnson in the shower to get him to snap out of his trance-like state. I started him, not knowing anything had happened. Johnson then went on to score about 20 points. For a guy who was just punched in the mouth, he played a tremendous game.

At this point we were 8-9, and I thought we might at least break even for the season. Then we lost seven games in a row. Four of those we easily could have won had the breaks gone our way. It seemed like every game was a last-second or an overtime loss.

But our players didn't lie down for the remainder of the season. We went on the road to Oklahoma State and beat them 60-58 after they had trounced us in Columbia. Then we finished off the season on a great note with a win over Nebraska at home. Nebraska had a sound team coached by Joe Cipriano. The final score was 91-70, giving us a 5-9 record in the conference; it just as easily could have been 9-5. We felt really good about finishing the season with two big wins, and we had some good players returning.

A new optimism took over the program. The coaches could feel it, the players could feel it, the fans could feel it. Everyone was excited about the basketball program again. We started playing before full houses, 5,800 fans packed into Brewer Fieldhouse. At the end of the season, they decided to throw a basketball banquet beginning a tradition we carry on to this day. It is one of the biggest events of the year for our program.

"It's a hell of a deal," Coach Stalcup quipped. "You win ten games and they're giving you a banquet. I won ten games once and they hung me in effigy."

Of course, Sparky virtually always had a winning year. Success tends to make the fans intolerant of anything less.

"Spark," I explained, "It's timing. You have to understand timing."

We began to add a key player here, a key player there. David Pike comes to mind. Pike was a junior college player about 5-9 or 5-10, but he was a winner. We recruited another junior college player — another winner — Henry Smith. When Pike and Smith played on teams, those teams won; I was counting on that bit of history to repeat itself when they played for us.

With Pike in the lineup his first year, the 1968-69 season, the transformation from a losing program to a winning one continued. Once again we opened the season with a big victory at Arkansas, 60-59. We started out 7-3, our only losses coming against Big Ten teams Indiana and Northwestern on the road and against Oklahoma State in Kansas City. We had turned the corner.

We managed only one more win on the road that season, but it was a memorable victory in Kansas.

We were big underdogs, and before the game, I said to my assistant that if we were to lose, at least we were going to have some fun. I told my captain, Tomlinson, to go to Kansas coach Ted Owens and request the end of the floor the Jayhawks were practicing on.

"Do that, and they'll beat us even worse," my assistant said.

Tomlinson carried out his orders to the letter. He went up to Coach Owens, and with his best Southeastern grin, told him he was the captain of the Missouri Tigers, and he would like to request the end of the floor that the Jayhawks were practicing on.

This was before the crowd came in, so I sneaked under the bleachers and watched Tomlinson carry out his instructions. Ted was very angry, but he moved his team as requested. I laughed so hard.

"By God, they'll beat us by 50 points," my assistant said.

It didn't happen. Tomlinson made two free throws at the end of the game, and we beat them by one.

The other road games were just as close. Three of our conference losses came in overtime on the road. Yet we still finished the season 14-11.

With the addition of Hank Smith in the 1969-70 season, I was thinking big. Everyone else picked us about sixth in the conference, but I thought we could win it. The first half of the season made it look like my confidence wasn't so crazy.

We beat Arkansas and Indiana at home and a solid Texas A&M team on the road. Then in the first round of the preseason Big Eight Tournament, we defeated Iowa State by two points. We were 8-2 going into our second-round game against Colorado, the conference winner the previous season.

It was another one of those heartbreaking defeats. We lost 75-73, but the conference noticed us. We were a team to be reckoned with.

We lost a couple of one- and two-point games in the second half of the season on our way to a 15-11 year. The 15-win season was an improvement from the previous year, but we had the same players back from that year, and we had added Smith. I was disappointed, however, I had to admit it was a much better season than anyone — anyone but me, that is — had predicted.

I remember one of the problems that year pertained to the players' wives. Four of our kids were married, and their wives fought all the time. It was an unfortunate sidelight to the season, which I think carried over to the players. Although they were a great bunch of people, the wives just didn't understand what their husbands were going through.

I adopted a new rule after that season: Don't recruit a married player.

10
A Super Tiger

With Smith returning, along with some other fine players, I knew we could contend. But the real key to our next season came down to the addition of a player named John Brown.

Brown was the first big-name high school prospect I recruited. He had an absolutely tremendous prep career, leading his Dixon High School team to an undefeated record and the Missouri state championship. There was quite a recruiting war for Brown's talents.

I tried to find out all there was to know about John Brown. Whatever insight I could learn about his life, I tried to use to our advantage. Many people from around the state showed an interest in getting Brown to Mizzou, including the governor.

Brown eventually had me on my hands and knees — literally. After one trip to Dixon, I couldn't walk upright because of intense back pain. I remember crawling through my front yard. I crawled to the door and took the key out of my pocket. I opened the door, crawled into the living room, then into the bedroom. While lying on the floor, I took my clothes off and actually climbed into bed. I didn't sleep very well, and I called the doctor the next morning.

This all led to surgery, but it was worth it: It also led to the signing of John Brown.

Brown came to the hospital with his mom and maybe his sister. With the television crews there, he announced that he was coming to the University of Missouri. Brown may have felt some sympathy for me, but I was willing to have surgery again if it meant signing someone like John.

He would bring us to another level. Freshmen weren't allowed to play at that time, but if they had been, John would have started. He had that much talent.

We would never lose ten games in a season with John. We went 17-9 his sophomore year, 21-6 his junior year and 21-6 his senior year. Brown became Missouri's first-ever first-round draft choice, in both the NBA and the ABA.

We started out like gangbusters during his sophomore season, winning seven of our first eight games. When the conference tournament rolled around we were very confident. But our hopes were shot down in the first round against Kansas which handed us one of my worst defeats, 96-63. Kansas had a tremendous team that year and would finish the conference 14-0. We still completed our conference season with a respectable 9-5 record, our best conference mark in 15 years.

In Brown's junior year, we won 12 of our first 13 games. Our only loss was a four-point game against Kentucky on their court. We swept the Big Eight preseason tournament for the first time. We went 21-6, the first time a Missouri team won more than 20 games. We finished second to Kansas State in the Big Eight, missing out on a berth in the NCAA. But our record attracted an invitation to the NIT, where we put on a great showing in our opener before losing to St. John's 82-81.

Brown surprised me one year by announcing that he was thinking about leaving Missouri. When I asked why, he explained his background; his mother worked in a factory. He couldn't stand it any more, and he wanted to help her. A smaller school in Missouri was offering him a quick fix. Brown mentioned $30,000, a job, and a car. For a guy 19 or 20 years old, this was an enticing offer.

I combated it the only way I could. I told him what his goals should be if he stayed at Missouri.

"You could make the 1972 Olympic team," I said to him.

I knew he was that good, plus Mr. Iba, who was in the Big Eight, was going to coach the U.S. team.

"You will be more highly recognized at Missouri and get a

better education. You can come out of this a No. 1 draft choice. At a smaller school, the competition is not as good, and it doesn't always bring out the best in you. It can be done, but it takes more motivation."

Brown elected to stay, and all of those things I said came true.

I remember getting the news that he had made the 1972 Olympic team. I was in Brazil for a basketball clinic, in a town near the equator. It was arranged for a ham radio operator to help me call another ham radio operator in Rolla, Missouri. A storm came in and they told me if I saw any lightning, I was to take off the earphones immediately. With those instructions in mind, I strained to hear the details of how John Brown had made the Olympic team.

A foot injury would prevent him from participating, but it didn't detract from the honor.

I made up my mind that I would never counter an attempt to steal one of our players with anything but the facts. Besides, even if I wanted to, I doubt I could come up with $30,000. It's a lot of money, even by today's standards. If I was going to stay in the coaching profession — and I wanted to remain in it as long as I could — I would select the means for building my team and keeping it together, and it would not involve any $30,000 offers.

Nonetheless, it upset me to think a guy would offer to buy a kid. That method and means are unattractive to me. I always thought the offer of an education — an offer that is legally and ethically sound — should be a pretty potent lure.

One of our best teams ever was during Brown's senior year, the 1972-73 season. We had Brown and Al Eberhard, another future first-round draft choice, at the forward spots. Mike Griffin and Greg Flaker were our guards. Mike Jeffries was the sixth man. If not for a preseason injury to center Bob Allen, there's no telling how far this team could have gone. Allen, who had averaged 13 points and 10 rebounds the previous year, had really come along in the off-season, but then he injured himself while getting in shape.

Sharing the spotlight with the team that season was our new arena, the Hearnes Center. Instead of 5,800 fans cramming into Brewer Fieldhouse, Hearnes could hold more than 13,000. It took some time to get the fans to fill it up. Hearnes can accommodate 5,800 people in the bottom two rings, and nobody wanted to sit higher up, because they didn't want what they thought was poor seating.

"You show me a place with more than 5,000 seats and I'll show you a place with high seats," I told them. "Somebody's got to sit there."

It was kind of unfortunate really, that our '72-73 ballclub, one of the best ever, one of the top ten teams in the country, averaged under 10,000 fans with a 13,000-seat arena. Then in 1975-76, with maybe the best Missouri ballclub on record, a team that made it to the final eight, we averaged under 6,000 fans. I thought this was sad.

Although it did take a while, the new $11 million facility eventually elevated the program. It is a nice athletic facility, and is much more than just a basketball arena. Only recently have we begun to fill it to capacity.

We put together a string of 12 victories to begin the season in 1972, including impressive wins against Purdue, Ohio State and Holy Cross. The national spotlight now shined upon us. Each week we crept a little higher in the ratings, No. 10 one week, then No. 5.

We won the Big Eight Classic championship by defeating a nationally ranked Kansas State team. Al Eberhard played one of his best games as a Tiger in the championship, scoring 33 points, and was voted the tournament MVP. Eberhard stood 6-5, but his defensive skills were good enough for us to put him on guys much taller. He handled Oklahoma's 6-9 Alvan Adams, and we gave him some minutes against Kansas State's 7-0 Steve Mitchell.

Eberhard was the epitome of the player who gives you every ounce of effort. Even today, though he's about 40 years old, he'll dive on concrete for a ball in a pickup game.

The greatest emotional story I have ever been associated with involves Al in a Big Eight Tournament game. He had a huge ankle. He sat up all night, getting iced every hour to try to reduce the swelling. We went over to practice and he couldn't even walk.

"Al," I told him, "we have already won this tournament in years past. This game is important, but let the other guys try to win it. Let's let your ankle rest so we can win the regular season."

"Let's wait until tonight," Al said. "I'll keep taking treatments."

So Al suits up for the game.

"Al, I'm not going to play you," I said. "Why don't you sit down and watch."

"Well, look," he said. "I've had these before. I know myself. If I run a little bit, it will loosen up."

"OK. You take a layup, and I'll watch." I swear, he couldn't even hobble. I said, "Come here. Sit down. This is stupid. Just sit down and watch; we'll be all right."

"No," he said. "Didn't you see me loosening up? It's starting to feel much better."

"You can't even walk."

But he wouldn't give up. He made another run at it and, by golly, it looked like it was loosening up. He somehow withstood the pain and he ran.

I think he scored 26 points in that game. It was the most courageous thing I have ever seen.

The Eberhards are a tough breed. Al's dad, Marvin, is a country guy, a hog farmer. They cut hogs, holding them up and castrating them in a matter of seconds. The hogs bite them and put up a hell of a fight, but they just cut one, and then grab another one.

Al had a summer job once rebuilding a clubhouse that had burned down. They had to tear out several posts and some old baling wire. Al cut his arm on the job once, and his supervisor, Tommy Stone, who was leery about hiring athletes because some of them wouldn't do any work, told him to go see a doctor. But Al just reached down, tore his T-shirt off, wrapped it around his arm and went ahead working.

Marvin used to play his son on a cement court they built on their farm house. They'd knock each other down on the cement, then pick one another up and keep playing. They are really close.

After Al's big game in the tournament with the swollen ankle, Marvin, who knew what he had been through, came back to the hotel where his son was staying. Marvin saw his son in the shower, walked inside and embraced him. In all my years as a coach, I can't recall a more emotional moment than that one.

Al works with the Missouri Governor's Office on the Council for Physical Fitness, and just recently was hired as the head of a new development program within the athletic department. Al will be a great representative. Marvin and Al's mother, Hazel, still come to the games.

We placed four guys on the all-tournament team in the

1972-73 season. Eberhard, Brown and Jeffries made first team. Orv Salmon, a guard, put in a scrappy performance and made second team.

We reached No. 5 in the UPI poll after a squeaky one-point win over Southern Methodist in Dallas. Brown passed me up on the list of all-time Missouri scorers in that game, and he made the winning basket as time ran out. But the game was won only after a big controversy.

SMU had a great player in Ira Terrell. They weren't ranked, but they were capable of beating anybody on their home court.

We entered their arena a couple of hours before the game, checked out the surroundings, familiarized ourselves with the court. I like to talk to the people at the scorer's table. More often than not, I would find myself at the table sometime during a game, so it was a good idea to meet the folks who worked there.

I met the timer and joked, "If we're behind, are you going to give us a fast clock? And if we're ahead, are you going to give us a slow clock?"

He laughed and said, "Coach Stewart, I want you to know that I'm from Marshall, Missouri, and I'll do as good as I can."

We led the entire game until the final minute. We're up by one point with 20 seconds left when SMU calls a timeout. I told our players that if they scored with less than 10 seconds in the game, we would immediately call a timeout. I told one of our players to tell the referees what we intended to do so they'd be looking for it.

They took the ball inbounds and ran the clock down to about eight seconds. Ira Terrell hit a little jumper on the right side, and they took the lead for the first time in the game.

I looked up at the clock and saw :08 left in the game when he shot it. Our guys called timeout like we planned. I look up again and the clock is still running. I'm going crazy. It goes all the way down to :00, and so the game (as far as the clock is concerned) is over.

I stomped on over to the scorer's table and said, "Wait a minute. They shot with eight seconds. We have some time left."

The officials decided we had two seconds left.

"Two seconds?"

"Coach, we're giving you two," the ref said.

"Well, I'll take the two."

During our timeout, we set up a play. I told my players that if we tried to throw the ball the length of the court, it would probably be batted out to end the game.

"Let's set up for one long shot. Throw in a shorter pass, and maybe get off one good shot."

Basketball players are always practicing the long shot before they begin a workout. This was one of those times where it could really pay off.

"Who can hit the long shot?" I asked.

For some reason, I picked this kid out, Steve Blind. I don't know whatever possessed me. About the only other thing I remember him for is leaving the team after alleged misconduct. But I picked him that night because something told me he could make the shot.

The clock is reset for two seconds; it won't begin, of course, until the ball touches a player inbounds. We throw the ball from under the SMU basket to the halfcourt line. Blind fumbles it, chases it down, bounces it once, and puts up an off-balance shot. Now I'm thinking the two seconds were up before Blind shot the ball. The ball doesn't go anywhere near the rim, and I'm thinking, game over.

But John Brown, who won't give up, runs over, grabs the ball out of the air about four feet away from the basket and throws it in, all in one motion.

You know that all of this takes longer than two seconds.

I looked up at the referee and he says it is good. I run out and hustle my players off the court.

"Let's go to the dressing room!"

As we did, a good friend of mine, Larry Lange, was with me. I knew Larry when I was in Iowa. As we ran off the court, a guy tried to hit me, but Larry beat him to the punch. As Larry turned around, another guy kicked him in the rear end, catching Larry in mid-air. So as we are running to the dressing room, Larry is suddenly airborne and he's flying by me.

When we got in the dressing room, Larry was laughing, explaining the whole situation to me. Meanwhile, the SMU fans weren't laughing. People pounded on our door for 45 minutes.

The basket counted, I found out later, because the timekeeper from Marshall, Missouri, forgot to reset the horn when he put the two seconds back on the clock. When time ran out, he didn't punch the horn, and there was nothing he could do about it.

Some people thought we should give the game back, but we didn't because we won the game. They took a few seconds away from us, and then they gave them back. Justice served.

You'll have games won and lost on calls now and then. It's the nature of the game. I don't like commenting on officiating, and as a rule I don't. We've had our share of calls go against us; we've had a number go our way. I don't think people want to hear excuses. I think they'd rather hear, "Well, we got beat by a better team."

I've made it a policy not to talk about officials because you'll say things after a game that ten minutes afterwards you'd like to swallow.

I have a similar rule about not turning in another school. I think your first reaction when you lose in recruiting is to say "they cheated." I think it's better to just let it drop. I figure if the other school cheated and the player accepted that, then I don't want that player in my program anyway. If he is willing to take a big short cut, then I don't want him around.

If you think someone has cheated, just go out and get another player. Some people seem to think a lot of terrible activities go on in recruiting, but I'm not so sure. Our program has been accused of doing some things, too. I've heard some disgusting stories, however, I'm still not convinced it goes on as much as people say. While you hear a lot, you can't prove it. Life is too short.

I think some people need to cheat, and some people need to worry about others cheating. One year, some Big Eight coaches were talking about another coach in the league. Jack Hartman and Joe Cipriano thought this coach had given a player a car.

"Wait a minute," I said. "What's the difference between a coach giving a car and another coach giving players a ride home or clothes?"

They said giving clothes and a ride wasn't as bad. They said that was a misdemeanor and what the other coach was allegedly doing was a felony. I understand this type of reasoning, but you shouldn't give a player something outside the rules, regardless of what it is, to induce him to attend a school.

I said, "Well, that's just by your definition. My definition is yours is a felony, because I don't give my players clothes and a ride home."

They said practically all coaches give players clothes and transportation. I told them I don't.

At the time of this conversation, Oklahoma State wasn't doing very well, so I said, "Maybe Oklahoma State ought to get to cheat two or three times, real big. You can't get anyone to go to Stillwater." Today, I'm sure with their recent success that the people in Stillwater are not having trouble recruiting athletes to come to their school.

Now I could use the example of Kansas State in football, another program that's been struggling. They ought to let K-State have three major violations so they can get even. Just kidding, folks. This is only a joke.

Unfortunately, in basketball the joke is, the NCAA always goes after the wrong schools. As Abe Lemon once put it, "The NCAA was so mad at Kentucky, they gave Grambling two more years of probation."

To return to the 1972-73 season, the win over SMU put us near the top of the national rankings. One of John Wooden's UCLA teams — they had Bill Walton that year — was No. 1. Maryland, Marquette and North Carolina State were the other teams ahead of us.

The conference season began and soon things got a little out of kilter for us. Like every year it was tough winning on the road in the conference. We lost four conference games on the road, as well as one at home in overtime against Colorado. This was our only loss in 13 games at the Hearnes Center that year.

Because of our difficulty on the road, we finished third in the Big Eight, eliminating our chances at the NCAA despite an overall 21-5 record.

The NIT invited us for the second year in a row, and for the second year in a row, we lost in the first round. Massachusetts beat us 78-71.

John Brown's mother came to New York for the NIT. She told me she remembered telling John a few years earlier, when he was considering leaving Missouri, "Whatever Coach Stewart tells you to do, do it." That meant a lot to me.

John was an All-American, destined to become a first-rounder. The timing was perfect for him: The NBA and the ABA were getting in a bidding war over the top players. Atlanta picked him in the NBA first round, and San Antonio took him in the ABA.

A funny thing happened then: San Antonio came to me and offered me their coaching job. At first I thought it was an effort to lure John Brown, but they showed me that it wasn't. They offered me a three-year deal, $35,000 the first year, $40,000 the second, $45,000 the third.

I didn't feel I was ready to coach in professional basketball. Plus, I really wanted to stay on the college scene. Anyway, the money they offered me was almost what I was making at Missouri, if you counted the 17 other jobs I was doing.

John, meanwhile, signed a contract with Atlanta for more than a million dollars. He earned it; he was somebody you wanted to see it happen to. It also didn't hurt our recruiting to tell prospects that our program produced one of the top six or seven college players in the nation.

11
The Magic Returns

After John Brown left, we fell off a bit, finishing the 1973-74 season 12-14. We started out at 10-3, but when the conference season began, we took it on the chin.

Still, Al Eberhard made the season memorable. He was an excellent senior. We gave him all three awards at the end of the year: Sparky Stalcup's Inspirational Award, the George Edwards Achievement Award and Most Valuable Player.

During the 1974-75 season, the magic returned, thanks to "Magic Man" Willie Smith. Willie had a terrific high school career at Edward W. Clark High School in Las Vegas, then played junior college ball. We recruited Willie with the help of a basketball official I had been associated with years ago.

In the late '50s, I was asked to officiate a high school basketball game. Not just any game, mind you. It was a game to determine who would go to the finals of the state tournament. The schools involved were great rivals: Jefferson City versus Jefferson City Helias, the public school versus the parochial school. I was told that I would be working with Buford Goddard, one of the best basketball officials in the state.

Some people at the University of Missouri were worried that I might make a controversial call that could upset a potential

77

recruit and wanted me to refuse. But I accepted the offer as a challenge.

When Buford and I got through the first half we walked off the court together. I told him, "I have a good game going, so when we get out there in the second half, don't screw it up."

I was joking, of course. Buford was such a high-caliber official he was about to jump to the collegiate level.

Naturally, it turned out to be a close one, and Goddard and I called a hell of a game. It came down to the final seconds, a one-point game, decided on a last-second bucket. When it was over, we shook hands, and we knew in our hearts we had done a good job.

The Big Eight called on Goddard to officiate a little later, so our paths would cross again. We ran into one another once and were talking about college basketball.

"You know," Goddard said, "there's this guard at a junior college in Oklahoma, and he's just what you need. He's a leader and he can play some defense. But he can't shoot."

I sent assistant Dan McCleary to Seminole Junior College to look at Willie Smith. After he saw him play, McCleary thought we might be interested in Willie, so I scheduled a trip to watch the National Junior College Tournament when our season was over. Willie's team wasn't playing, but I would meet him there.

Gene Hawk coached Willie, and that was a big plus for us — Hawk had played for Mr. Iba.

When I met Willie in Hutchinson, Kansas, he approached me wearing a fur coat, and he had some kind of apparel on his head. When I walked up to Willie, he started giving me some unorthodox handshake. The soul shake was in vogue then.

"Willie, I don't have time for that," I said. "I don't understand it, I just don't know anything about it. I'm here to talk about you coming to the University of Missouri to play basketball."

Apparently I struck a good note with him; he told me he thought I was honest. I wasn't going into any rigmarole to impress him or pretend that I knew all about black culture. Willie said he was signing a letter of intent to come to Missouri.

I still recruit the same way I recruited Willie. He's a great example of how you don't have to cheat to get a player. It's a pleasure to meet a kid's parents and help him make one of the most important decisions in his life. If other schools were going to play dirty, I would rather lose games than get down to that level.

In September, our assistant Gene Jones walks into my office and says, "I got a phone call from Willie Smith."

"Yeah? What did he want?" I said. "What do you think he wants?" Gene then started to laugh.

I said, "You tell Willie Smith that if he wants to play for Norm Stewart, either get on the damn highway and hitchhike, or take a bus. He's getting here on his own."

Gene laughed again, and said, "Well, I knew that's the way it was going to be."

Three days later, here comes Willie Smith.

During the first three days of practice I was disappointed. The way Willie was performing was not good enough to cut it. I called Dan McCleary in Houston where he had started a new career in financial counseling. I gave McCleary a lot of static, telling him that it was a good thing he had quit, because after seeing Willie in practice for two or three days, I might have fired him.

When the season opened, Willie began averaging 20 points a game. Dan called me from Houston and said, "Would you be hiring me back by now?"

I told Dan that Willie was really a great player and that he was going to get better. The funny thing was, we recruited him as a defensive guard and a leader, and he did both just as we had hoped. But when we showed him all he had to do was tuck in his left elbow when he shot, he became a heck of a shooter, too. Willie's scoring average would top all others in school history.

His junior year we went 18-9. We played in an offshoot postseason tournament, the National Collegiate Commissioner's Tournament, where we lost to Purdue 87-74. Despite that disappointment, we looked forward to Willie's senior year. The "Magic Man" had brought winning back to the program.

The 1975-76 year was another special season. Willie Smith, Kim Anderson, Jim Kennedy, Jeff Currie, James Clabon and Scott Sims were big contributors. But Willie was the headliner. It was not uncommon to see him score 30 points in a game.

Willie put on a great show against Toledo in the second game of the season. He sank a shot from halfcourt at the first-half buzzer. Willie kept us in the ball game during regulation and he put our team ahead for good in overtime. He wound up with 30 points.

We went to 6-0 after an easy win over South Dakota State. Willie dazzled the crowd with an assortment of great one-on-one moves during that game. He racked up another 30 points.

UCLA knocked us down a notch with an 83-71 win on their court, and then we traveled to Hawaii. Jet lag may have played a part in our splitting two games with the University of Hawaii; we should have won both of them. We didn't play with our usual intensity. But Jim Kennedy played a superb game to lead us in our win there, scoring 28 points.

In the Big Eight Preseason Tournament, we played like the team I knew. We swept by Oklahoma State, Kansas State and Kansas for the title and brought our record to 10-2. Willie captured the tournament MVP award.

By now we had run up an 11-game winning streak and reached 17-2. You had to go back to the 1920s to find a Tiger team that had started off this well.

Smith's heroics — a basket with 12 seconds remaining — gave us a one-point victory against Oklahoma State, 72-71. Our record climbed to 19-3.

We started to feel confident about winning the conference. Missouri hadn't had a share of the league title in 35 years and hadn't won it outright in 46.

Kim Anderson kept us in the Big Eight race by sparking us to a 95-84 overtime win over Nebraska. He scored 25 points, had 14 rebounds and led the way in the overtime with a flurry of points. He took the spotlight away from Smith, who still managed 31 points.

The spotlight returned to Willie in our win over Kansas State in Manhattan. He was absolutely phenomenal, scoring 38 points. The win gave us a tie for the conference lead.

I had told Willie about an old play where you throw the ball inbounds off the back of a defensive player, step inbounds and catch it before he wakes up, and put it in the basket. He executed the play to perfection. After the game Willie asked me, "Where did you learn that play, Coach? In the professional ranks?"

"No," I said, "the little town of Shelbyville. It's one of those things they teach you: Never turn your back on the ball."

There was an amusing sidelight to this victory involving my mother. The game was televised regionally, and my mother was watching it back in Shelbyville. When it ended, I was at an emotional high: I had coached a team that clinched at least a tie for the Big Eight championship and had a chance to win it outright for the first time in almost half a century.

As I walked off the floor, the cameras on me, I ran into Susan Reiter. Her husband Bob, a former teammate of mine and a leading scorer for Missouri, had died of leukemia within the past year. Bob and I had become very good friends after our playing days, and Virginia and I would socialize with them. As I walked off the floor, Susan was the first person I saw, along with her son.

It occurred to me how your life can be filled with such highs and lows. She had just been through a traumatic time, but she was there and happy for me. She came up to me and we hugged one another. So when I came home from the game and my mother called to congratulate me, at the end of the conversation she asked, "Who was that girl you were hugging?"

I've always teased my mom so I said, "Oh, mom, I have a girl in every town. That was just a girl in Manhattan who always comes to the games." I figured she knew I was joking, so I let it drop.

The next day my mother called me back, and again after talking about the game, she asked, "Now who is that girl?"

At this point I became a little peeved and I told her the truth. I guess the way we were brought up in our family, you didn't embrace anyone but your wife, your sister or your mother. I had always been subdued in my reactions until this win at Kansas State. Here I was 40 years old, and my mother was really curious about who I had hugged after a game.

The big win came over Colorado. We clinched the championship, ending many years of frustration and earning an automatic berth into the NCAA. We'd had clubs that came close, that should have been there, but this club was the first one for me. For that reason, it was a very special team.

The NCAA field that year consisted of 32 teams compared with today's 64. You only had to win one game to make it to the Sweet Sixteen. If you won three games, you became one of the Final Four. Making the NCAA Tournament was much more of a distinction back then.

When the NCAA Tournament began in 1939, I think they only allowed nine teams. Even in the 1960s only about 20 teams were selected. You couldn't get into the tournament unless you won your league. It was hard to get in, and the NIT wasn't easy to get into either.

What made the 1975-76 year even more special was the involvement of C.J. Kessler, my old high school coach. I would sometimes have him on the bench with me during those early years.

One year we played in Columbia in the final game of the regular season. It was 1970-71, when we just started to really compete. We had a chance to go to the NIT if we won the game. Kessler was on the bench.

"How long have you coached?" I asked him.

"About thirty years."

"That's a long time," I said. "You know, if we win this game, I've been thinking, we'll need somebody to go to New York just to make all the accommodations and do all the scouting."

Kessler was scouting teams back when Shelbyville went to the state high school tournament. He would sometimes send a friend of his from Indiana, Pat Patterson, to do the scouting. I was really impressed that he would go to such a length in high school to prepare for a tournament game. Not too many coaches did that back then.

I turned to Kessler again and said, "We're going to need someone in New York to watch my team and really take care of things. You know, make sure there's enough ice in the bucket after the games, things like that."

Kessler really hadn't responded much in the past when I talked to him about coaching, and how important I thought a game was. But when I started to include him, saying that he was probably going to go to New York with us, he edged up on the front of his seat. A different look came over his face. It was like a current going through his body, and he said, "Damn, we gotta win this game!"

Well, we didn't win that game. We lost it in overtime, 71-69, and we didn't get selected for the NIT. But from then on, when we had good teams, like the 1975-76 team, I'd ask Kessler to come down and watch them.

Kessler came several times in '75-76. He watched a game or two in Columbia during the middle of the season, and he returned at the end of the season when we were about to win the Big Eight championship.

He walked into the dressing room right before the Colorado game, the one we needed to win to take the conference outright. I'll never forget what he told the players:

"You know, I was with you in the beginning of the season, and helped you get started. I came back and checked you out in the middle of the season. And now I'm here to watch you win the championship. And I didn't come to watch a loser."

We simply creamed Colorado, 95-60.

We didn't know just how good we were that year. We knew we had a fine team, but it's always hard to tell how far a team will go.

We beat Washington 69-67 in the first round of the NCAA to jump into the Sweet Sixteen. We beat Texas Tech 86-75 in the second round to advance to the regional finals.

Now we went up against Johnny Orr's Michigan team. Rickey Green was a star for the Wolverines that year. We played in Freedom Hall in Louisville, Kentucky; a win there would put us in the Final Four for the first time.

I sequestered the players in a meeting room and got Kessler on the phone. He talked with several of them. I felt this was something that could enhance our chances for success, and I wanted Kessler to feel like he was part of our success, despite his not being there with us.

Willie Smith just dazzled the crowd in Louisville. He led a dramatic comeback after we fell 17 points down in the first half. We took a five-point lead with about seven minutes left in the game, but some missed free throws down the stretch really cost us and we lost.

Smith ended his career at Missouri with a bang, scoring 43 points, just three shy of breaking the school record. In my opinion, Willie was the best guard in the country.

I was sorry to lose the game, of course, but I think I may have been more disappointed for Kessler's sake than my own. I'm glad he got to share in our glory, anyway. He made a lasting impact on many lives.

Kessler had the marvelous ability to get people to accept one another. He knew how important it was for someone to be accepted and recognized. I can remember him in Shelbyville bringing a student into class and acknowledging her because she was the best at shorthand. Another person was praised before the class when his scholastic efforts won him a trip to Chicago.

Kessler knew how to build up a person's confidence. We all know what reward does for us, and as a superintendent, he built that into the school system.

Every now and then, the people he touched would throw a dinner for him, C.J. Kessler Night. Never any invitations, it was just word-of-mouth. I was astonished by the number of people who showed up from all over the country. People came from Alaska, Florida, and California.

The first time they did this was after Kessler's retirement. I was at Northern Iowa, and they asked me to come down and speak. About 500 people showed up. Doesn't sound like a big crowd, you say? Well, remember, there were only 600 people in the whole community.

The last time they threw a party for him, I was coaching at Missouri, and another 400 or 500 people attended. He had touched a lot of lives.

The last time I saw him, he was in a nursing home in Quincy, Illinois. I don't think he recognized me except for a brief instant. As much as I loved Kessler, I didn't want to see him anymore. Selfishly, I just wanted to remember him as the vibrant person he had been, and the excitement we shared during the 1975-76 season. He just recently passed away.

We still had Kim Anderson, Jim Kennedy and Scott Sims returning to Mizzou the next season. They put in a great season for us — all three were drafted by the pros — and we finished 21-8. The highlights that season included beating Illinois in the Show-Me Classic by one point, and winning the Big Eight Conference Preseason Tournament. We finished the regular season in a tie for second in the Big Eight, so we missed out on the NCAA.

After the 1976-77 season, we hit another lull. The next two seasons were down years.

The 1977-78 season was a strange one. We finished sixth in the conference, but the Big Eight had started playing a postseason tournament to determine the automatic NCAA berth. To everyone's surprise, we swept the postseason tournament and earned a berth in the NCAA with a 14-15 record. Someone in the Eastern press said we were like a mule in the Kentucky Derby.

The Missouri mules provided some excitement in the first round of the Midwest Regional. It took two overtimes for Utah to beat us 86-79.

I served on a committee that formulated the idea of moving to a postseason Big Eight Tournament. By moving the tournament to the postseason, we picked up two more regular season games at home. The administrators liked the idea because it saved money. On top of that, the ACC was very successful with its postseason tournament.

In 1978-79, our team once again won less than half of our games, but we almost took the Big Eight Tournament for the second year in a row.

This was the second season in a row where we played both a preseason and a postseason tournament, so it was possible to play a Big Eight team four times. This particular season, Jim Killingsworth's Oklahoma State team beat me the first three times, and we were faced with playing him a fourth time in the postseason tourney.

I remember talking to him before the fourth contest. I said, "Killer, I want you to do me a favor. If you beat me again tonight, will you allow me one more chance. We could go upstairs to the practice gym and play one more game, and I know damn good and well you can't beat me five times in a row."

Fortunately, they did not beat us. We beat Killingsworth on our court in Columbia, but we lost in the tournament semifinals to Kansas in Kansas City by three points. We came close to gaining another NCAA berth with a .500 record.

Instead we finished the season 13-15. It would be my last losing season. The decade of the 80s produced some wonderful players and Missouri teams.

12

The Stipanovich-Sundvold Era

The St. Louis media make a big fuss when we don't have a player from St. Louis. On the one hand, yes, I agree, we should have a player or two from the biggest city in the state. On the other hand, if you look at the players that came up through St. Louis and count the big-time college players, there just haven't been that many for that population.

We got the best in Steve Stipanovich. The 7-footer would help lead us to four consecutive conference titles. Other teams in the Big Eight recruited big men just to match up against him.

We were coming off two losing years, but the nucleus of a good team was returning for 1979-80. We had Larry Drew and Ricky Frazier, perhaps the best competitor we ever had, and another great freshman recruit named Jon Sundvold.

Stipanovich had a tremendous career at DeSmet High School, a private Jesuit school. I watched Steve throughout his high school career and saw him play practically every game. I observed personal as well as athletic growth between his sophomore and junior years, the only summer he attended my basketball camp. As I watched him, everything seemed to fit. He was what we needed. We knew we would have an outstanding team with him on it.

By the time his senior season began, every basketball fan at Missouri knew who Stipanovich was, and wanted him to be a Tiger. The Antlers, a student cheering group, came out with a button that said, "I love Stipo." It was the students' idea, not ours, but as a result, the NCAA made a rule prohibiting buttons like that for recruiting. It's one of those peculiar rules I find hard to understand.

This was a fun time for the basketball program. We would take a group of people to see one of Steve's high school games, driving in buses and reserving seats so there would be space in the gym for us.

The rules weren't so strict then, therefore we could see a lot of Steve. I even went to every one of his all-star games so he could not have any doubt about our interest in him. Now you can see just so many games and go to so many practices.

His was a fun recruitment, not a pain. Steve and I got off to a good start because we could talk, with no malarkey. We were going to do everything possible to get Steve, but not in an underhanded manner; we didn't have to offer anything else. We still maintain a good relationship with Steve's mother and father.

The high school had a rule about visiting practice: We could see him just once a week. When we showed up, we'd see coaches from Notre Dame, UCLA, North Carolina, and Kentucky. I remember seeing Digger Phelps of Notre Dame there. I think Digger always thought he was going to get Stipanovich.

Dean Smith called me one day in the middle of all of this. He asked, "What do you really feel about Steve Stipanovich? Will he actually come to your place?"

"We have not lost a player of his stature since I came to Missouri," I told him. "If we do our work properly, he will come."

From that point on, North Carolina really stopped recruiting Steve, except for what we call "maintenance work." If Steve started looking elsewhere, they would still have their hat in the ring.

Kentucky tried hard to get Steve. All their people attended one ball game, including Joe Hall, the head coach. It was really quite a show.

I think I won over his relatives at one of his all-star games, the Dapper Dan Classic in Pittsburgh. Steve has a lot of relatives in the Pittsburgh area, and as far as they were concerned, they had to approve of Coach Stewart if Steve was going to go to Missouri.

The morning of the Dapper Dan we met at a motel. I'm thinking about how Steve is going to do in the ball game, but his relatives had their own game plan: They were checking me out.

They began drinking boilermakers, a shot of beer and a shot of whiskey, a popular drink in Pittsburgh.

"I don't make a habit of drinking whiskey in the morning," I said, "But I will have a beer with you."

We stayed and talked basketball for three or four hours. We had some laughs, some good conversation, talking about all the teams Steve played on and everything he had already experienced in his career. All the while, they drank boilermakers and I drank beer. I'm sure they thought, "Ole Norm, he can fit in. He'll be all right. He can handle Steve."

Steve came to me at the end of a high school tournament in Columbia after his senior year.

"Coach," he said, "I'm thinking about coming to Missouri. But I want to make sure you know my family and their background. I work hard at basketball and school, but my family likes to have a good time."

I said, "Just as long as it is in the framework of moderation. Our family does the same thing. That should be the least of your problems."

We had a banquet in Columbia with about 200 people paying for their own dinner, all to help recruit Steve. These were folks who didn't necessarily have a lot of money, but they could give their time. They got a big kick out of seeing recruiting at this level. We made sure that just about every situation was in control and had everyone who could influence Steve on our side.

I think it all boiled down to these factors: We made a great effort to recruit Steve, his parents could see him play, and he could accomplish anything here that he wanted to during his college career. We also convinced him that with a big man like himself, we could be a national contender. Steve believed we had an opportunity to win, and sure enough, he helped make it come true.

The confirmation that Steve would actually come to Missouri was a story in itself. I happened to be at the Final Four in Utah with my son Lindsey Scott. I remember sitting in a meeting room when Lindsey came over all excited.

"Dad," he said, "it's Stipo on the phone. And he's going to tell you he's coming to Missouri."

I got on the phone and Steve made his announcement to me.

"Well, that's outstanding," I said. "I'm really looking forward to working with you. I don't know when I'll get back, but I'll make arrangements immediately."

"You don't have to leave," Steve said. "There's no reason."

So I stayed.

About ten minutes later I get another phone call. Lindsey comes running in again, even more excited.

"It's Jon Sundvold!"

The first time I saw Jon play for Blue Springs High School he scored 50 points. The second time I saw him play, he scored 49. Ninety-nine points in two games.

Sometimes you see people who score points like that, and that's the sum of their game. Jon did the other things, too. Besides the picture-perfect jump shot, he could pass the ball. He was just one outstanding high school basketball player. I think he would have come to Missouri no matter what Steve decided, but he wanted to wait until after Steve made his decision before announcing his own.

This was the easiest declaration time I ever had. We had pounded the pavement for these guys for a long time. Now I'm at the Final Four, taking it easy, and these two outstanding players call to tell me they are coming to my school.

I'll never forget Steve's first day of practice at Mizzou. In those days, we ran at the conclusion of practice. Now we run every 25 to 30 minutes, conditioning as practice goes along, but back then, we ran hard at the end.

The guys were running pretty hard and Steve became ill. We kept boxes of sawdust behind the baskets and Steve walked over and vomited into the sawdust pit. I came over shortly afterward and said, "Tough day. Come back tomorrow and we'll really get 'er cranked up."

Steve said, "No, I'm not done yet."

"No, go on in and get some water. Take a shower and replenish yourself."

"No, I haven't done all of the running. The other players did more running than I did and I need to finish up."

Steve got up and ran as hard as if someone was running along beside him, maybe even harder.

When he finished, I said, "You just solved a couple problems."

"What do you mean?"

"No one can accuse me of either babying you or showing any favoritism. You are also willing to work harder than anyone else."

From that point on, he was the hardest-working player on the squad. This really influenced the team, especially the reserves. Here was the best big man around, giving it his all in practice. The reserves knew they really had to put out if they wanted some playing time.

We won our first ten games during Steve's freshman season. The highlights included wins at Illinois and against USC on national television.

Then we proceeded to win the Big Eight Conference regular season with an 11-3 record. We lost to Kansas in the semifinals of the Big Eight Postseason Tournament.

We still made the NCAA field, however, and surprised a lot of people. After easily disposing of San Jose State in the first round, we went up against heavily favored Notre Dame. Mark Dressler scored 32 points in this game, a real heroic effort. Larry Drew set a record for most assists in a game with 12. We won in overtime, 87-84.

In the next round against Louisiana State, we stayed in the game but lost 68-63. We finished the season 25-6, and Steve was voted the Big Eight Newcomer of the Year. The Stipanovich-Sundvold era had been ushered in. We lost one key player, though: Larry Drew, who had set the school record for career assists, was drafted in the first round by the Detroit Pistons.

I remember telling one of my assistants, "This will be one of the most difficult years we ever have."

"Why's that?"

"Because when we've come off the best successes we've ever had, it's difficult for them to get back up there, even though you can do it." Sometimes I'm right when I would rather be wrong.

That was Stipanovich's sophomore year. You have to remember his high school senior year. His team had won 60 in a row, their second straight tournament, and he was highly recruited. Steve played in nine all-star games, was the most valuable player in some of them, and he was always put up against Ralph Sampson, Sam Bowie and Antoine Carr. Then he came to Missouri and everyone had high expectations, despite his having had ankle surgery at the end of his senior year.

All of this would have demoralized a normal guy, but he delivered. He was the only new starter on the ballclub until Sundvold forced his way into the lineup in the second half of the season.

At the end of his freshman year, Stipanovich was tired. People wanted him to play on the 1980 Olympic team, but he didn't want to. I told him, "I understand."

The various pressures and problems had taken their toll on him. But I said, "When you return from summer vacation, let's be ready to go again."

Well, we weren't, and not just because of him. Nobody was ready to play.

We were going to be a step slower in the 1980-81 season with the loss of Drew, although we still expected to do well. Then before the season began, Mark Dressler hurt his knee while playing on a synthetic floor. He was lost for the entire season.

We were a good team occasionally that season, but sometimes we were just average. The low point of the year was getting whipped by Louisville 71-49 on national television.

There was an even lower point for Stipo, an episode that attracted a lot of media attention and became a distraction for us.

I was down at the Lake of the Ozarks with my wife and football coach Warren Powers and his wife for New Year's Eve. I got a call at 6 o'clock in the morning and rushed back from the lake. In fact, Warren drove back; I think he set a speed record. I met with Steve at my house and we went through the entire episode.

He got shot in the arm and first said it was an intruder in his room. I think he was embarrassed. Then he came out with the real story that he accidentally shot himself.

There was a big media flap, and the fans really harassed him, but Steve handled the situation pretty well. I used to tell players that they were at an advantage over me because the fans on the road always got on me but rarely them. And if they didn't get on me, all I had to do was get up a couple of times to attract their attention. Well, we were at Oklahoma one game after Steve's accident, and the fans there were shooting pop guns.

I told Stipo, "You know what, I really appreciate your team effort. Usually we come down here, and all 10,000 are yelling at my ass. But you got about 2,000 of them on you now." He came out of the game a little later, with the fans yelling and the pop guns going off, and he's laughing.

"You know what?" he tells me, "You're right."

We were 4-3 in the middle of the conference season, and I called the team together and said, "I expect us to win the next seven games. And you do whatever you want to do the rest of the season. We're the best team in this league."

We won six of the last seven conference games and finished 11-3.

We captured the Big Eight title again, earning a berth in the NCAA. The season ended on a sour note, though, when we lost in the first round of the tournament to Lamar, a team we had beaten handily earlier in the season.

From that point on, those kids never gave up. The squad regrouped before the 1981-82 season and was ready to perform to its capabilities.

We were selected to win the Big Eight. I told the team not to get too cocky because they hadn't given us the damn trophy yet. The preseason polls ranked us 15th in the country.

The team was on a roll at the beginning of that season, putting together a long string of victories.

Illinois provided a hard time for us in St. Louis, but we took care of them in overtime, 78-68.

Three games into our conference season, Nebraska gave us all we could handle, tying the score with 11 seconds left, 42-42. We called timeout and called a play for Ricky Frazier to get the ball. Frazier got the ball, but instead of shooting, made a great pass to Prince Bridges for a basket as time ran out. Our record was 13-0, 3-0 in the conference.

Our next big challenge was Louisville on national television. Louisville had been ranked as high as fourth earlier in the year because they had four starters returning. Their seniors had played on the 1980 national championship team. We took care of the Cardinals in St. Louis 69-55. We were 14-0.

There was no shot clock then, though there had been some experiments with it in the early '70s, so sometimes it became advantageous to go to a spread offense.

Against Kansas in our next game the spread offense was a key. The Jayhawks' zone was very tough to penetrate, so when we got the lead, we held it. During the second half we held the ball for more than six minutes. Marvin "Moon" McCrary did an outstanding defensive job in this game. Marvin didn't score very many points, but he knew how to play defense. We won the game 41-35. The 41 points were the fewest we had scored since 1959. Not the most exciting style for most fans to watch, however, it won games.

This type of ball game reminds me of a recruiting story. My assistants Rich Daly and Bob Sundvold arranged a recruiting trip for me. They would usually embellish something about a player's height or ability. They were always telling me a player was 6-5 when he was 6-3. On this occasion, they told me that the recruit's mother was one of the best-looking women they had ever seen, and I should be forewarned because I was going to be distracted.

We do a very good job of preparing for these recruiting visits because a bad presentation can cost you. I thought Daly and Sundvold were setting me up, that this woman would not be attractive at all.

When I got to the door and met her, I saw a very attractive woman, just as Daly and Sundvold had said. I wasn't prepared, and I gave the most marble-mouthed presentation you would ever hear. But the funniest thing about the trip came at the end, when I asked her if she had any questions.

She said, "Do you have that game plan, where you're ahead by ten points at the end of the game, and you hold onto the ball, and you let the other team get close? I call it pissing away a lead."

In those days, you didn't hear that language much in public, and I certainly didn't expect it from this woman. My mouth dropped open at first, and then I recovered.

Finally I said, "Why yes, quite honestly, I invented that game."

The coaches laugh about it now. We didn't get the player, but at least we have the story.

In our next game against Oklahoma, we went to 16-0 with an 84-64 win. North Carolina suffered its first loss that week, to Wake Forest, and afterward The Associated Press and United Press International voted us No. 1 in the country. It was the first time a Tiger team had been ranked No. 1, and the first time a Big

Eight school reached the top since 1959. I think this went a long way toward improving the image of basketball in the Big Eight.

Now we could bask in a little glory. And now everybody would be gunning for us.

We beat Iowa State 86-73 at Ames, then played highly regarded Kansas State on their court. The Wildcats were ranked as high as 13th in the polls. They were definitely our biggest road challenge to date.

We had a 51-45 lead and were running our spread offense, when Prince Bridges gave us an even more comfortable lead with a slam dunk. But we missed several free throws in the next few minutes to allow the Wildcats to close the gap to 57-56 with about 30 seconds to go.

The clincher came when Sundvold was double-teamed and saw Stipo wide open near the basket. Steve slammed it home to give us a 59-56 lead, and we held on to win 59-58. The regionally televised game showed we could play well as the No. 1 team under the national spotlight.

We maintained the top spot for another week after defeating Oklahoma State to go 19-0. No other Missouri team had gone this long undefeated.

Then Nebraska turned the lights out in the next game. We played lethargically and shot poorly. Nebraska beat us 67-51.

We rebounded for four more conference wins, but none of them came easily. At 23-1, we were ranked fourth in the country and were scheduled to play the 12th-ranked Georgetown Hoyas next.

The Hoyas had Patrick Ewing starting as a freshman. Eric "Sleepy" Floyd also played on that team. Georgetown coach John Thompson wouldn't let us work out the day before the game; he claimed he needed the gym three hours. We then played poorly before a national television audience. Seventeen turnovers and weak shooting helped defeat us, and Steve got in foul trouble guarding Ewing, eventually fouling out. We were beaten 63-51.

Although we followed this loss with another one at home against Kansas State 57-56, we still took first in the conference. We were the undisputed champions for the third year in a row, the first time that had been accomplished in the Big Eight.

Fortunately, the situation turned around for us in time for

the Big Eight Tournament. We swept our way to the championship, earning a first-round bye in the NCAA Tournament. Next
we beat Marquette 73-69 to advance to the regional semifinals
against Houston.

Houston had 7-foot Akeem Olajuwon at center and Clyde
Drexler at forward. Olajuwon was still a little raw then, but his
shot-blocking ability made the other team alter many shots. We
knew he would affect our game, so we had practiced by shooting
over a towel taped to a long stick.

I could see that we were intimidated with Olajuwon in the
middle. The Cougars took a 38-32 halftime lead. We made a run
on them in the second half, thanks to some great scoring by
Frazier, who finished with 29 points. But they took a 79-74 lead
late in the game and held on to win 79-78. Our dream of reaching
the Final Four once again was stalled. We finished the season 27-
4.

They named Frazier the Big Eight Player of the Year.
Frazier and Sundvold grabbed first-team all-conference honors,
while Stipanovich and McCrary were named to the second team.
We lost Frazier and McCrary to graduation, and both were
drafted by the pros — Frazier in the second round by Chicago
and McCrary in the fifth round by Phoenix.

This great season and all the No. 1 attention enabled us to
have more exposure on national television. During the 1982-83
season, when Stipanovich and Sundvold returned for their senior seasons, we would play eight times on national TV.

We opened the season against North Carolina on CBS in St.
Louis. This game has become a great TV match-up. We always
play an exciting game against the Tar Heels, and this one was no
exception. We beat them 64-60, with a big boost from Barry
Laurie, a guard from Versailles, Missouri, who had been in Jon
Sundvold's shadow. During the late stages of the North Carolina
game, Laurie hit two baskets that were really crucial for us. After
the game, Dean Smith said, "I knew who Jon Sundvold was, but
who is that other guard?"

Barry was a kid who put in a lot of practice time but didn't
experience the continuous highlights some of the other front-line
players knew. A ball game like that is important to a player like
Laurie. It gives him a moment in the sun, and, more important,
it gives him confidence. You like to see it happen to everyone on

the team at some point. Usually it happens if they stay in there and persevere.

We won seven in a row before going on a trip to Washington and Hawaii. Hawaii had invited us to play in their Rainbow Classic along with some other great teams. It was going to be an enjoyable trip. We may have been thinking about Hawaii when we played Washington. At any rate, the Huskies beat us 55-48 in Seattle.

We won our first two games in the Rainbow Classic against Arizona State and Hawaii. Then North Carolina avenged our earlier win with a 73-58 win in the finals.

We would play five overtime games that season, three on national television. And we lost all three.

Marquette beat us 60-59 after we had beaten them in the NCAA the previous year. Iowa State beat us in overtime in Ames, an ESPN game. Then in the finals of the Big Eight Tournament, we lost to Oklahoma State in two overtimes in another CBS game. Our record on the tube was 4-4.

But we won the conference for the fourth year in a row and received another NCAA bid. We were paired against the Iowa Hawkeyes, who eliminated us 77-63.

This wasn't the best way to end the senior season for Stipanovich and Sundvold. But they had brought us a lot of national attention. We went 26-8 for the season, and during the four years with Stipo and Jon, Mizzou went 100-28, with four straight NCAA bids.

Steve was named an Academic All-American; Jon was a first-team All-American. Both went in the first round in the pros, Stipo going second overall after Ralph Sampson. Missouri would retire both players' numbers, making them the first players so honored since Willie Smith.

They created more than a winning tradition at Missouri. They reinforced what the 1975-76 team had accomplished. National recognition. Competitiveness on a national level. It's a tradition that still exists.

13

The Mischievous
Chievous

It is rare that a high school player will decide on a college based on his educational pursuits. Fortunately, though, that's just what happened with a player who would become the school's all-time leading scorer.

Many people choose not to believe this, suspecting something more under the surface. But the fact is we found a player from New York named Derrick Chievous who wanted to come to the University of Missouri because of its journalism school. For a time, it looked like Derrick would change his mind and attend a Big East school, but thanks to his high school coach, Derrick kept his goal of going into journalism.

Education is a big part of our recruiting. I want to talk to players who want to be the best player on the team, but I also want them to value an education.

I'm a professional once I enter a recruit's home, because that's my job. But occasionally I have some fun with it. Once I went into a home where the mother asked me, "How many students do you have?"

It's a good question, because everyone wants their son to have personal attention.

I answered, "Three."

"Three!" she shouted.

"Yeah, three students and 24,000 other retards that don't know why they're there."

It was an exaggeration, but I made a point about how few serious students there are in college. I knew we weren't going to get the player, anyway, and you don't waste a lot of time with players you don't have much chance of getting. If I couldn't get the player, at least I could try to find some humor. I thought it was comical and so did her husband. She wasn't laughing, however. One of my assistants stepped in and said, "Let's go home."

When we recruited Derrick, I wasn't playing for laughs. I remember going to New York to meet him and his mother. His coach thought it might be a good idea to hold the meeting at his house, but when I got there, no one showed up. I waited and waited and finally left.

On my way back to the airport, I gave Derrick's mother a call. She picked up the phone and it soon became evident that there was a problem. The situation mystified me.

I told her it was unfortunate that we offered Derrick just what he wanted in a school, and yet there was this misunderstanding. We had an excellent journalism program and a basketball program where he could achieve whatever he wanted to achieve. She asked if I would return in a week. She assured me I wouldn't end up walking the streets of New York.

When I saw her the next week, I found her to be a very cautious woman. She wanted to make sure everything was just right, that the journalism program was indeed one of the best and that the basketball program was everything it was billed to be. Furthermore, she seemed to want me to act as a sort of parent away from home if Derrick decided to attend Missouri.

Derrick's coach stepped in and reminded him about his original standards for selecting a school. Journalism and basketball was the package. So Derrick stayed in the boat and came to Missouri.

Derrick was a phenomenal player, the No. 1 scorer ever at Missouri, the first to score more than 2,000 points in a career. But his biggest impact on the program was in bringing us a different style of basketball. No one wanted to forget Stipanovich and Sundvold, but in college basketball if you want to maintain your program, you have to change with the times. We scored more points with Derrick, and we attracted more fans to the arena with him. Derrick helped us win a league championship and get a lot of national coverage.

Chievous had some peculiarities. A strikingly unusual attitude made him a challenge to handle at times. He was completely different from the norm, pun intended. But you have to recognize individual differences — and give them a little leeway sometimes — to have your best ballclub.

I told the rest of the team a story about a player who did exactly as I wanted but didn't achieve the results. Then there was another ballplayer, like Derrick, who did nothing the way I liked, but got tremendous results. I pride myself in being this intelligent — I didn't play the one who didn't get results.

Some of the differences about Derrick were just those between New York and Columbia. Down deep, I thought he was a good guy, and I tried to make sure he knew that.

When he was a sophomore, Derrick did something that really impressed me. Lynn Hardy was supposed to give a clinic at a school, but he couldn't make it because of an academic requirement, so he asked Derrick to take his place. The coach and others in the community called to report that Derrick did an outstanding job. He took time to talk with the youngsters and encouraged them to play fairly and do a good job in school. When I heard this, I told Derrick from then on, he wasn't going to bug me.

I still benched Derrick on occasion. He hadn't played well in a game against Nebraska when we lost a big lead and the game during the last three or four minutes. When we came home I said, "We're not holding one individual responsible, but we are going to make some changes."

I sat Derrick on the bench for the start of the next game against Iowa State. Derrick never said a word while he was benched, he understood and accepted it. While he sat there, the team jumped out to an incredible lead in the opening minutes. Before the first half was over, we were up by about 30 points.

I looked at Derrick and said, "They're doing pretty good, aren't they?"

"Yeah."

"Do you want to play?"

"Well, sure."

I said, "I want to see the same type of effort that the other players are putting out. I want to see that all the time."

I played him about twenty minutes and he scored 30 points, so I thought this was working pretty well. We went to Oklahoma State and I didn't start him there either. We won that game, too.

This whole episode brought the team together. Derrick realized we would do what was in our best interest first, and we would try to do what was in his best interest, too.

From 1984-88 Derrick would play in 130 games and break many school records. He scored more than 2,500 points. He set the school record for best career three-point field goal percentage, 45 percent. One year he sank 28 consecutive free throws. Derrick was an all-around player, leading the team in rebounds and steals, as well as scoring. When it was all over his senior year, Chievous became an All-American and a first-round draft choice of the Houston Rockets.

Our team had hit another lull after the graduation of Stipanovich and Sundvold in 1983. We went 16-14 in 1983-84 and did not play in a postseason tournament.

Derrick made an immediate impact as a freshman the following season. He was first-team all-tourney in the Big Eight Tournament. Our record improved slightly to 18-14, and we earned a berth in the NIT.

His sophomore year we were 21-14 finding ourselves in the NCAA again. We went 24-10 in 1986-87, and 19-11 his senior year.

In that 1987-88 season, we were coming off a Big Eight championship and an NCAA tournament berth. A lot of people were returning, and Doug Smith had been added. We were anticipating everything and anything.

The recruitment of other players from Detroit helped us attract Smith out of MacKenzie High School. Smith knew about the others and watched them do well. I liked watching him play and talking to his mother and grandmother. That was basically all there was to it: Smith said he was coming to the University of Missouri.

The highlight of that season was the game at the University of Nevada-Las Vegas. It ranks right up there as one of our best wins ever. We went into the game 15-5. UNLV was 21-2 and ranked seventh. They had a 70-3 record on their home court.

Before the game I had one of the best interviews I ever had

with Billy Packer with our own television crew for my coach's show. I asked him how he perceived the ball game and how we were going to win it. Packer said we needed to handle their press, go inside and control the tempo.

Packer said something else that made a lot of sense. UNLV had this fireworks display that was kind of intimidating.

"Why not take the team off the floor after the introduction, before the fireworks?" Packer asked.

"I think that's a good idea," I replied.

I'm not too much into psychology, however, I understand and accept sensible advice. There's no reason to stay and watch a fireworks display going off in the Thomas and Mack Center while 19,000 people are going crazy.

Derrick fouled out of the game with just under two minutes left, but he played brilliantly, scoring 26 points. The game stayed close throughout. Byron Irvin hit two free throws to give us an 80-79 lead with about a minute to play. It was insane during the last 60 seconds. They didn't get the good shot, and Lee Coward was fouled with about 30 seconds left.

I remember standing on the court next to our former player Willie Smith, who lived in Las Vegas. I asked him if he thought Lee would make the free throws. Smith said, "He'll make the first one."

He made the first one and missed the second, just like Willie predicted. We're up 81-79.

UNLV ran the ball up the court, first looking inside to tie. Then Karl James tried a three-pointer but missed and we ran out the clock.

Hardly anyone goes into Vegas and wins. We really felt great getting out of there. We had maybe two thousand fans travel with us, and at a post-game party everyone came together. These events usually don't excite me, but this one brought out the best in everybody. The university, the team, and the fans had a great time in a great setting.

When we came back to our hotel we walked by the crap tables and the roulette wheels. Everything stopped. For about fifteen seconds they stopped shooting crap and they stopped spinning the wheels to applaud those kids.

I told the players it was an insignificant point as far as the world is concerned. But when you become a little older, you are going to remember that for one day, people in Vegas, the high rollers and the tourists stopped to recognize you. A moment in the sun.

After that game, we didn't work together very well. We won only three of the remaining six games and finished 19-11. Still, the win over Las Vegas really stood out.

By the time Chievous graduated, our team had reached an exciting level of playing that attracted a record number of fans to the Hearnes Center. Our average home attendance went from 9,000 to about 13,000 people during his senior year, and Derrick was the major factor.

But we also had some other key players who helped improve our level of play in that era. Greg Church, Byron Irvin, Lee Coward, Nathan Buntin, Gary Leonard, Mike Sandbothe and Doug Smith all would return. In fact, this next group was so talented, they would win more games than any other in school history.

14
Eye of the Storm

We appeared to be headed for a dream season in 1988-89. It was a season in which we would record my 500th career win. We would reach the top three in the polls. Then the walls would start caving in.

I would collapse on a team plane bound for Oklahoma. The NCAA would begin an investigation into reports of rules violations. The media would brand me and members of my coaching staff as "cheaters." While combating this criticism, I would have an even bigger fight, with cancer. The challenges ahead were great. I would find out what life was like in the eye of the storm.

The season began with our playing in the Dodge NIT. We beat Southwest Missouri and Xavier in Columbia in the first two rounds to earn a trip to New York to play North Carolina in the semifinals.

The team just blew things open against North Carolina midway through the second half, to run an 18-point lead. The final score was 91-81, putting us in the tournament final against Syracuse. This was a milestone, it was my 500th career victory.

I was caught in the excitement of the season so I couldn't pay a whole lot of attention to it. But looking back, what a way to reach the milestone: during the semifinals of a national tournament against North Carolina, and its coach, Dean Smith, a man recognized as one of the all-time great coaches. At the time, though, I was thinking about Syracuse. A reporter noted that I appeared nonchalant after the win.

Syracuse beat us 86-84 in overtime in the final of the NIT, nonetheless our season was off to a great start. People considered us a top ten team.

We were scheduled to play in another tournament after the NIT, the Diet Pepsi Tournament of Champions. The three other schools in this tournament were North Carolina, Temple and Arizona. Pretty heady competition.

There was a great deal of promotion surrounding this tournament during the summer, including a sold-out media advance that I attended. A day after the media event, a Charlotte newspaper ran a picture of the coaches. It was supposed to include John Chaney of Temple, Lute Olsen of Arizona, Dean Smith of North Carolina and Norm Stewart. But instead of my picture beside the others, there was a lady who was identified as me. I have no idea who she was. It was simply a mistake the newspaper made.

When we arrived in Charlotte for the tournament, a big banquet was held for the coaches. I thought this was a chance to have some fun. People attend these functions to kick back. They don't want to hear some malarkey from coaches about how good or bad their teams are. They want to hear some funny stories. I thought it would be great to poke a little fun at the newspaper for the mistake it had made in the summer.

So when they introduced me at the banquet, I went up to the podium wearing a wig I'd brought along for the occasion. To say it went over well is an understatement. People really got a kick out of it. So I just left it on as I made my presentation about our team. I also gave a tribute to Dean Smith.

It was a hit.

I've had a lot of fun with people in coaching and have shared this side of my personality with the public many times. Sometimes I think the media ignores this part of my identity. I hope some of the fun and laughter gets out occasionally. It's part of me, so it should be included in my image.

North Carolina beat Arizona in the first round of the tournament, while we beat Temple 91-74 in double-overtime, with Byron Irvin scoring 33 points. We had earned the right to play North Carolina again, only this time, it was in Charlotte, North Carolina. Two weeks before, we had taken care of them on a neutral court in New York; I knew they wanted to even the score badly.

I walked out on the floor for warm-ups. I wanted to see what the mood was among the North Carolina players and their coaches. I'll never forget the look in their eyes.

I watched our players in warm-ups, too, and there was a different quickness in our step.

"Are you ready?" I asked our guys.

They said they were.

"You had better be ready, because North Carolina is really ready. In fact, after looking at them and their coaching staff during practice, I'm going to have (trainer) Ron Dubuque tape my ankles."

We went out and played well, but North Carolina undressed us. We were down 15 or 20 points in the first half. The Tar Heels beat us 76-60.

I've really enjoyed the series with North Carolina. We've played them eight times through 1990 and split with them. That's one of the records I'm really proud of, a strong indication of how well we compete with the best teams in the nation.

We won our next four games to run our record to 10-2 going into our annual game against Illinois at St. Louis. We had trouble winning this game throughout the '80s. I can't really give an explanation for this other than Lou Henson has had some great teams. It's almost always a very close affair. There are always a lot of Illinois fans at the game, even though it's considered a neutral court. We lost this game 87-84, but our problems off the court were just about to begin.

In December, coach Bob Sundvold came into my office and told me he had loaned $135 to P.J. Mays.

"Have you lost your F------ mind?" I blurted. It was shocking because I thought he would know better. He said he didn't think it was a violation at first.

I'll go over more details about this matter later on. The fact is, Bob came to me when he realized it was a violation, and I immediately told him to self-report it, which he did, after consulting with a former NCAA enforcement officer.

You simply do not give money to an athlete under any condition. I wasn't overly concerned because I felt our program was sound. It's not based on inducements to get players to come here or to get them to stay.

After the Illinois game, we started a string of victories and moved up steadily in the polls. But about that time some stories appeared raising questions about our recruiting success in Detroit.

Another disturbing bit of publicity centered on an allegation by a reporter who said I made the statement that I knew someone who could "take care of" his one-year-old child. This was absolutely false. I did engage in a heated discussion with that reporter about his newspaper's coverage of the team, but I never threatened his child.

I've figured out that the best thing is to ignore press criticism. I think some people are just waiting for you to explode so they can pounce on the opportunity to expose a weakness. One of the best years I had with the media was the 1989-90 season, when I hired a press advisor. We had a fabulous year, and I never went off. It was almost like a placebo. If a certain negative question was asked, I would look at my press advisor and I could continue. He kept me abreast of the questions that might be asked, and we went over what we wanted to get across. We were prepared.

Looking back, when I've had any trouble with reporters, it has been with either young reporters or student reporters. I can remember one such incident with a youthful reporter 14 years ago.

The man had been out of school for only a few years. He had graduated from Missouri, but his writing appeared to favor Kansas State. At that time he was covering the Big Eight Tournament. Both of my sons attended the games. They have always enjoyed the games and were very vocal. This reporter came over to one of them and said, "You should conduct yourself better at a game."

Now it seems to me that if it's your job to write about a game, you're spreading yourself a little thin trying to serve as a substitute parent at the same time.

My son replied, "Why don't you just go ahead and write about Kansas State. That's what you like to do."

I'm sure that angered the reporter. It implied he wasn't objective.

The reporter then remarked to my son, "If you don't change

your behavior, I'm going to write a story about what a poor job your father has done raising you."

My son turned to the reporter and retorted, "You do, and I'll kick your ass."

After the game, my wife came to me and said, "We need to talk to the boys. Something has occurred." I sat down with both of them and heard their version of the story. I tried to give the writer the benefit of the doubt.

"There are advantages and disadvantages to this job," I told the boys.

"The advantages are, I can afford to take all of us on trips, like the one to South America we just came back from. If you want to enjoy some of the advantages, you have to put up with some other things."

I wanted to balance the books, so my son wouldn't hold anything against the reporter. But when I was through, my older son said, "Dad, I listened to every bit of it, and no way was my brother at fault."

That put me on the spot. Now it appeared I wasn't protecting my son.

So I said, "What should we do? Go over, the three of us, and take all of them on? There are several of them. We could go over there and kick the shit out of all of them, if you want to do that."

They laughed and said, "No, we just wanted you to know the truth about what actually happened."

It was preposterous that a reporter, representing the newspaper, should try to intimidate a youngster who is rooting for his father's team. I always remember this incident whenever I read an article criticizing me.

One article that did upset me was a commentary by a columnist. After we defeated Roy Williams' Kansas team 91-66, it was reported that I didn't even bother to shake the hand of the man I had "embarrassed." This columnist wrote that my team rudely ran off the court immediately after the victory. I was told I needed to grow up. However, he never asked me or Coach Williams about the story before he wrote it. If he had, he would have discovered that I did indeed shake hands with Williams after the game.

He later retracted his story. Of course it was on the bottom of the third page following a front page column. He's no longer a columnist. This reporter made no effort to obtain any background information. When we had visited Kansas in the past, we were often showered with flying objects and derisive comments as we entered and left the court. Roy Williams has changed the attitudes of KU fans a great deal since he took over, but they used to throw Cokes and spit on the players.

In this respect, one night I remember a coat falling down. I picked it up and walked around in front of the stands and said, "Someone dropped their coat." I gave it back to someone who appeared to be a student.

About fifteen years later, this same man came up to me to tell me he was an attorney in Kansas City, and that he was sorry for some of the comments he had made in the stands.

"You shouldn't be too dismayed," I told him, "Because when you're 18 or 19 years old, those are the kinds of things you do. If you are still doing them now, then you have a problem."

Some more background that the columnist at that KU game didn't know was, before the game we learned Virginia had a tumor and was going to have surgery the next day. We did not know then whether the tumor was benign or malignant.

I had made up my mind I would get the players so well-prepared that I would not have to attend the game. I said to Virginia the team would win the game with or without me, but of course she insisted that I go to the game.

The last practice before the KU game I had told the players, "Everything is ready. You know how you are going to play the game. Now I'm going to show you how to leave the floor. As soon as you win the game, you turn, and you run off the court."

I wanted my team prepared for the game against KU, and as an added psychological touch, I was putting an image in their minds, not only how they would win this game, but how they would leave it.

After the game, people commented on how relaxed I had looked as I sat on the bench, even when the game was close. I was so relaxed because of the preparation, and in turn, one of the reasons we were so prepared was that I wanted to be with Virginia.

Some people were calling this one of the best Missouri teams ever. As we climbed to the No. 3 spot in the polls, the state's two major newspapers intensified their investigations into possible NCAA rules violations. In early February, the papers were beginning to report what Bob Sundvold had already self-reported to the university in late December, that he had given an improper loan to P.J. Mays to fly back to his high school to check out problems with his transcript.

The first set of interviews with the players for the NCAA investigation could not have come at a worse time. It was in February, one day before our game with Oklahoma, which had been ranked No. 1.

Virginia was recuperating from two major operations. The procedures had been a success, but they made my life additionally stressful in conjunction with everything else that was happening.

Then, while traveling to Norman, Oklahoma, I collapsed on the team plane. When they told me I had cancer, I just stopped thinking about basketball for a while. Life took on a different perspective.

15

Life or Death

After surgery, when doctors removed a tumor from my colon, I couldn't really follow the progress of the team. Members of my family would visit me and sometimes talk about the games. I knew Bob had been suspended. Rich Daly was appointed interim coach, and they brought in Al Eberhard, who had been a great player for us, as an assistant coach. Al made some real contributions in a tough situation.

There was one game no one talked about. No one ever said a word to me about the Iowa State game, and I didn't read the paper. I could just feel that we had lost.

Because of some of the complications I experienced, I was really confined to the hospital. I couldn't follow the team closely, nor did I have the desire to. I just tried to concentrate on getting well.

I'm sure there was a destabilization on the team. There's an emotional disruption in losing your coach for the season. Rich eventually stabilized things, and they went on to win the Big Eight Tournament going three deep in the NCAA. But there was trouble for a while.

After I got out of the hospital in March, I wanted to come over to the players and say, "I'm OK, you're OK." They had lost a few games, including a Kansas State game on a tip-in, something that never should have happened. I had called that one, I just felt it: "We're going to lose on a tip-in." It was simply one of those things, I suppose.

In any event the team came back to Columbia after the loss to Kansas State. The seniors were about to play their last home game against Colorado. I wanted to meet with the players before that game.

However, the NCAA has rules governing situations like this. Here I am, the coach of the team, recovering from surgery, and the NCAA has a rule that may prevent me from visiting my team. Since Rich was interim coach and Al was hired as an assistant, I could no longer be involved with the team. In some instances, this rule makes sense; in this case, it was asinine. Did they think I was going to come out on the floor and give us an extra advantage?

So I came over to see the team, not to talk to them as a coach, but just to say, "Hi, I'm OK." I wanted to wish them good luck.

While I met them in a conference room, I couldn't finish my talk. It was too emotional and I had to leave.

"Look," I wanted to say, "You all work hard for Rich and stay together." That's all. But I couldn't get the words out. This wasn't doing the team any good, and I finally decided to just walk out. It was terribly frustrating.

Here were guys I had recruited, and I only wanted to say something to motivate them. They had fluttered a bit and were having some trouble both on and off the court. Some of the players were challenging Rich. I thought I could change things, but it didn't work because I was too emotional.

A few days later there was a story going around that one of the players, unhappy with his playing time, had refused to sit on the bench when he was taken out of the ball game, actually sitting in the crowd for a while. This player didn't realize that there had been many pro scouts at the game; he looked very unprofessional to them. This was right before conference tournament time. I knew I needed to meet with the players once more.

This time I would be prepared. But I had to sneak out of the house; Virginia didn't want me anywhere near the team. I had to trick her. I told her I was feeling a little better.

"I think I'll take a ride," I remarked to her.

I asked Laura to drive. When we got into the car, Laura said, "Where do you want to go?"

114

"To the Hearnes Building," I replied.

Laura didn't say a word. She would do whatever I asked, and vice versa.

I think we drove all the way to the floor of the Hearnes Building after driving through some big doors. I walked in and assembled the players. There were no theatrics involved in what I had to say. It was what I felt. If I don't feel anything, I don't say anything. I remember saying something like this:

"The last time I was here, I wasn't prepared. I assure you, now, I am prepared. I want to tell you that you've got just a few things to do before you complete your season. It's as simple as this: You have two games to lose. You've got the Big Eight Tournament. If you lose, you have had a good enough year to go to the NCAA, so your season will not be over. You'll have to lose another game before it's all finished.

"So, go ahead, play out your season, and in the meantime, I want you to shut your f------ mouth. If Coach Daly asks you to stand on your head and crap through your nose, you stand on your head and blow."

I don't know where I got that last line. But that's what came to my mind. Then I proceeded to talk to each of them individually. I think I praised only one player and hammered everybody else.

I was very pleased with the team after that because they won five games in a row. What did my talk have to do with it? Who knows? I think part of it was that Rich really asserted himself and stabilized the team.

One unfortunate misunderstanding came from this meeting. A player who had left the team, a guy probably upset with his playing time, accused me of trying to stop them from talking to the NCAA. He mentioned my telling them to shut up, when what I meant was to be quiet while Coach Daly tried to do his job.

I wasn't following the NCAA investigation. I was too sick to really care. I had to go to M.D. Anderson in Houston for a second opinion about my post-operative treatment. One of my scans showed a spot on my kidney. The doctors didn't like the scan. It made for an anxious trip to Houston. There were some people who held onto a glimmer of hope that perhaps the tumor that had been removed was benign. But then you could go in the other direction: Maybe it was a lot worse than the doctors thought.

Four of us flew to Houston. A good friend, Carolyn Hawks, came to be with my wife. My good friend Don Walsworth came to be with me. Dr. Jack Jensen, who used to be a resident in Columbia had made the arrangements for the trip together with some good friends, Stan and Ann Kronke and Bill and Nancy Laurie.

Jack's wife said we were the four sorriest looking people she had ever seen when we stepped off the plane in Houston drained and exhausted. Fortunately, we had some time to recuperate from the trip before going to the hospital.

M.D. Anderson is one of the top medical facilities in the world. Everyone should spend one day there. It can be depressing, but you'll learn that cancer shows no prejudice. If you smoke, a visit there may be a way to get you to stop. Carolyn Hawks described our arrival at M.D Anderson as almost a religious experience. When you walk into the huge lobby, you encounter a new perspective. Here's a place where you'll find every type of cancer patient. One floor just has breast cancer patients, another floor is reserved for colon cancer, while still another floor only contains prostate cancer patients.

As we sat in the lobby, waiting for my name to be called, an elderly woman sitting nearby, yells, "Aren't you Norm Stewart?" She had what I thought was an Oklahoma accent.

I said, "Why yes."

"Well, I'm so sorry you're sick. You know, one of my daughters is here with cancer." She went on to tell a rather upbeat story about her daughter's treatment and prognosis.

When she was through I said, "I just know you must be a Cowboy or a Sooner fan. Which one?"

"Cowboy. That Billy Tubbs plays no defense."

Her comment broke some of the tension.

Fortunately, the doctors at M.D. Anderson confirmed everything we'd heard in Columbia: The spot on my kidney was just a cyst.

The doctors recommended chemotherapy as a safeguard. When you have different types of cancer, you fall into several different categories. They put me in a 70 percent category. I was told that I had a 70 percent chance of living five years, and they said the chemo would raise the percentage. I always say, it doesn't matter what risk group you're in, as long as you fall in the right one percent. I was still at ten times the risk of having a recurrence of cancer, no matter what.

I asked the doctors what they would do. They said they would have the chemotherapy, and I replied, "Okay, that's what I'll do."

I realized now I knew my opponent. I knew a little bit about the odds, and I knew how it would be treated. For a guy who likes to be in control, this was a great relief.

At some point, we took a walk in a park behind the hotel connected to M.D. Anderson, near the Rice campus, where our son Lindsey went to school. It was comforting to be in familiar surroundings. Virginia and I had some very good memories visiting him here. It was springtime, and the grass had just been cut. There were kids playing nearby; the place was alive. I began to feel a little stronger.

When we had some spare time, a few of us went to a Houston sports bar and got the bartender to change the channel to the Big Eight Tournament. We returned to the bar the next night, but he wouldn't let us watch it. I think it was because of a Southwest Conference Tournament game. On the third night, we watched Missouri win the tournament championship game. This victory made me feel great. I was proud of the kids.

The team went three deep in the NCAA. They beat Creighton and Texas before losing the regional semifinal 83-80 to Syracuse. I admired their effort and the way Coach Daly took over, but I had more important matters to think about.

The chemotherapy was an intravenous treatment combined with a vitamin. They hook you up with a little bag and put a needle in the back of your hand. It didn't take very long for each session. I would go into the doctor's office five days in a row, then I would be off for three weeks, afterwards, resuming another five consecutive sessions. This was my routine for three months. Next I progressed to five days of treatment followed by four weeks away from it. I did that for three months. Throughout this period, I was checking with the oncologist. After those five-day treatments, I'd go in for blood tests on the following Thursday, keeping track of my vitals and blood count.

The doctors gave me good information about diet and rest, but I still don't know if there is anything written about doing exercise while you are on chemotherapy. I followed the diet explicitly. When someone calls me now to say that they are going to be on chemo, I tell them to be sure to make a solution out of baking soda and salt. You need to keep this with you at all times to rinse your mouth out to prevent sores.

At first, I was very frightened. The chemotherapy sessions left me feeling rather ill. Afterwards, I would read a little bit and rest. I did get one reward after chemo, however, a milk shake. That drink got me through.

My days following treatment were quiet. I was very passive, which suited me just fine. Although I did not exercise much that first week, I liked to take brief walks.

During the second week, I increased my activity. The doctors said I shouldn't expose myself to the sun while on chemotherapy. Well, I thought there was nothing to this treatment and there was no reason why I couldn't play golf.

I had a terrible reaction. Sores developed in my mouth and I became very sick. I'm a little hard-headed, but I stopped playing golf for a while. After the third week, I felt worse.

But throughout the fourth, fifth and six weeks, I became a very good patient. And after taking the chemo, I didn't get sick.

Meanwhile, they were testing me every week, watching the blood counts, which could give an indication of a recurrence. At the end of six months the doctors took a couple of scans. Any time there was bleeding in my stools, they would do a check. I had a colonoscopy again. Now I have one every year, sometimes every six months. I'm a believer: By age 50, everyone should have had a colonoscopy, probably before that.

I also do hemocults. You take a sample at home and send it in to a lab for results. People should do this at least once a year.

There was a lot of anxiety as the six-month evaluation approached. Will it be there or won't it? How are you going to accept it if it is? I was reminded daily that I could have a recurrence, although I tried not to think about it. Virginia and I talked a lot. I really thought we showed considerable strength during that time. I knew it was on her mind. All I could do was make sure I took care of myself and that everything was in order.

We always had a strong family, and now it became even more sharply focused. Everything in my life became more sharply focused. Our relationship with friends grew more important. I looked forward to going on little walks with Virginia just around the neighborhood.

After taking chemotherapy through Thursday, I would be given permission to travel. The first time our friends Dick and

Carol Savage invited us out to Palm Springs, California. I didn't think I would play golf, but I did take my clubs along.

One day I told Dick, "I don't believe I can take a full swing, but why don't we go out and play? I'll just play in from a hundred yards; that way, I won't have to take a full swing."

My surgery scars were still quite evident. I played two or three holes from a hundred yards out. Then I decided I would try to drive. I took the driver out and took a practice swing. When I finished, I had to look down the front of my shirt to see if I was still together. I thought I might have split open, but it wasn't bad, so I continued to play.

When I got back from the trip to Palm Springs, I asked my doctor, "What do you think about my playing some golf?"

He said, "Uh, it would be all right."

"That's good, because I've already played some."

Our second trip was to Marco Island, Florida. We stayed at Hall and Helen Trice's beautiful home. My wife and I were quite fortunate to have friends invite us to their place. People simply made their residences available.

We went to Florida again with the Walsworths. Another time we traveled to the Lake of the Ozarks. The golf and the vacations helped me recover. I couldn't put the clubs down. I owe some of this to the guy who hired me at Northern Iowa, Jim Witham. He gave me a set of clubs and I started playing at age 26. I never had a lesson. Now I play to a 12 handicap, but I enjoy myself.

Some people close to me asked whether I had considered quitting coaching. Well, there just wasn't anything to consider yet. My rationale was that you can't decide on anything until you find out what you can do. I had to wait for the results of the examination at the end of six months of treatment. There was no reason to think, "What if this happens or what if that happens?"

I had nothing to do for six months except get well and make sure I was doing everything I could to still live a normal life. It bothered me, of course, that death was a possibility if the cancer spread, but I thought, "If I'm going to die, I won't have to worry about coaching."

When the six months of chemotherapy were over, I took the complete round of tests and waited to hear from the doctors. I was back at the office when the doctor called with the results. This was the big moment of anticipation. My future would be laid out before me with just a few words from my doctor.

"It's okay," he said.

Unless you've gone through the same thing, you can't imagine the incredible relief.

He arranged for what we needed to continue doing. I had to see the oncologist every three months and also had to continue with the hemocult tests. Now I make my family take them too.

Colon cancer is hereditary, and I asked everyone in my family to have colonoscopies. For Christmas, I gave each one a family health record book put out by the Mayo Clinic. It tells how to treat various diseases and helps you keep track of shots and illnesses. People have gotten away from taking good care of themselves. We've forgotten how. It didn't use to be this way. The health record book may not be as popular a gift as a good tie and socks, but it certainly is a more valuable one.

16
On Court and Off

With a clean bill of health, it was time to turn to basketball again. In October of 1989, we began another promising year, my 23rd season at Missouri. I began it a little lighter, a little balder, and we still had the NCAA investigation hanging over our heads. But as I told one reporter, I was just happy to start the season on the right side of the soil.

Yet as the season commenced, I received a list of allegations and possible violations of NCAA rules from my attorney. The NCAA would not supply me with a list of allegations so my attorney had to construct a list from newspaper articles. I was interviewed by the NCAA in late November. Their investigation would cause several disruptions, but it would not detract from the great things we were accomplishing.

Nothing could diminish what Doug Smith did during his junior season that year. The 6-10 forward averaged about 20 points a game, but did everything else too: rebound, block shots, pass the ball. If I could pick out the most outstanding individual ever to play for us, Doug Smith might be it. Not just one of the best players, one of the best individuals. He's a great player as well as a great person, and he knows how to share the limelight.

Fans only see one side of Doug. He looks older than his actual age. He doesn't smile that much on the basketball court, always looking the same whether he's doing well or not. This is valuable in basketball where the ups and downs can get to you.

Doug was voted onto the Missouri All-Decade Team toward the end of the year. We were playing in Columbia that day and he scored 44 points. At the very end he missed a layup that would have tied Joe Scott for the record for most points scored by a Tiger in one game.

The All-Decade players were introduced during halftime and Doug's name was the last one read. He instinctively walked down the line and shook hands with every player, including the returning players — about 60 men. To me, that's just Doug Smith.

Doug's decision not to go pro at the conclusion of his junior year amazed a lot of people. He refused a fabulous amount of money. ESPN's Dick Vitale was saying throughout Doug's junior year that he wasn't coming back to Missouri. I told Dick I didn't believe that this was true, and he backed off a bit but at the end of the year, Vitale reiterated his previous opinion saying that Doug was going to turn professional.

Dick says a lot of things. He's done a great job of increasing interest in college basketball. But because he speculates, he makes a lot of mistakes. This was a classic one.

The newspapers also pushed Doug to turn pro. It was as if they were trying to make him leave, and when he didn't go, they wondered why. When I talked with Doug, I recalled my experience as a student-athlete, when I had the opportunity to sign a baseball contract at the end of my junior year. I thought it was better to remain in school and finish my degree. Doug realized that he would be in a better position to get his degree if he stayed his fourth year. He might not finish in four years, but he'd be that much closer.

Many people don't understand the athlete, especially educators. They think that athletes should graduate in four years, but recent surveys show a low percentage of *all* students graduate in four years. More are graduating in five years. There are several reasons for not graduating or taking longer than four years to get your degree. First of all, a person may run out of funds. Next, they may find employment an attractive option. And finally, they may discover they just don't have the ability or the interest.

An athlete who doesn't get a degree in four or five years may be better off getting some experience in the job or the sports world and then returning to school. This is particularly true of athletes who have trouble with school work. Barring serious injury, Doug will obviously play pro basketball and make an inordinate amount of money. He'll also gain all kinds of experience. Later, he can come back, get his degree, and give himself more protection against losing all the money he's earned. Right now, all everyone seems interested in, is if the athlete gets his degree in four or five years. Well, it's obvious you want them to graduate, but different circumstances surround every individual.

Doug weighed everything and thought he should insure himself against injury if he decided to stay at Mizzou. I wrote for an NCAA rules interpretation on the matter. I told the NCAA, "Doug Smith is a good person and student. The opportunity to turn pro at the end of his junior season was an attractive option. Doug has indicated he would return to Missouri if he could insure himself against a disabling injury. Question: What is the mechanism for this?"

The NCAA answered that the student-athlete may borrow against his future earnings potential from an established commercial lending institution for the purpose of purchasing insurance against a disabling injury that would prevent him from pursuing professional basketball. The stipulation was that the athletic department or any representatives cannot be involved in the arrangement.

Doug obtained his coverage through Lloyd's of London. He wanted to be with his teammates, and he wanted to return on my behalf also. It was a great gesture on his part and I think a good decision too.

Our 1989-90 season began without four starters from the previous year: Greg Church, Mike Sandbothe, Byron Irvin and Gary Leonard had graduated. But due to great playing from Doug, Anthony Peeler, Lee Coward, John McIntyre, Nathan Buntin, Travis Ford and Jamal Coleman our team would steadily climb to the top of the polls and stay there for several weeks.

Players at this time were being questioned about the NCAA investigation during the most inopportune moments. I thought it was remarkable how they could concentrate on what we had to do and just forget about all the other problems. We would win the Big Eight and reach the No. 1 ranking in the nation.

We won our first nine games, including big wins against Louisville, North Carolina and Arkansas. We lost the annual border war with Illinois, 101-93, then reeled off 12 more wins to go 21-1.

We were scheduled to play Kansas, the top-ranked team in the country, on January 20, my 55th birthday. They were ranked No. 1 and we were No. 4. You'd think that a match-up of Nos. 1 and 4 would be about as exciting as it could get, but the game turned out to be even more dramatic due to what happened behind the scenes.

Right before we were to play KU, the administration came to the coaching staff and said the players were ineligible because of an arrangement we had made to allow them to spend more time at home for the Christmas holiday. This had been approved in advance by the Big Eight. On December 27, right in the middle of the break, we had a game at Memphis State. Normally, we would ask the players to return to Columbia on their own before the Memphis game, and then the team would travel round-trip together to Memphis, the school picking up the costs of transportation.

On this occasion it was approved by the Big Eight Office to allow our players to fly round-trip from their homes to Memphis. There would be no added benefit for the players. They would just fly one less leg of the trip. Our coaching staff asked our compliance officer, who then asked the Big Eight, which said "OK." And that's the way many of the players traveled to Memphis.

But, it turned out that the Big Eight had been wrong. The university attorneys discovered that even though we had Big Eight permission, the flights were an NCAA violation. The university self-reported it to the NCAA, much to our own detriment. Now just before the Kansas game, with the No. 1 ranking on the line, the players are told to pay for part of their round-trip air fare to Memphis or they wouldn't be able to compete against Kansas.

When the business manager checked on the price for the air fare, he didn't go to the players to find out what they had paid. One player had found a ticket for just twenty-four dollars. Without bothering to check the lowest fare the students had paid, the school asked some of the players to pay more than a hundred dollars.

The situation was totally unreasonable. First of all, it wasn't the players' fault; they'd been told it was alright. The administrators asked if I would ask the players to repay the money. I said, "No." They inquired why. I replied that I always advise my players the same way I would advise my own child. If my child got caught in something like this, I would tell my child to tell them to learn how to run their business. You should not have to pay one hundred and twenty-five dollars for something that cost twenty-five dollars.

I then received a call from Mike Slive, an attorney for the administration. Slive said something to the effect (and I'm paraphrasing) "Why don't you go to those kids and say, 'Look, pay the money. Get this behind us. And let's beat Kansas' ass.'"

"First of all," I replied, "I don't talk to my ballclub that way. And second, I don't give them advice like that. Furthermore, I don't pay attention to outsiders who try to give me bad advice on what to do."

Slive said, "Well, I guess that's the end of the conversation."

"Not really," I retorted. "You're the one who called me. Tell me if you have anything to say."

He was trying to have me appeal to my players asking them to pay. If I had followed that advice, I don't think I would still be coaching. There are times when players really rely on you as an adult to fight for a just cause. When you show them you will fight for their interests, that is when they will support you. This is how you build loyalties. Slive did give me one piece of information that was helpful: He suggested the prices for the air fares could be negotiated.

Dick Tamburo, the athletic director, asked if he could talk to the players about this matter.

"Dick, you don't have to ask me," I said. "You're the athletic director. You can meet with my players at any given time you'd like to." So we arranged a meeting one day during practice.

Tamburo came, along with Gary Zwonitzer, director of business affairs, and Carl Settergren, our faculty representative to the Big Eight. They asked the players to repay the money. These men said there was no way they could negotiate the price, and that the NCAA had ruled them ineligible. Unless they paid for the airfares, the team would remain ineligible.

Some of the players looked at me and I inquired, "What do you want to do?"

A few of them said, "Hey, I can't pay that. I don't want to pay that. It's not my fault, not my mistake."

They wanted one player, Bradd Sutton, to pay about one hundred and forty dollars back. He had just gotten married and started a family. He needed every dollar he could get.

I told the players, "Give us a little time. I will see if we can come up with a solution."

Well, I knew we didn't have much time. Kansas was arriving and we couldn't practice. This was the overriding issue.

As the players were stretching, one of them said to an administrator, "Why don't you give us the money you cheat us out of on meals, and we will give you money back for the tickets."

I got a charge out of this, but of course, it just infuriated that administrator. The players aren't stupid, and they know what's going on. They'll challenge you every now and then if they feel they're being mistreated. Some of the players believe they're getting a raw deal on meals. They don't like eating in the dining hall all year long. It becomes repetitious. What's more, meals aren't served on Sunday, so they get per diem: a dollar and something for breakfast, two dollars for lunch, and two dollars and fifty cents for dinner. Where can a big, strapping athlete eat on five dollars a day?

The player's comment gave me an idea how to solve the problem. Even though they received very little money for meals, guys would still prefer it over eating in the dining hall. I told the players, "I think I can get them to lower the price they're asking you to pay for those air fares. If you don't eat in the dining hall anymore, we can increase your scholarship check to pay for your meals. Now if I let you have your food money would you get this behind you?"

We may have won the Kansas game with this plan.

They went crazy. The guys wanted out of that dining hall. Moreover, they saw someone on their side working for them now. They put their hands together and then practiced for about forty minutes. When we left the building, I said to myself, "We just won."

Going into this game, the national press had flooded Columbia. The hype for it was fantastic: No. 1 vs. No. 4.

We started the game relaxed, maybe too relaxed. In the first half we went at the KU team like they were a barber college. We didn't concentrate or take our time on offense. When we threw up shots, our attitude seemed to be, "If we miss, we'll get the rebound." They jumped out to an early lead and led at halftime by about three points.

We settled down once we realized we were attacking them at random. We pushed the ball inside and got some balance in the offense. We blocked out and didn't give them any cheap baskets. It was a great game, as good as the pre-game hype. Four guys scored more than 20 points.

The final score was Missouri 95, Kansas 87. We climbed to No. 1 in the country because second-ranked Georgetown and third-ranked Oklahoma both lost. We remained there for two weeks, beating Rutgers, Colorado twice, and Iowa State.

We lost to Kansas State in Manhattan to fall in the polls, but we regained the top position after knocking off Kansas again, beating them 77-71 in Lawrence, another sweet victory. I can still hear Dick Vitale saying before the game, "They're going down in Lawrence, baby."

The game in Lawrence was much better than the one in Columbia from a basketball purist's standpoint. The Jayhawks had won 14 in a row there, and everybody thought the home-court advantage would take us out of the picture.

John McIntyre was the feature player. He had some tremendous runs during this game. There would be a loose ball, he'd grab it, step back beyond the three-point line and launch one. Under most circumstances, this wouldn't be a good shot, but he was so hot I think he could have thrown a BB through a lifesaver.

Despite our success, toward the end of the season the team fell apart. We hit a real slump, first with a big loss at Oklahoma 107-90.

Meanwhile, there were more off-court distractions. Someone from NBC told me that they were going to have a review of the book *Raw Recruits* during halftime of the nationally televised Missouri-Notre Dame game. The book contained allegations against Missouri, and Al McGuire wanted to know if I would go on at halftime when one of the authors was being interviewed. I thought about it for some time. Here I am coaching a big game, and I have to come out and take a defensive posture on a book that contains I don't know what. I didn't like the idea.

I called my attorney, Steve Owens, and we worked late into the night and through the early morning of game day deciding what to do. Finally, I had to stop and let Steve continue to work matters out. He finally negotiated an arrangement that made sense.

Bob Costas became involved in it, and once I heard that, I relaxed a bit, because he is really a great professional. He knows the subject matter and is a great interviewer, a rare combination. I thought if he got involved, our program would get the fairest treatment it possibly could.

So there we were talking into the early morning hours the night before a nationally televised game. Costas and his producers were in New York; McGuire and his producer were in South Bend; my attorney, who was visiting his in-laws, was in a farmhouse in Monett, Missouri; I am in South Bend. Meanwhile, my staff and players overhear a lot of these conversations as they filter in and out of my hotel room for pre-game instructions.

Notre Dame trounced us in South Bend 98-67. Some people wonder how we lost so badly. Given all the distractions, I am surprised we even scored.

I had Virginia tape the game so I could see how our program was discussed at halftime. I was initially pleased with the content because I thought it was well-handled for the most part. Then I was a little surprised to see that they let the interview run into the second half of the ball game. I had never seen a ball game pre-empted for that type of thing. Maybe I was over-sensitive, but I couldn't help but be sensitive; you never know what viewers will believe.

Alex Wolff received plenty of air time to promote this book, but how much in it was new information? Most of the allegations in the excerpts had already been reported in newspapers. The NCAA had investigated all of the allegations Wolff was making. The NCAA did not bring charges on any of them, except one, which was later determined not to be an infraction. When it's the same old charges repeated time and again, there is an increased chance of making an error or airing a falsehood. It became a tiresome, repetitive process to deny these accusations that hurt our program.

One allegation about assistant coach Rich Daly was absurd. An unnamed source alleged Daly offered Detroit Cooley High coach Ben Kelso $20,000 to influence a player to sign with the Tigers. We joked that if Daly had $20,000, he'd keep it. I had always heard the rumor that Kelso expected to receive $5,000 or $10,000 to sign a player, but it was only a rumor. Why publish or broadcast rumors or quote unnamed sources without any supporting evidence?

Another allegation in *Raw Recruits* was that Doug Smith had a standardized test score falsified. Again, the book cited unnamed sources; someone just said it, so it was printed, without any evidence. This was just street talk, like the Daly allegation. The NCAA didn't find any foundation to either charge.

Wolff covers college basketball for *Sports Illustrated*, and in at least one article, he has recommended readers to take a look at *Raw Recruits*. A lot of people might question Wolff's journalistic integrity, when he can advertise his book in the middle of his own report on college basketball.

There was another round of NCAA interviews involving me and my staff two days before the Big Eight Tournament. If you had to pick the worst times for those talks, you couldn't have succeeded any more.

We were favored to win the Big Eight Tournament, but we lost the opening round to Colorado, which had finished last in the conference. Then, in the first round of the NCAA, we were defeated by my former school, Northern Iowa, 74-71.

Nonetheless, there were some postseason accolades for Smith and Peeler. Smith was named Big Eight Player of the Year. Peeler made first team all-conference. Both of them earned All-American honors. But the season ended on a low note, and now we waited for the NCAA to finish its investigation, one of the most thorough in its history.

17

Judgment Day

I grinned when I walked before the cameras into the hearing with the NCAA Committee on Infractions on September 28, 1990. If the press ever catches you with your head down or your hand on your forehead, that is the picture they will print out of a thousand. So you try to make sure your head is never bowed.

The night before the Infractions hearing, the university attorneys, Slive and Glazier, and some of their associates stayed at the Kansas City Marriott Hotel at the university's expense. Members of the NCAA's enforcement staff also stayed at the Marriott at the NCAA's expense. What I thought unusual about all this was the fact that everyone on the NCAA staff lived in Kansas City. I also know that Glazier lived in Kansas City at the time. Apparently, the NCAA doesn't have to watch its pennies as closely as the athletic programs it investigates.

My attorney Steve Owens said to the Infractions Committee during his opening statement, "This would be a good time to send a message to people both inside and outside the room that the NCAA is a fair group." Steve repeated this line in his closing statement. David Berst, the NCAA executive director for enforcement responded, "We're not here to send a message outside the room," as if the NCAA wasn't concerned about its image.

During the first break, my attorney and I watched as Berst grabbed a plate of brownies and cookies, walked out of the hearing room, and personally passed the plate around to members of the media. I got the impression the NCAA was a little concerned about its image, and it preferred to deal with it by handing out brownies and cookies to members of the press. I guess you could say the media was literally spoonfed by the NCAA.

I had told the Infractions Committee I could have done a better job in conducting my program, but I drew a parallel to winning a game by 25 points, then telling your team afterwards, "You could have done better." I honestly feel that I've done a good job over a long period of time. Sure we can make improvements, but when you consider the fact I had four athletic directors in about six years, I think I've been able to hold everything together pretty well.

The NCAA's final report came after 21 months of investigating a period between 1985 and 1989. The experience was educational.

A book called *Undue Process,* written by Don Yaeger and published before our 1990-91 season, in many ways sums up my experience with the NCAA's procedures. Yaeger produced a revealing look at the questionable methods used by the NCAA during its investigations. The system needs to change. It can be arbitrary and unfair, as evidenced by allowing UNLV in the NCAA Tournament after initially banning them from postseason play.

I'll touch on some of my ideas for reform in a later chapter, but now, here's a chronology of events leading up to the day of judgment. This chronology was put together with the help of remarks found in the university response to the NCAA.

CHRONOLOGY

About October 22, 1988
Assistant coach Bob Sundvold loans former student-athlete P.J. Mays $135 for an airplane ticket.

About November 16	Chris Sinatra-Ostlund, member of Total Person Program, informs Sundvold the loan is a possible violation.
About November 17	Sundvold discusses this matter with a former NCAA enforcement officer and decides to self-report.
November 18-December 3	Season begins. Two tournaments on the road. Sundvold works on rough draft of self-report.
Early December	Sundvold shows a rough draft of his self-report to Sinatra-Ostlund. Athletic Director Dick Tamburo is busy looking for new football coach.
December 27	Sundvold says he informs Tamburo as Tamburo prepares to leave for Orange Bowl. Tamburo asks for finished report by January 5.
Early January, 1989	University says it self-reports the loan to NCAA.
February	Newspaper reports appear concerning the Mays airline ticket.
February 8	University suspends Sundvold.

February 9	I collapse on plane flight and am soon diagnosed with cancer.
February 20	The NCAA enforcement staff says it receives Missouri's written report of the Sundvold loan.
March 7	NCAA issues what it calls a Preliminary Letter of Inquiry to the university, though it does not appear to meet the NCAA's own requirements for a Preliminary Letter.
After March 7	NCAA investigation continues.
May 2, 1990	Receipt of Official Inquiry. NCAA's allegations.
May 6	Press conference regarding Official Inquiry.
May and June	University and coaches draft separate responses to Letter of Inquiry as well as response to follow-up investigation.
July	Supplemental Letter of Inquiry charging Norm Stewart with unethical conduct.
July 18	Norm Stewart calls news conference to respond to Supplemental Letter.

Mid-September   Pre-hearing conference
                                 with university and NCAA
                                 staff.

September 28   Hearing before NCAA
                                 Committee on Infractions.

November 8   Release of Infractions Report.

Many people have wondered why it took so long for Bob Sundvold's self-report to reach Dick Tamburo's desk. A number of circumstances delayed Bob from getting it to Dick sooner. There were season-opening tournaments in New York and Charlotte, Tamburo was looking for a new football coach, and there were holidays and bowl games. The process of compiling the self-report began in November.

An important issue raised by my attorney, Steve Owens, concerned the date the university received the Preliminary Letter of Inquiry. Owens pointed out that while the university received a letter on March 7, 1989, by the NCAA's own definition, this wasn't a Preliminary Letter. This argument was based on the NCAA's own rules for notifying an institution of a preliminary inquiry. Bylaw 32.2.2.4 requires that a Preliminary Letter "state that in the event the allegations appear to be of a substantive nature, an official inquiry may be filed in accordance with the provisions of 32.5, or in the alternative, the institution will be notified that the matter has been closed."

The letter the school received left all of this out, and it did not identify itself as a preliminary inquiry. Why is the date of receipt of the letter so important? Because the NCAA has set a statute of limitations for its investigations; it can go back only four years from the date of the preliminary inquiry. Why is this time period important? Several of the major allegations concerned Curtis Kidd's return from his official paid visit on April 7, 1985. If the school didn't receive a preliminary inquiry by April 7, 1989, then the NCAA couldn't charge them with any violations on or before that date.

In August of 1989, my attorney wrote university attorneys Mike Slive and Mike Glazier, asking whether they received a Preliminary Letter of Inquiry. They responded that they had not.

Therefore, in my attorney's opinion, we had no reason to defend allegations about a trip to Detroit in April of 1985, because they didn't fall within the four-year statute of limitations. Nonetheless, the NCAA investigated the hell out of the April 1985 trip to Detroit. It appears that while the universities are required to follow the letter of the law, the NCAA is not required to follow such strict interpretation.

The first thing a coach finds out when his program is under investigation is how the university attorneys will position you. In our situation, they made sure the administration was set in one corner, the coaches in another corner, the press in a third corner and the NCAA in a fourth. The attorneys for MU made certain that we couldn't talk to our players, we couldn't talk to our administrators, we couldn't find out what they were investigating, and we couldn't talk to the press.

Throughout the investigation, the Board of Curators and the Intercollegiate Athletic Counsel were periodically briefed by Slive and Glazier. I was never asked to appear before either of those committees to brief them or tell them my side of the story. Based on the information they were getting, who knows what impression was left with those committees?

After the investigation was over and I was trying to analyze what my responsibility was and what was done by the university, I couldn't help but feel that the attorneys for the university did an outstanding job in one area: They protected the people who hired them. Athletic Director Dick Tamburo was insulated from the investigation. His name and the chancellor's name were absent from any of the violations listed in the Infractions Committee's final report, yet some of the major allegations concerned their duties. They are the individuals who are supposed to exercise "institutional control" over the athletic program. However, the chancellor was never interviewed by the NCAA, and the athletic director was interviewed only once on a minor matter. They certainly were not interviewed in the same manner as the coaches. I'm not finding fault with any individual, just the system and how it was used.

I think many people failed to realize that it wasn't just the coaching staff who was being judged by the NCAA. Theoretically, the administration was also on trial. After all, when the NCAA alleges "lack of institutional control," who controls the institution? Under NCAA rules, it is supposed to be the chancellor and the athletic director. The administration hand-picked the attorneys. Nearly a half a million dollars in university funds were paid to these attorneys, while the coaches had to hire their own lawyers. The chancellor and the athletic director remained nameless throughout the entire investigation; the coaches became the target of the investigation, and two of them resigned. Many people question this system.

We were told not to "meddle" in the investigation by attempting to get information on our own. This proved particularly true when Bob Sundvold tried to find out who had established a preseason conditioning competition known as "Tiger Olympics." He called a former strength coach, Rob Rogers, to find out what he knew about Tiger Olympics. Rogers said he was the person who set it up, and Bob then told him to make sure the NCAA understood that. But when Rogers testified to the NCAA that Sundvold had called him and asked him to report that he was responsible for establishing Tiger Olympics, the NCAA accused Bob of tampering with a witness. Under this process, you are damned if you do, and damned if you don't.

When I was first interviewed in November of 1989, I was not supplied with a list of allegations or interview topics. As a result, I wasn't prepared to answer all of the questions; I couldn't think back and remember exactly what had happened throughout those years. Once we received the Official Letter of Inquiry in May of 1990, at least we knew what we had on our hands.

I personally produced more than 1,000 pages of documents during the investigation, supplying information the NCAA had not obtained. I felt my whole staff was very forthright to the investigators at all times.

I have set out in the Appendix, the Official Inquiry we received in May, 1990, and the Supplemental Letter of Inquiry we received in July, 1990. The Supplemental Letter included an unethical conduct charge against me. You'll notice there are a lot of allegations in the Official Inquiry, however, look at them closely. I've seen this happen in other NCAA investigations. It's the old story of throwing a bunch of cow dung on the wall and seeing what sticks.

The sheer number of allegations got the attention of the media, and the public reaction was, "These are a lot of allegations; something must be wrong here." But some of these charges are so asinine most rational people wouldn't consider them. I think the idea was for the NCAA to come up with a large number of allegations to accompany their major violation, which was self-reported and then let the media do the rest. I believe they knew from the start that only five or six violations would stick.

In July of 1990, we received a Supplemental Official Inquiry. This letter added two more charges, including one that jeopardized my job. I've included this Supplemental Inquiry in the Appendix.

I was charged with providing false and misleading information. This new unethical conduct charge became well-publicized and smeared my reputation. On July 18, 1990, I called a news conference in Kansas City. My complete statement is also located in the Appendix. Most readers will remember it because it was highly publicized. Secondly, it played a pivotal role in the case. It put the NCAA on the defensive because the public was informed about the skimpy evidence the NCAA was relying on to bring forth the charge of unethical conduct.

After the news conference, I received an overwhelming positive reaction from fans and the media (believe it or not).

The night before we met with the Infractions Committee in November of 1990 to hear their findings, we were informed that part of the charge against me for allegedly providing false and misleading information had been dropped. The NCAA had the audacity to publicly charge me with unethical conduct, then several months later quietly say it had made a mistake. They didn't notify me, they just called the university attorneys, as if, "Oh, that's nothing. We do this all the time."

When Steve Owens, my attorney, told me this charge had been dropped, we simply had to laugh. We could only laugh at a lot of things throughout this investigation, no matter how infuriating they really were.

Steve said he was having trouble with the case because it was not a law case. Even though you have the facts, that doesn't mean anything. For example, during the hearing we were told that an affidavit, signed and sworn by a witness, does not carry any more weight with the Infractions Committee than a memo of an interview with a witness, prepared by the enforcement staff, which the witness has verified as accurate.

This proved to be particularly troubling because one witness, the father of a former recruit, had told the NCAA that he had seen Coach Daly and I in Detroit on an Easter Sunday and that we had been assisted in recruiting by Vic Adams. This individual, who had an ax to grind with me and the university, was later interviewed by Steve Owens and Coach Daly. When face-to-face with Daly, this individual did not recall seeing Daly before. Furthermore, he identified my attorney as the one who had recruited his son in 1985. Needless to say, this individual was not very credible to begin with. But in order to rebut his accusation that I was in Detroit on Easter Sunday, we obtained 14 signed, sworn affidavits from witnesses, as well as records from the university and a local business, indicating that I was in Columbia on that day.

So the evidence boiled down to this: We had 14 signed, sworn affidavits and documentation placing me in Columbia that day. The NCAA had one interview memorandum of a witness who had an ax to grind, who could not identify Coach Daly, and who identified my attorney as the person who had recruited his son. The evidence seemed overwhelmingly in my favor, but given the Infractions Committee's statement that a signed, sworn affidavit carried no more weight than an unsigned interview memo, I was still uneasy.

The Infractions Committee made another statement that concerned Steve and me. The Committee told us that it did not place much weight in "subsequent interviews" — interviews of a witness that take place *after* the NCAA has interviewed the witness. The apparent reason for this is that the Committee feels a witness may be pressured into changing his earlier testimony, so the first interview is more reliable. While I understand their concern, it's not fair to schools or coaches because the NCAA almost always interviews the witness first. Its whole process is designed that way. It interviews witnesses first, then it issues its official inquiry, setting forth the allegations, and invites you to conduct your interviews; and based on your investigation you are to respond to allegations. Therefore, interviews conducted by a university or a coach will almost always be "subsequent interviews." You provide your information based on your interviews and the Infractions Committee then tells you it places very little weight on it because it is based on subsequent interviews.

It arose in our case like this: The investigators interviewed a witness and claimed he had said one thing. We later went out and interviewed the witness and he said another thing. During our interview the witness became angry at the way the investigators were portrayed in his final interview. He had his own attorney draft a statement correcting any misimpressions. Nonetheless, the Infractions Committee told us that they placed very little weight on our interview of the witness because it was a "subsequent interview."

The whole thing made me wonder, what were we to do? The NCAA asked us to go out and conduct our own investigation. If we do, our interviews are given little or no weight because they are "subsequent interviews." If we interview a witness who has not been interviewed before and ask the witness to put his testimony in the form of a signed, sworn affidavit, we are told that that affidavit carries no more weight than the investigator's unsigned, unsworn memo of another witness. The whole process made me feel virtually helpless.

By the way, none of these things was set out in the NCAA rules. There is no rule that says the enforcement staff's interview memos, even if unverified by the witness, should be given as much weight as an affidavit signed and sworn by a witness. There is no rule saying subsequent interviews should be given less weight than initial interviews. It is simply part of the folklore of the NCAA process.

In this regard I kind of get a chuckle out of some of the movements to reform the NCAA's investigation rules. As long as the NCAA rules can apply unwritten standards, like the ones just described, without answering to anyone, what difference does it make how the rules are reformed? Besides, what's the assurance the NCAA will follow the new rules? For example, the NCAA currently has a rule requiring investigators to take their interview memos back to the witness so the witness can make any necessary corrections and sign the memo to verify its accuracy. In my case, of the 36 interview memos I was allowed to see, only 13 had been corrected and signed by the witness. But the memos were used as if they were entirely accurate. There shouldn't have been any trouble locating the witnesses to get them to correct and sign the memos because three of the unsigned memos involved interviews of me; one involved Coach Daly; one involved Coach Sundvold; and several of the other unsigned ones involved players who were still on our team. Surely the NCAA knew where we were and, as members of an NCAA institution, we had to sign the memos once they were corrected.

So I am very skeptical that changes in the written rules

above will achieve our goals of reform. What really needs to be reformed are attitudes and mentality—but more on that in a later chapter.

The allegation that I wasn't forthcoming regarding another matter still hung over my head. But I knew it wouldn't hold up because it was ridiculous. This charge involved the letter of intent for Daniel Lyton and the alleged involvement of Vic Adams. If it stuck, I was going to file a lawsuit.

I didn't sleep any easier knowing part of the ethics charge against me remained. I tried not to be bothered by it, but my frustration level varied from day to day. I wondered, with the rumors they had, could the NCAA just say, "Yeah, he knew about Lyton's letter of intent?" I decided to maintain the posture that I always had: We ran a good program.

In the end, the unethical conduct charge was dropped, however, I was still named in an allegation for lack of institutional control. As you can see from their response, even the university found it hard to believe a coach can be responsible for control of an institution.

The wording in the Infractions Report is a bit harsh and misleading. For instance, the report said most of the violations concerned recruiting, because as far as the NCAA is concerned, a player is a recruit until he enters school. But most of the athletes involved already had signed their letters of intent when the incidents occurred, so there couldn't have been any recruiting involved.

There is also reason to suspect that the university's attorneys, Mike Slive and Mike Glazier, negotiated with the NCAA on the particular wording. The language in many cases is more lenient regarding the university administration than the coaching staff. When you are in this position, you begin to hear all sorts of stories. Some people were telling me the chancellor wanted to fire me, and Slive and Glazier's work did little to disprove that.

One story had the chancellor asking a relative of the president of the national Missouri Alumni Board, "What would happen if I fired Stewart?" There was a similar rumor from one of our faculty members. He said the chancellor had told another chancellor in the Big Eight that he had a basketball coach he could not control, and it was a great concern. You can imagine what was going through my head as I heard these stories. I couldn't talk to anyone to verify or discredit them. I wasn't allowed to speak with the administration. When we did meet with the administration later on, it was at my insistence. I was in limbo. I'm sure the administration was hearing its share of rumors also. That was the sad part: The coaches and the administration could not talk, and the media loved it. Rumors and innuendo were printed and reprinted.

Every time there was a story supporting the administration, a "high ranking source" in the administration was quoted. We were told by reporters that high ranking officials were having lunch with other reporters during the investigation. Eventually, the university-owned television and radio stations did an extensive poll to find out how much support there was for me. I was told a poll of this nature cost up to $25,000. The poll was conducted at the end of the investigation, when you might expect my popularity to be at a low point, but it turned out that about 80 to 85 percent supported me. The radio and television stations called me for comment. The story aired, although it wasn't played as high as if it were a poll showing a lack of support. And it just so happened they didn't use my comments.

I still wonder who wanted the poll conducted. Even though I had the public's support, I knew where all of this was heading. We were going to be penalized. The NCAA's record on such issues is pretty clear: You are going to lose. I think members of the NCAA enforcement staff liked the idea of getting a veteran coach's scalp. It would earn them more respect in the eyes of their boss.

I've talked with another coach whose program is going through the final phase of an investigation and the NCAA is finding some of the same things wrong with his program. He agrees with me that we are virtually incapable of conducting programs without minor violations. However, when the NCAA holds an inquiry, it will not distinguish minor rule infractions from major ones.

The best you can hope for is to soften the blow. But when the report was released, it didn't seem mild. I've included the NCAA Infractions Report in the Appendix.

Now it's time to review these charges. I want to analyze them one by one. You be the judge of how serious the violations were, who should have borne responsibility, and whether the penalties were fair.

At five years of age.

Virginia and me at an early Christmas—a stud, even then.

Shelbyville, Shelbyville, you are it! We finished 2nd in the state finals (I'm in 1st row, 3rd from right).

The official was a great friend, the late Alex George. Number 22 is yours truly.

Here comes the pitch, but where is it going?

Some members of my first MU team in 1967-68. Standing: Tom Johnson, Tom Miltenberger, Gary Frazier, Gene Jones. Sitting: Dave Bennett, Henry Pinkney, and Jim Chapman.

The 1975-76 Tigers, a great ballclub, one of the top five teams in the country. Notice the attendance.

Courtesy of Univ. of Missouri Sports Information Office

With Willie Smith(left) after winning the Show-Me Classic. Also pictured is Mark Anderson, who became an assistant at Providence, and the late Herb Schooling, then MU Chancellor.

Courtesy of Univ. of Missouri Sports Information Office

Courtesy of Univ. of Missouri Sports Information Office

Our first outright Big Eight Championship (1975) in 46 years.

Winning the Big Eight became commonplace, with four consecutive wins.

Here's an early public relations photo.

ur 1979-80 team hoto. This team et an NCAA field bal shooting ecord, hitting for a 73 percentage. he record still ands.

Doug Smith—1988-89-90-91. A great player and an even greater individual.

Steve Stipanovich—1980-81-82-83. The best player to come out of St. Louis.

Derrick Chievous—1985-86-87-88. A phenomenal scorer, he brought the big crowds to the Hearnes Center.

Jon Sundvold—1980-81-82-83. He had the picture-perfect jumpshot, and so much more.

Ricky Frazier—1980-81-82. One of the best competitors we've ever had.

Larry Drew—1977-78-79-80. A great team leader, he holds the career record for assists.

John Brown—1971-72-73. A great player from Dixon, Missouri, and the first nationally prominent player to play for me.

Willie Smith—1975-76. He took the team one game away from the Final Four in 1976, the closest we've ever gotten.

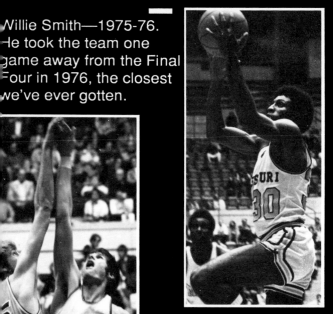

Al Eberhard—1972-73-74. He won all three team awards in 1974. What an inspirational player.

Kim Anderson—1974-75-76-77. The Player of the Year in 1977, now he's a coach.

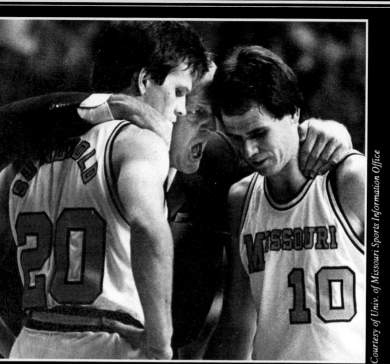

Calmly getting my point across to Jon Sundvold and Barrie Laurie.

Courtesy of Univ. of Missouri Sports Information Office

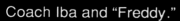

Coach Iba and "Freddy."

At Lindsey and
Susan's wedding.
Front row: Laura,
Kathleen, LuAnn,
Jennifer, Jeff. Back
row: Me, Susan,
Virginia's father
Barney, Lindsey, and
Virginia.

The Coach and
the Boss.

18

The Trouble with P.J.

The most serious violations, according to the NCAA, concerned our treatment of P.J. Mays, who signed a letter of intent to play for us in 1987. He was awarded institutional financial aid, although he was ineligible to receive such aid. During Mays' first semester of his senior year in high school, when he signed the letter of intent, we thought he had met the 2.0 minimum grade point requirement. The NCAA said the Missouri coaching staff ignored a letter that Mays was ineligible for athletics and allowed him to practice three or four times.

This statement is very misleading and damaging to the coaching staff. The "letter" — which none of the coaches remembers receiving — was an internal memorandum from a member of our Total Person Program to the coaching staff.

The Total Person Program was established by former athletic director Jack Lengyel and current athletic director Dick Tamburo. It's an academic counseling unit that's supposed to help the total development of a student-athlete. There is one division that is supposed to monitor the eligibility of student-athletes.

The memo from the Total Person Program didn't say anything about Mays being ineligible. Furthermore, the NCAA's own rule allows a player to practice for two weeks while a school checks his grade point average.

Mays was not a highly recruited high school basketball player, he would not make or break a team. A 6-3 guard, he was not among the top 50 players in the country, or even the top 100. He was just a good player from Cincinnati, Ohio's Purcell-Marian High School, a private school.

His junior year Mays had a knee injury and was a border-line prospect. We felt he had recovered from his injury, although not many teams recruited him. He played for Jim Stoll, an outstanding high school coach. I had watched the kid play and I liked him.

On at least one occasion, in the fall of 1987, I talked with Stoll and the Mays family about admission requirements, especially Proposition 48. I didn't discuss Mays' grades during a home visit because I was impressed with the guidance he was receiving from his coach and his mother. Yvonne Mays seemed to be a good parent. Greg Jones was P.J.'s surrogate father, a man P.J. had known since he was 2 years old.

I obtained much of the following information concerning the university's response to the NCAA investigation through my lawyer. I didn't get the chance to talk to all of the individuals involved about their participation, so these answers came from the university's investigation.

According to university attorneys, Assistant Coach Bob Sundvold said he returned to Ohio a week after my visit to check P.J.'s transcript. Sundvold recounted talking with Stoll and Mays' high school guidance counselor, Sister Virginia Ann. Sundvold reviewed the sixth-semester transcript and said Mays appeared to be on track to qualify, based on his calculations of the projected grade point average.

University documents show Mays said there were no improper offers and the coaching staff limited its recruiting discussions to reasons why he should attend Missouri.

Mays signed a letter of intent to come to Missouri during the early signing period in his senior year. Once a player signs a letter of intent, his admission is determined by the Registrar's Office. The Total Person Program follows this process and keeps the athletic department informed of any eligibility problems. P.J. went on to perform well on the basketball court, averaging about 24 points a game, but we did not know then how poorly he was performing in the classroom, especially his final semester.

The University Director of Admissions, Gary Smith, said that a transcript dated February 4, 1988, showed Mays' grades through the seventh semester and accompanied his application received in June. Smith stated that Mays' transcript, which included his class rank and an ACT score of 18, met the qualifications for admission under normal standards. His admission was subject to verification by his final transcript.

This was not unusual. As many as 800 other incoming freshmen were admitted the same way. If a student never submitted a final transcript, the school would remind him or her on October 1 that a transcript was needed.

P.J. did a terrible job in his last semester of school. I am convinced he knew this. I don't know what he thought was going to happen when we found out. Maybe he thought we'd just let it go, or maybe he thought he'd be ineligible but still on scholarship.

According to the university response to the NCAA, Mays' high school guidance counselor said he met with P.J. during the final weeks of his senior year and told him he didn't see how Mays could achieve a 2.0 in his core curriculum to meet the scholarship requirements. But an unusual circumstance would prevent the university from finding out soon enough. Purcell-Marian would not release his final transcript to the university until his last semester's tuition was paid. Mrs. Mays hadn't paid it upon P.J.'s graduation.

I did not know his transcript had been withheld. I assumed the Registrar's Office had done its job of checking transcripts for admissions. This is not the coach's job, nor should it ever be the coach's job, to handle or review a new recruit's transcript. Schools don't want coaches involved in this, and I don't blame them. It just leaves you open to more suspicion. That's why we have the Total Person Program evaluate things.

P.J. arrived in Columbia in June for orientation. No one from the coaching staff had yet heard of any problems about his grades. University records show that Mays was authorized for scholarship in July, with a housing revision in August. I had nothing to do with the process.

The man in charge of evaluating the certification and eligibility in the Total Person Program was John Little. Little, according to the University response to the NCAA, said he first saw

Mays' seventh-semester transcript around July. He said he didn't carefully evaluate it because the university had already admitted Mays as a normal student.

Little said his first priority was checking on the eligibility status of the football and cross-country teams, which started practice in late August. He would check on the athletic eligibility of basketball players later because they didn't start practice until October. Little stated the Big Eight Conference deadline for certifying basketball players' eligibility was not until October 1. I'm sure he felt he had plenty of time to find out about P.J.'s athletic eligibility.

Little reported that he recalled telling Assistant Coach Sundvold in July that he needed Mays' final transcript, but Little wasn't overly concerned because many athletes don't get them in until late summer. He observed the next time he was aware the final transcript still had not arrived was about September 9. Little said he sent a letter to me and the other coaches telling us the school needed a final transcript for Mays to certify him for practice and competition.

We don't remember receiving the letter, but the university provided a copy for the NCAA. Even if we had received this letter, it did not say Mays was ineligible. It simply said (and this is taken straight from the memorandum supplied by the university) "We are missing a few things on the scholarship freshmen that we will need in order to certify them for practice and competition."

The memo listed these three items: a final transcript for P.J. Mays, a Normandy High School NCAA Core form (48-C) for Mike Wawrzyniak and an ACT test verification for Anthony Peeler.

Even without the transcript, it still would have been within the rules for Mays to practice because of the 1988-89 NCAA Bylaw 5-6-(b)-(1), allowing a player a maximum of two weeks of practice while his school determines his high school grade point average. My attorney brought up this grace period rule in the NCAA hearings.

The NCAA countered by saying it would try to prove we violated an internal university rule. "You do have rules on these matters, don't you?" the NCAA asked at the hearings. University officials, afraid of looking like they had none of their own regulations, nodded their heads. So the NCAA found we had violated our own internal rule and placed this "violation" in its report. But no one has since found any university rule forbidding a two-week grace period to check out a player's eligibility. The university rules, as far as we have discovered, merely reflect the NCAA rules, which allow for a grace period. We still don't know whether the grace period applies to future athletes.

The NCAA made an issue out of the fact that we let Mays practice after receiving the Little memo. It appeared as if the coaches were ignoring the rules. But in the end the coaching staff was criticized not for breaking an NCAA rule, but for breaking one of our own rules we can't even find on our books.

According to university documents, Little said that on September 9 or 10, Sundvold discovered that the reason Mays had not been able to obtain a final transcript was because he owed his high school $450 for his last semester. Sundvold told Little that Mrs. Mays assured him she would pay the bill promptly and the university would get the transcript.

Little recalled that it was in early October when he said to Sundvold that Mays' transcript still had not been received by the university. Mays' status crossed his mind again when practice began on October 15. Little testified he was surprised Mays had practiced with the team.

University documents state Yvonne Mays said her son called her on October 12 to inform her that the university did not have a final copy of his transcript, and that he wouldn't be allowed to play unless it was delivered. Mrs. Mays said she then called the high school and learned she would have to pay the outstanding $450 bill before the school would release the final transcript. Mrs. Mays claimed she borrowed the money and sent the transcript Federal Express to Missouri.

Little said next that he went to the Admissions Office to review Mays' admission file after he found out practice had started. During this evaluation, Little apparently made a rough calculation of Mays' projected core grade point average. He suddenly realized two different grade scales had been used during Mays' high school years. Little said he thought at this point that Mays might not qualify based on his grades. There was a possibility the wrong scale had been used to calculate Mays' grade point when he was admitted.

University documents show that Mays said he received his transcript in his dorm on October 15 but didn't give it to the coaching staff until a few days later. Mays stated he forgot to bring it to practice and that Sundvold eventually drove him to his room to pick up the transcript. The university documents said this is when Mays was declared ineligible and was withheld from practice.

The NCAA investigators and some sports writers would rip the coaching staff apart for allowing Mays to practice after we received this "letter" notifying us he was ineligible. But again, I'm not sure we received the letter, the letter didn't say he was ineligible, and I still maintain we had a grace period to allow Mays to practice.

Although Mays was awarded financial aid without the minimum grade point average — a violation of the rules — I didn't have anything to do with certifying him. I can't assume any responsibility in certifying an athlete for school, and I've met with the chancellor regarding this point. Moreover, I don't want my assistants involved in transferring materials from a high school to the university, because if you are going to have any problems, that's where they are going to occur. The chancellor and I are in complete agreement about this.

Our Total Person Program believes it is the coaches' responsibility to obtain the transcripts from the high school because they can't do it. I have struck a middle ground with them by saying we will encourage people to send them transcripts, but not the official one. The official one must be transported from the high school to the University Registrar's Office without our involvement.

I will say this about the Total Person Program. They have some people who try to do an outstanding job. But the old system is better. When you reach the point of doing so much for the kids, they rely on you too much. Student-athletes should bear more responsibility for their education. This will ultimately make them more motivated, better students.

Who does the university blame for the scholarship aid that was awarded to Mays? In its report, it cited the failure of two systems, the certification of eligibility and the financial aid administration. From now on there will be a new procedure requiring positive certification of eligibility before athletic aid is credited to a student-athlete's account.

When the coaching staff realized Mays wasn't eligible, we dropped him from practice and told him he would have to pay his way. Unfortunately, this wasn't the end of our troubles with P.J.

On October 22, 1988, in the parking lot outside the Missouri basketball office, assistant coach Bob Sundvold handed Mays $135. The money was a loan to help Mays buy an airline ticket to review his high school record. When the money exchanged hands, a violation was committed.

This was a gesture you just never do, even for humanitarian reasons, such as in Mays' case. Bob thought different rules applied because Mays was no longer a student-athlete, having been ruled ineligible due to his grades. It would have been fine, for instance, if Bob loaned $135 to a student who wasn't an athlete. But Mays was still considered a "recruited" athlete, so such loans are prohibited.

Bob Sundvold made a mistake, but not nearly as big a mistake as reported by the media and the NCAA. First of all, it wasn't a recruiting violation; we weren't gaining any advantage over other schools by this loan. Secondly, Bob began the self-reporting process once he found out it was a violation. There was no effort to cover up the incident or let it slide, contrary to what the NCAA or the media implied.

Since I had no direct knowledge of this incident at this time, here are fragments of what transpired around the time of the loan, according to the university's response to the NCAA.

On October 20, 1988, Sundvold met with university eligibility coordinator John Little. Little's review of Mays' high school transcript revealed he was not eligible. In the university response to the NCAA, Little claims Sundvold took responsibility for the problem and expressed concern about what my reaction would be. However, Sundvold told the university he never assumed responsibility. Sundvold felt — and I agree — that those matters were the responsibility of the Total Person Program.

Little and Sundvold apparently weren't totally convinced at first that Mays' core grade point was under 2.0. An issue in question was a class called "Introduction to Physical Science" that P.J. took his freshman year. It was not included in Mays' list of core courses on the transcript, possibly because Mays attended a different high school as a freshman. If Mays' original high school considered "Introduction to Physical Science" a core course, then it could be used to calculate his final core grade point average.

Little said that if P.J.'s freshman physical science course applied as a core course, and if it could be added to the original grade scale, Mays would have a total core grade point above 2.0 and would be eligible to play basketball.

The university's documents state that Little told Sundvold these issues needed to be resolved with officials at Mays' high school. The school would need to give the University Admissions Office a letter saying whether the physical science course could be considered a core course. Little said this is when Sundvold got the idea of sending Mays back to Cincinnati to talk with people at his high school.

That night, Sundvold telephoned Yvonne Mays to tell her P.J. was ineligible. Like all mothers, she was trying to arrange the best opportunities for her son. When she found out about his ineligibility, Mrs. Mays was shocked and did not want to believe it.

Yvonne Mays, according to the university response to the NCAA, was very angry at Sundvold and the university because no one had examined her son's final transcript for two full months while he was enrolled there.

Sundvold reportedly said P.J. didn't appear surprised when he was informed of his problem.

Mrs. Mays may not have known how bad her son's grades were, because she did not have a final transcript from Purcell-Marian. If she had been able to pay for his last semester, then we could have learned the truth long before P.J. attended his first class at Missouri.

Every student knows, athlete or not, that when you receive a poor grade, you have an opportunity to discuss it with the teacher. Maybe there was a chance the teacher would re-evaluate P.J.'s grade. Maybe he could do some extra work to improve it. And just maybe the teacher made a mistake. I've run into very few people who were never in this position; I had been in a similar position as a student too. You may expect to be turned down, but who knows? It can't hurt to ask.

This was Bob Sundvold's suggestion to P.J., that he go back to his school and see what he could find out.

Sundvold said he called Yvonne Mays again on October 21 to console her because he felt bad about what had happened. During this phone call, it was decided P.J. would return to Cincinnati to meet with high school officials. Sundvold recalled

Yvonne wanted him to talk to the officials at the school because she held him accountable. Sundvold replied that he couldn't do that.

On October 22, P.J. Mays and his roommate, Jamal Coleman, were cleaning their room when Sundvold gave P.J. a call. Mays said this is when he first heard of Sundvold's idea to resolve his grade problem.

According to the university response to the NCAA, Mays said he told Sundvold he didn't have the money to pay for the flight to Cincinnati, so Sundvold responded by asking him to borrow it from Jamal. Mays said he put the receiver down and pretended to request the money from Jamal, even though he didn't. Then he told Sundvold that Coleman couldn't lend him the money. Mays said Sundvold subsequently told him to call the airlines and arrange a flight to Cincinnati.

Mays made arrangements to fly from Columbia to St. Louis to Cincinnati at a cost of $138. Mays claims he told Coleman that Sundvold was going to pay for it, but Coleman told the university that Mays knew Sundvold expected Mays to repay the loan. Coleman reported that Mays said, "I'm not going to pay it back."

Jamal Coleman drove P.J. Mays to the athletic office parking lot. Sundvold said Mays stepped out of the car and the money exchanged hands. He told Mays this money was a loan, and Mays was expected to repay it when he got his Pell Grant. Later on Sundvold discovered that Mays had actually received his $415 Pell Grant a week earlier.

Sundvold said Mays commented that he needed another three dollars to cover the cost of the ticket to Cincinnati. Sundvold told Mays to borrow the three dollars from Coleman.

Yvonne Mays was informed by her mother at work that the university was sending P.J. home and that the school wanted to know whether Yvonne had the money to pay for his airline ticket. Yvonne said she told her mother, "Tell them, hell no."

Mrs. Mays stated she called Sundvold when she came home from work to find out what was going on. She said Sundvold explained how P.J could possibly be ruled eligible again. During this conversation, she asked Sundvold how P.J. was going to return to Missouri. She claimed he was only concerned at that moment about getting him home, and he hoped she and P.J. could figure out a way he could get back.

Mrs. Mays said she argued that since Sundvold was sending P.J. to Cincinnati, he should arrange for his return to Columbia. However, Sundvold told her he was not to blame for the matter. She then said that he agreed to have a prepaid return ticket prepared by Canterbury Travel in Columbia and that she could decide how to pay for it later.

According to the university response to the NCAA, Mrs. Mays replied, "Fine, just get my child back in school." The travel agency explained that with prepaid tickets, it simply extends credit to the person traveling.

Travel records show P.J. Mays left Columbia at 4:10 p.m. on Saturday, October 22, and arrived in Cincinnati that night.

The university's report states Mays claimed that Sundvold woke him with a phone call on Monday, October 24, the day Mays was to meet with high school officials, and was upset that Mays was still in bed.

Mays said he got up, dressed and called the school after Sundvold called him, then he went to meet with Don Loos, his former guidance counselor. Mays alleged he had received some written instructions on how to conduct himself with school officials.

Loos reportedly said he was asked whether a life sciences and a physical sciences course on Mays' transcript could be considered lab courses. If so, this would favorably affect Mays' core grade point. But Loos told Mays in both cases these were not lab courses.

He said Mays' only other question was whether the grading scale that was in effect when he first enrolled at Purcell-Marian could be used to calculate his entire grade point average. According to Loos, the old grading scale was used to calculate grades before June 1987, the new scale thereafter.

Loos stated that Mays did not pressure him. The guidance counselor also said that Sundvold called him as well to discuss the same issues. Sundvold didn't exert any pressure either or ask Loos to change a grade.

Mays flew back to Columbia that evening on the prepaid flight. Mays said he told Bob his high school did not see any mistakes in the transcript.

Mrs. Mays called Chris Sinatra-Ostlund, the director of our Total Person Program, on November 15 to discuss a number of matters, including how much money Mays owed the school due to the cancellation of P.J.'s scholarship. Sinatra-Ostlund said Mrs. Mays mentioned a letter indicating her son owed $144.

Apparently recognizing the money from Sundvold was only a loan, Mays reportedly remarked, "Oh, that must be for the ticket Bob bought to send P.J. home."

Sinatra-Ostlund inquired, "What ticket?"

Mrs. Mays then explained the details of P.J.'s trip to Cincinnati. Sinatra-Ostlund said this was the first time she realized something might be wrong. The $144 bill, incidentally, was actually for books P.J. had charged to the athletic department.

According to the university report to the NCAA, Sundvold said the first time he realized the $135 loan was an issue was when he spoke with Sinatra-Ostlund the next morning. He told Sinatra-Ostlund he would call his friend, a former NCAA investigator.

Meanwhile, Bob was trying to collect the money from the Mays family, without any success.

The university report claims that Yvonne Mays stated she bought equipment to tape a telephone call with Sundvold because she was concerned about his intentions. Sundvold said he had talked with P.J. regarding repaying the debt, and that P.J. told him to talk to his mom. When Sundvold called, Mrs. Mays taped the conversation.

The transcript of the conversation was supplied to the university. Several times during it, Bob tried to get Mrs. Mays to agree to repay the loan. But each time, she said she didn't understand it to be a loan.

At one point, it appeared Bob may have asked Mrs. Mays to tell Sinatra-Ostlund that the loan had been repaid.

The university asked Sundvold about this part in the phone conversation. Sundvold said he wasn't asking Mays to lie, but that he was setting up a scenario for Yvonne so she could understand that as soon as the money was repaid, he would be in a better position. He did not want Sinatra-Ostlund or Yvonne Mays to think the $135 was a gift, because it wasn't.

Another big issue with the NCAA was the length of time between Sinatra-Ostlund's telling Bob this may be a violation and the university reporting it to the NCAA.

We played in two tournaments on the road during this time, which was around the Thanksgiving holiday. We had the NIT in New York, then the Diet Pepsi Tournament of Champions in Charlotte. It was a very busy period for the coaching staff.

Sundvold stated he called his friend, the former NCAA enforcement officer, the day Sinatra-Ostlund told him about the probable violation, but his friend wasn't there. He said he didn't talk with faculty athletic representative Carl Settergren or Joanne Rutherford, a staff member in charge of interpretations, because he felt his friend would be more knowledgeable.

Sundvold said he finally got hold of his friend that night in Cincinnati, and his friend's testimony agrees, saying the call came in to his hotel room around 10 p.m.

According to his friend, Sundvold got to the point quickly, explaining that he lent some money to a non-qualifier who had been removed from the basketball team and was no longer receiving financial aid. Bob's question was, does a loan to someone who is no longer an eligible player constitute a violation?

Bob's friend, the former NCAA enforcement officer, answered that the player remains a student-athlete and thus remains subject to the extra benefit legislation. The loan was a violation.

Sundvold said he then asked his friend what he should do. His friend explained the self-reporting procedure to him and advised Sundvold to self-report to Dick Tamburo, the Missouri athletic director. Bob's friend said he explained several steps Sundvold should take to prepare his self-report. He recalled Sundvold mentioning he would rather deal with it now than let it hang over his head.

Bob had two or three more conversations with his friend, the former NCAA enforcement officer, on how to write the self-report, and he wrote it up in about two to three weeks. Much of the delay was due to the back-to-back tournament schedule.

Sundvold, according to the university's report, said he showed Sinatra-Ostlund a draft of his self-report during the week of December 7-14.

As I've already explained, when Bob came in to tell me, it was the first time I was aware of the loan. I was shocked.

I said, "We will report this to Dick Tamburo."

I think we walked across the hall to Tamburo's office at that time, and he wasn't there. Tamburo was busy looking for a new football coach then.

Sundvold said he finally contacted Tamburo in person about this matter on December 27, just before the AD was leaving for a trip to the Orange Bowl. Tamburo apparently asked to have a written report on his desk when he returned from the Orange Bowl on January 5.

Yes, it did take a few weeks for this problem to go from Chris Sinatra-Ostlund to Bob to Bob's friend, back to Bob, then to me, to Tamburo's office, and finally to the enforcement staff. But there was no effort to cover up the situation, as some people have insinuated.

This was an infraction we're indeed guilty of, however, it was self-reported. The university conducted its own internal investigation, and the university suspended Bob.

The NCAA called it a major violation. Bob Sundvold, who had given us 13 years of loyal service without any prior rules problems, eventually thought it was in everyone's best interest to resign over a mistake he self-reported.

The university has taken some extra steps to make sure this doesn't happen again. Travel agencies have received specific conditions under which tickets may be arranged by staff members for student-athletes, prospective student-athletes and their parents. We've given the coaches a complete interpretation of extra benefit legislation that pertained to the loan to Mays.

Mays attempted to stay in school as a normal student by receiving financial aid that was available to any other student. The Financial Aid Office helped Mays apply for a Pell Grant of $875 per semester, a NDSL Perkins Loan of $550 per semester, a Stafford/GSL of $1,312.50 per semester and an SEOG Grant of $300 a semester.

Here was another administrative goof beyond my control. The university report says the Total Person Program did not communicate with the Financial Aid Office about NCAA restrictions that still applied to Mays. He was not eligible for the SEOG. This constituted another violation.

While the school was learning the truth about Mays' transcript in the fall of 1988, questions came up about his ACT score. According to the university response to the NCAA, Mays reportedly said he received a letter from the ACT board notifying him his score was being challenged because it doubled from the fall of his senior year to the spring. Mays said that the ACT board reported a handwriting and thumbprint discrepancy.

It's important to note that Mays had said he did not receive any help on his ACT test from people connected with the University of Missouri. He had taken this test in Cincinnati.

Mays had the option of taking the ACT again, but he decided to leave the university and enroll at another school that did not require an ACT score for admission. Because he did not appeal the ACT challenge, his score was invalidated.

The university interviewed P.J. and Mrs. Mays at length about the ACT matter.

Yvonne said the ACT board found that P.J.'s signature on the answering sheet did not match his other signature on record with them. According to the university report, Yvonne claimed P.J. had injured his hand the evening before the test and wore an ace bandage to the test site. She wrote a letter requesting the test proctor to fill out the answer sheet information because the injury prevented P.J. from writing. But Mrs. Mays said P.J. told her he had someone sitting at his table fill out the personal information sheet for him.

P.J. stated that the answers on the sheet were his own. He said his score had improved so much because he took a course to help him understand the test better.

The question that now arises is, how could the school give an athletic scholarship to a person whose ACT results doubled? Shouldn't that have raised some questions? The coaches bore the brunt of the penalties and the criticism from the NCAA investigation, but I don't think responsibility in these areas fell in the realm of the coaching staff.

The university currently has taken the position that it will investigate a five-point jump in an ACT score. This would equate to 200 points on the SAT. The Coordinator of Eligibility will examine all test scores and will notify the Compliance Coordinator of any inconsistencies. It's now written that coaches will share the responsibility of monitoring the scores.

19
Motown Tigers

The NCAA and the media focused a lot of attention on our recruiting in the Detroit area. It started with some newspaper articles about Assistant Coach Rich Daly, dubbing him "Doctor Detroit" for his success signing players there.

Detroit is an important town from a recruiting standpoint. I think the number of players from Detroit on college teams is more than 100. A recent first-round pick named Derrick Coleman was from Detroit. We tried to recruit him, but he chose Syracuse.

I love Detroit players because the kids will go to school and do well. Success in school is one of our prerequisites. I think their upbringing has something to do with it. Families in Detroit love sports and put a high emphasis on education, too.

There is such a wealth of players in the Detroit area that the University of Michigan can't take all of them. We recruited players Michigan and Michigan State passed up, and we got some good ones: the Lynn Hardys, the Lee Cowards, the Nathan Buntins. Rich Daly was primarily responsible for getting these players. They weren't the first-round picks or can't-miss prospects, and weren't highly sought. We like to say, "Anybody can see a ruby in a goat's rear end, but after that, it takes a professional eye and some luck to pick a player who can play."

Rich Daly has the ability to do that as well as anyone in the country, so we started taking players from Detroit and succeeded with them. I'm sure the press reminded Michigan State coach Jud Heathcote of this fact, since he was supposedly getting the better pick of athletes in his area but wasn't winning games. I don't doubt that Jud tried to do whatever he could to keep us from recruiting in his territory. Daly was embarrassing him.

When Michigan recruited a player, we would drop out, because we felt they were going to get that player. Michigan State was a little different because its program wasn't doing as well. A player might look at Michigan State and say, "I may do better at Missouri."

We needed to find someone knowledgeable about the top programs in Detroit just as we had done in California and Washington, D.C. Rich made many phone calls to people who are on the inside in areas where there is considerable basketball talent.

In Detroit, one of those people is Vic Adams.

When you go to a game with Rich Daly, you get a lesson in how to work a crowd. I would walk into a gym with him, and the next thing I know he's sitting in the front row with the cheerleaders. Then I look up and he's in the back row talking to someone else in the stands. Next he moves on to a group of coaches. A few minutes later I might see him in a corner by himself, looking like it's a pain to even be in the gym. But he won't leave until he finds out who's who in Zooville.

So it was inevitable, with Adams' knowledge of Detroit basketball, that Daly would develop an association with him.

One of the big questions in the NCAA investigation concerned Adams' involvement in our recruiting. Was he a representative of the University of Missouri's athletic interests, or was he just a person with a lot of knowledge about players in Detroit, knowledge he shared with many schools?

The NCAA has rules against athletic representatives assisting in the recruiting of prospects, but on the other hand, it has a rule allowing a scouting service or agent to distribute personal information about a prospect to universities. Vic Adams, in my opinion, was neither of these.

When we recruit a player, we want to know what that athlete is thinking and who is going to influence his decision making. This may be his coach, it may be a girlfriend, perhaps his best friend. Vic Adams might be able to tell us who this important contact was. We are always looking for someone who has an association with a player. If we have this information, then a phone call or a letter at the appropriate time — perfectly within the rules — can be a key in the recruitment of a player.

It was alleged that Adams acted as an athletic representative and assisted us in the recruitment of two players, Curtis Kidd and Daniel Lyton.

The NCAA deemed Adams a representative of Missouri's athletic interests based on the number of phone calls Rich Daly made to his house, but we checked Rich's phone records and found five other people he had called more than Vic Adams. The NCAA's logic escapes me. The NCAA has specific rules delineating what conduct will make someone an athletic representative. There is no rule that after so many phone calls to an individual he becomes an athletic representative of the university. Yet at the Infractions Committee hearing, the Committee dubbed Adams our athletic representative because Rich called him so often.

Adams was a guy who hung around Cooley High School's summer league and high school basketball games. According to the university response to the NCAA, Kidd told investigators Adams would give several area players rides to and from games. Kidd reportedly said Adams first visited his home in his sophomore or junior year to give him a ride to practice. This was long before we showed any interest in Kidd. On top of that, Kidd's mother was reported as saying Adams and her daughter knew each other from high school, and he would often visit this daughter when he stopped by the home.

Kidd's father reportedly told investigators that Adams' relationship with his son preceded the university's recruitment. He said Adams happened to be a good friend of his son who was looking out for him. He also mentioned Adams discussing other universities besides Missouri.

How could this mean Adams was an athletic representative for Missouri? Doesn't it sound more like he's trying to be a representative for the best interests of Kidd and his family?

This is a different picture from the one you get in *Raw Recruits*. That book quoted unnamed people as saying Adams was beginning to do everything with a "black and orange" twist. At least the author could have gotten the school colors right. They're black and gold.

I first met Vic Adams at a basketball game in Detroit, where I was watching a player named Demetrius Gore. Gore went on to have a very successful basketball career at Pittsburgh. Demetrius' father was with one of the major car manufacturers and moved to St. Louis. Because his father lived in the St. Louis area, there was some interest expressed in Demetrius' attending the University of Missouri.

I had just encountered Vic when someone in the stands recognized me and asked, "Who are you watching?"

I was kind of surprised anyone would recognize me because it was one of my first visits to Detroit. I simply looked down at the program and picked out a number 15. I had seen number 15 on the court and he obviously was not going to log very many minutes.

"I like number 15," I said.

This guy went absolutely bananas. He couldn't get over it, that I'd come all the way from Missouri to watch a guy who wasn't going to play anyplace other than Joe's Pizza Parlor.

Vic got a kick out of this, and we had a fun relationship after that. It was just a casual acquaintance. I called him on occasion because he had good information about players, and he was amusing to be around. Rumor claimed that Adams had performed with the Winans, a gospel group, and once sang as a backup for Stevie Wonder. One time he gave me a record he had cut. That was about the extent of our relationship.

Vic had actually coached at one of the schools and helped a lot of athletes go on to play in college. To my knowledge, he never wanted money, he was only interested in seeing players get to school and play basketball. One of those kids was Curtis Kidd.

Kidd's coach at Cooley High was Ben Kelso. When we went after Kidd, we were familiar with this school because we had recruited Lynn Hardy when he played there.

Kidd ended up at Arkansas-Little Rock. Sometimes a player will choose a smaller school because he wants to make sure he'll play. Most athletes don't look at the educational aspect, which is unfortunate.

Unbeknownst to me, someone on our staff turned in UALR for alleged recruiting violations involving Kidd. The call to the NCAA caused Ben Kelso a lot of anxiety because the NCAA had given him a very hard time one summer. The NCAA apparently looked into Kelso's connection with college coaches. There was never any action taken on UALR or Kelso by the NCAA, although the Michigan High School Activities Association reportedly penalized Kelso later for violating some association rules in an unrelated case.

Kelso then turned around and started talking to the NCAA about us. I think it was in retaliation.

Kidd alleged Daly and I flew back with him to Detroit following his official campus visit in April, 1985. Then after we landed in Detroit, we were met by Vic Adams, who drove us to Kidd's father's house, where all of us encouraged Kidd to attend Missouri, according to Kidd.

This story was an attempt to show that we asked Adams to assist us in the recruitment of Kidd, thereby making him an athletic representative. NCAA rules state an athletic representative is prohibited from making in-person on- or off-campus recruiting contacts.

Much of this allegation is based on statements allegedly made by Kidd, and the odd thing is, he would not sign a written statement for the NCAA. In fact the NCAA would only have one signed statement for the allegation. That should tell you something about its credibility. After Kidd enrolled at UALR, he was convicted of forgery and theft and then transferred to another school. A lot of the investigation was based on what people supposedly told the NCAA but wouldn't swear to, or confirm in writing.

Records show Kidd probably flew in a private charter on his way home from our recruiting trip. The plane was owned by Floyd Riley, a friend of the university. The question involved whether we were on the plane and once in Detroit, whether Adams accompanied us back to Kidd's house. When the university investigated the allegation, the university attorneys made an issue out of the flight's not being paid for, reporting this as another violation.

Why did the university make such a fuss about this free flight? The NCAA currently has a rule that says the use of a free private charter is allowed only if the university is aware of it and it is documented as a charitable gift. The administration took the position that it was never told about the use of this private charter, and therefore the coaching staff was violating the rules.

I had to get signed statements from previous athletic directors, going back to Don Faurot, Dan Devine, and Dave Hart, to prove that the athletic directors and the administrations were aware of this practice in the past. The day before the final meeting with the NCAA Infractions Committee, the NCAA dropped this allegation about the free use of a private plane because someone discovered an unpublished interpretation of the rule prohibiting free flights. This interpretation, available only to the administration and faculty reps, allowed the flights during the time in question.

Before this disclosure, I had no access to this interpretation, nor did my attorney. It was particularly frustrating to know interpretations existed that were kept secret from the coaches demonstrating another example of the lack of direction on the part of the university and the NCAA. How many other unpublished interpretations were there?

But with that charge relating to the free flight, we were still left with Kidd's allegation that Adams had accompanied us back to his house.

Another thing we can't determine is, why we would have put Kidd on a private plane? Our records show we had a ticket for him on a commercial flight. What we think must have happened is that when we went out to the Columbia airport his flight was overbooked, which happens frequently on weekends. If this was the case, we would have gone next door to get a charter to fly him back, calling a friend, Floyd Riley, to ask if we could use his airplane. Floyd's plane was available so that's how Kidd flew to Detroit. The ticket for the commercial flight was turned back in by the university and refunded.

Kidd originally claimed I was on the plane with Coach Daly. The flight log listed "Norm Stewart" in the entry under the category entitled "Passengers-Title-Company or Customers and Company Visited." When I was first asked about this by NCAA investigators in 1989, I could not recall being on the flight. I told the NCAA that it was possible, but I didn't remember. I was not trying to mislead investigators to avoid an infraction.

The flight had occurred almost five years ago. During those five years, I estimated that I had flown on more than 200 non-commercial flights. This flight had occurred on Easter Sunday. I had a difficult time believing that I would have flown to Detroit on Easter Sunday, and I tended not to accept the accusation because it came from Kidd, whom I felt had a motive to fabricate a story.

The NCAA issued a Supplemental Letter of Inquiry in July, charging I had provided false and misleading information during the November interview. To make matters worse, the university's attorneys came to the conclusion that the weight of the evidence supported the allegation that I was on the plane with Daly.

In my response to the NCAA, my attorney supplied a sworn statement from the pilot explaining that the notation was a generic term, and didn't mean I was actually a passenger on the flight.

Another area pilot swore the same thing. He said pilots often use generic terms. For example, if someone from Governor Ashcroft's staff was a passenger, he might record "John Ashcroft" in the flight log, even though Governor Ashcroft was not a passenger. He testified he would do the same for Norm Stewart.

My attorney found other evidence that "Norm Stewart" was a generic term used for other flights. During the recruiting of another player, an entry in a flight log read "Norm Stewart." We proved I was not a passenger on that flight, that it was Bob Sundvold who was on the plane. That is Sundvold's recollection, and the recruit, as well as both his parents, confirmed under oath that I made only one visit. University records indicated I traveled to the recruit's home with Sundvold on a date other than the one shown in the flight log.

I think anyone who is 55 years old will understand the difficulty in remembering what you were doing on an Easter Sunday five years ago. One thing for sure, I was not going to stand still and be called a liar because I couldn't recall being on a plane.

Finally, my wife searched and provided records to show I was in Columbia. We had 14 people who signed affidavits saying they had Easter brunch with me. I think this was the key to my whole defense.

My attorney also located phone records indicating I was in Columbia for a least a portion of Easter Sunday and all of the next two days.

Rich Daly stated that he couldn't recall for sure whether he was on the flight with Kidd, but at the same time he did not deny it. He verified that he was in Detroit on that date, however, he had no firm recollection how he got there. We went over the people we recruited over the last few years, and it is a long list. I think he spent 55 nights in Detroit, and sometimes recruiting trips blend together. Additionally, Rich filed an expense reimbursement form for expenses showing he was in Detroit that day. Now, if Rich was in Detroit doing something he shouldn't, would he have filed that reimbursement report? It was for only $30 to $40. One thing Daly was positive about: He was never transported by Vic Adams for any recruiting purposes.

At the end of the hearing, the Enforcement Staff concluded that I was not on the flight, and withdrew the charge, but not until I had fought a long battle.

This leaves the question as to whether Vic Adams is a representative of our athletic interests.

It's possible that he was working without our knowledge to bring athletes to Missouri. Although it is against the rules for someone to contact a player on the university's behalf, this rule is unenforceable.

If you're going to call Vic Adams an athletic representative, then you probably want to do the same for Sam Washington, who made it possible for Detroit players to play at St. Cecilia's Gym. When you went to this gym, you saw all the great players in the area. If you didn't know Sam Washington, you weren't going to get a player from Detroit. Sam didn't want anything except to know that you had a good program, that you were interested in kids and wanted to take care of them. When Sam died, we wore black arm bands on our uniform because he gave many of our kids a chance to improve their skills and play. His son is now running St. Cecilia's.

The NCAA rule prohibiting a representative from contacting a recruit can be a bit ridiculous at times.

A guy walking down the street could come up to a high school player and say, "Hi, I'm a Michigan grad. I hope you go to Michigan."

That's a technical violation. How are you going to enforce it? Is anyone going to turn that guy in?

You bring a kid to the campus and someone walks up to him and says, "I'm a graduate of 1948, I hope you come to Missouri." A violation. You can imagine how many times this rule is broken on every campus in the country. But there are exceptions. Generally, if someone is close to the family of a ballplayer and has a long-standing relationship, he can persuade the player to attend a certain university.

You're supposed to send representatives rules on how to act. We didn't send Vic any rules because we didn't see him as an athletic representative.

Raw Recruits underscored the rumors that Vic was having players over to see a Missouri highlight tape. The section about Missouri (approximately six pages long) was full of information supplied mainly by newspaper reporters and given to the author, but we can't find anyone who will testify that he saw this videotape. One player who purportedly said he viewed the tape was contacted and denied making such a statement.

Wolff defends his work by saying something to the effect, "Hey, that's what the newspaper reporters told me." The newspapers, in turn, reported that this book had uncovered major improprieties. I think all the book did was pull together a lot of rumors from unnamed sources. That's not journalism. Absolutely none of the major allegations in *Raw Recruits* was substantiated in the NCAA investigation of our program.

When I approached Kelso during the recruitment of another one of his players, Daniel Lyton, Kelso expressed some anger about our getting the NCAA on his back. He said we were responsible for one miserable summer. As I have stated previously, I wasn't aware that someone had called the NCAA, and I assured him I hadn't turned him in.

I believe Kelso did everything he could to prevent Daniel Lyton from attending our school. He reportedly advised Lyton to avoid Missouri and its coaches.

Kelso is a close associate of Charlie Parker, an assistant under George Raveling at the University of Southern California. USC had a verbal agreement with Daniel Lyton. When Lyton turned around and signed with us, it infuriated Kelso and USC. Raveling called me and threatened to turn us into the NCAA.

I let him talk, and when he finished, I said, "George, since you've already made your statement, let me make mine. I have never turned anyone in to the NCAA, but whether the kid signs or doesn't sign with us, I'm going to turn you in. Because Daniel Lyton was driving Charlie Parker's truck all summer long. Do you want to get ready to answer that question, along with some others I'm sure we'll be able to come up with?"

After I said that, I thought about it some more. I'm not going to turn in an individual. I never have, I don't believe in it because I don't think it works. The system they have now has too many glaring weaknesses within it. Nothing is corrected by informing on a colleague. You only wind up ruining one another.

The NCAA investigative process is a highly flawed system. Anyone who has been involved in it, any attorney, any learned individual, can see it is a highly questionable system and provides inconsistent penalties from school to school. I know of a highly visible football coach who did the same thing Bob Sundvold did, but did not self-report it. Why wasn't this football coach charged with unethical conduct and forced to resign?

Lyton signed a letter of intent to come to Missouri, but when it was time to show up, he didn't appear, so we waited to get some word or an explanation. Finally, I received a call while I was in Kansas City at Raytown South High School. An individual who identified himself as Lyton's uncle was on the line, asking whether I still wanted Daniel to come to Missouri. I told him I did. I said that we would work with Daniel, and he should understand he would be behind in school. I told him we wouldn't hold that against him if he came out for basketball.

Lyton enrolled on the last possible day. Then he withdrew from school on the very last day you could withdraw. I didn't think anything about it at the time, but now I believe he was trying to see whether we were going to violate a rule, any minor rule, in regard to preseason practice or workouts. We didn't violate any of those rules.

The NCAA talked with Lyton in the presence of Ben Kelso and other members of the Lyton family. They were not interviewed separately, so they were permitted to hear one another's answers. This is contrary to usual NCAA procedures.

Lyton was told by the investigators that if there was something improper in his recruiting and the national letter of intent, then he could be released and go to any school of his choice without losing eligibility. Otherwise, he would have to sit out a year to transfer. Immediately after that, Lyton came up with something improper, claiming we had Vic Adams pick up his letter of intent. Lyton appeared on a Columbia television station saying that he wanted the University of Missouri to go on probation so he could be released from his obligations under the letter of intent.

The Lyton family and Kelso did not tell a cohesive story. Lyton's first version was that we called him and told him Vic would pick up his letter of intent. Lyton claimed I called him three times. We checked my phone records and discovered I called him only once, the customary phone call to say congratulations.

The NCAA went back to Lyton and said, "Coach Stewart has only one phone call to your residence in his records."

Then Lyton changed his story, saying I didn't call, but that Coach Daly or some other assistant called and gave me the phone. The NCAA allowed Lyton to change his story.

I countered by saying, "If that did happen, how did I arrange for the letter to get picked up?"

They said I called Vic Adams.

We looked at my phone records again and found that I hadn't talked with Adams in a year. The NCAA permitted the Lytons and Kelso to change their story several times, with all of them in the same room.

Initially, Lyton's mother said she knew it was Vic Adams who supposedly picked up the letter, but I am told she later said she had never met Vic Adams before. She then amended her story and said she had met him previously, when a Providence coach was leaving her house, but the coach she identified swears he never saw Adams at or near their residence.

Another big discrepancy concerned the time the letter was signed. Lyton and his mother claimed it was signed in the evening shortly before it was picked up, but the letter itself shows it was signed in the afternoon at 2 p.m.

This is where the NCAA is wrong. I'm a member of their group. If they are working with their own membership, they should be trying to prove their members innocent. Instead, they were doing everything they could to find me guilty.

After Kelso and the Lytons modified their story even more, the NCAA alleged I arranged for the letter to be picked up. After more discussion, they said, "Well, it's obvious you didn't arrange for the letter to be picked up, but we think you knew about it."

Now, how could I fight them any more? I had given them all the information I knew to show that I didn't arrange it and still they thought I wasn't telling the truth.

We have a record showing that the letter of intent was sent to Lyton by overnight mail. It was then signed and mailed to the university. The question seems to boil down to how it was picked up and put in the mailbox. Just think about that for a second. Who cares who puts it in the mailbox?

We always send letters of intent out by some same-day service. We put a self-addressed, stamped envelope inside, so all the player has to do is sign it and send it back.

Why would we arrange to have somebody take the letter from his house and put it in the mailbox? I would never make such an arrangement. In my 35 years of coaching, I've never considered it. It would be within the rules for me to send an assistant coach to pick up a letter of intent as long as he didn't have contact with the recruit, but what an expense to retrieve a letter.

This allegation involving the Lyton letter of intent was dismissed in the end. However, it shows just how far the NCAA may go to prove one of its members guilty.

20
Sound and Fury

Some of the rules that the NCAA found our program had violated sound quite reprehensible, phrases like "unethical conduct" and "lack of institutional control," appear in their report. But in our case, the crimes mainly were either not as serious as they sounded, or the charges were not even appropriate to level at a coach.

Unethical Conduct

In charging Bob Sundvold with unethical conduct, the NCAA said he knowingly violated rules. In the case of loaning P.J. Mays money, Bob told me he thought it was okay because he believed Mays was no longer a part of our basketball program. Although he retained some doubt, he was trying to help this kid. Bob also admitted he gave some players a free meal, and on another occasion a free ride. But these weren't recurrent violations.

Here's another example of the sort of thing for which the NCAA found Bob at fault: It's raining or snowing outside, and a student-athlete is walking along the road towards campus. You drive by and he waves to you. You haven't called him or pre-arranged a trip, you just happen upon him by the roadside. If you pick him up, it's a violation.

The NCAA is saying, "Hey, you know the rules. You can't provide transportation."

And we admit, "Yes, we did know it was a violation, and we picked him up."

Here's another example: A kid is in a bit of trouble. He's not passing his schoolwork and he's also not doing well in basketball. This kid is homesick, and his girlfriend is mad at him. He's in a mess. You find him feeling incredibly sorry for himself one day, so you say, "Hey, let's go for a sandwich."

You take him to lunch and you try to comfort him. That's a violation, and you know it's a violation, but you do it anyway because it feels right in your heart.

This was basically what Bob admitted.

The NCAA still apparently deems Sundvold a good person. They didn't ban him from coaching, as they could have, nor was he asked to resign.

With Assistant Coach Rich Daly, the unethical conduct charge was different. The NCAA claimed Daly wasn't forthcoming in his answers. They cited lapses in memory and repeated use of the phrase "I don't know," when asked about a recruiting trip to Detroit.

I was at the hearing, and only one time do I remember Daly saying, "I don't know. I don't remember."

I remember his counsel telling the Infractions Committee, "Gentlemen, that is an answer. It is an answer that is accepted in all courts."

There are a lot of legitimate reasons why you might not remember something. Maybe it was too long ago, maybe you didn't do it, or maybe you simply don't have a good memory.

It's silly to expect someone to recall everything that happened five years ago on a given day. I make 150 flights a year, and I know questions about travel are difficult to answer. You have to check your records.

One time an attorney named Bob Smith called me and said I had flown with him to Kansas City to work on responding to a newspaper story. I said, "Bob, this really disturbs me. Maybe something has happened to my mental faculties, because as I recall I have never been on a plane with you."

Smith made the comment at the time the NCAA was saying

I had flown to Detroit with a recruit, another flight I couldn't recall.

I put the phone down and talked it over with my wife. Virginia said she didn't recall my telling her about this Kansas City flight. It bothered me all night.

I went to the office the next day and talked with Bob Sundvold. I said, "Throughout the investigation, I've been a little concerned about my memory because I've taken some medicine to help me sleep that may have caused some memory loss."

I told Sundvold what Smith said to me, and Bob started laughing.

"Norm, you didn't go on that trip, I did."

I said, "How do you remember?"

"I remember because I was mad that you sent me," he said. "You didn't want to go, so you sent me."

Now I wanted to call Bob Smith.

"Bob, I was not on the plane," I told him. He was still unconvinced. "Bob, you are really getting to me now," I said. "Look at your records and see what they say."

He called back in an hour and apologized. "You were not on that airplane," he said. The point is that you can't always remember the specifics. Sometimes people (like Bob Smith) who don't spend a lot of time on planes can't remember the specifics. It all blurs together sometimes.

The questions Daly couldn't answer concerned the recruiting of Curtis Kidd. The question was whether Daly or I was on the flight with Kidd to Detroit. Daly said he was in Detroit, but didn't remember the details of how he got there. This response didn't satisfy the NCAA, and Daly was found guilty of unethical conduct. He later appealed, and the unethical charge was dropped. I'll talk about that more in a later chapter.

The NCAA alleged I provided false and misleading information during an interview about an alleged trip to Detroit with Kidd and regarding contacts with Vic Adams during the recruitment of Daniel Lyton. In both cases, I successfully defended myself. My attorney provided evidence that I was not in Detroit, and we convinced the NCAA Lyton had strong motives to fabricate a violation so he could transfer to another school without losing eligibility.

The night before the Infractions Committee announced its findings, all the coaches received a phone call. Everyone was summoned to the administration building. There we met with the chancellor, Bob Ross, Mike Slive and Mike Glazier, Dick Tamburo, and I believe Carl Settergren (my memory may be failing again). We didn't finish until morning, just in time for us to meet with our own attorneys and write our reply.

Our press conference was scheduled for 10 a.m., therefore we had to make decisions late at night without much thought. This was another part of the whole process which should have been handled differently.

I was told my salary was frozen for the period of probation, and Sundvold and Daly had to resign. The NCAA had not demanded any of those actions.

The university wanted to punish the assistants. I gave them this choice: If you want to stay in the profession, you resign; if you don't, you can have a tough time finding a job. They resigned.

The curious thing is that the university had originally supported the assistant coaches. The university response to the NCAA disputed the charges of unethical conduct. Even though the NCAA found the coaches guilty, the Infractions Committee "did not believe that their actions . . . warranted imposing individual restrictions on their coaching activities." The NCAA left it up to the university to decide what restrictions would be imposed on the coaches. So why did the university decide Sundvold and Daly had to leave?

Lack of Control

The NCAA said the nature and scope of the allegations demonstrated a lack of control in the administration of the basketball program by the institution and the head coach.

In citing me for "lack of control," the NCAA referred to the NCAA Constitution 2.1. If you read that article in the *NCAA Manual*, you'll find that there's no mention of a coach's being responsible for controlling the administration of the basketball program. To quote Article 2.1.1., "The institution's chief executive officer is responsible for the administration of all aspects of the athletics program, including approval of the budget and audit of all expenditures." Yet the NCAA used this article to hit me with a violation; they just interpret the rules any way they want to.

Obviously, a coach is a part of the institution. I share the responsibility for operating the men's basketball program in compliance with NCAA rules, and I feel I've done an adequate job of monitoring what I had under my control. But even if I hadn't, the NCAA has no business—according to its own bylaws — finding a coach guilty of failing to exercise institutional control.

I suspect Slive and Glazier were involved with the wording of this violation which put me and not the administration on the firing line. Remember, these men did not work for me, yet they were the ones with direct contact with the NCAA.

Also working against me throughout the investigation were news leaks supplied by a high-ranking source to a certain member of the media. We were told that an important official was sitting down with a reporter and being guaranteed off-the-record status.

The writers whimsically went back and forth in their commentary about the way I handled my job. One day I was this guy with my finger on everything, every player, every person working at the school. "Stewart U," one writer called it.

But on another day, the writers would say I didn't know what was going on, that people were running amok because I didn't oversee them closely enough. Did these articles have any effect on the NCAA's rulings? I don't know, but they couldn't have helped. I know the NCAA officials read the newspapers.

The truth is, I delegate responsibility to my subordinates, and I think they did an acceptable job of carrying out those responsibilities. My job is to get the best performance from my coaches and players, and to that end I give them a certain amount of freedom. Sure I sit in an overseer's position. But at what point do you step in and say, "Hey, wait a minute. What is going on?" True, I failed to detect some violations, however, they were generally spontaneous, isolated, one-time incidents and nothing that indicated a lack of control.

The NCAA said I failed to adequately supervise my assistants or maintain a regular rules and compliance program. It is not my responsibility to run education and compliance programs. That is the job of the athletic director and the compliance officer.

If every coach at this institution ran a compliance program, they'd all be different. You don't want your coaches directing the compliance program. You have to have consistency. I am involved only in that I have a basic understanding of the rules, and I see to it that my assistants go to those programs and that they are familiar with them.

My staff and I regularly attended presentations by the Big Eight Conference concerning rules and compliance. I instruct my staff to be aware of and follow NCAA and Big Eight legislation. I have sent letters to representatives of the university's athletic interests to remind them of their limitations in recruiting.

When a violation is detected, as when Bob Sundvold told me he had loaned money to P.J. Mays, I told him to self-report it.

The NCAA stated I did not monitor the use of recruiting money. I don't have any recruiting money, nor am I in charge of its administration. If you need a cash advance, you go to the university. When you return from your recruiting trip, you fill out an expense form, and the money is reimbursed, less your cash advance.

The NCAA also said I didn't monitor student-athletes who came to the university the summer before their enrollment, therefore "almost assuring rules violations," such as people supplying the kids with free meals and free rides. The summer orientation sessions for freshman-to-be athletes are very beneficial in preparing them for college life. I can't watch their every move on and off campus, nor should I. But I agree that such sessions might present risks for infractions, and I told the university and the NCAA I would discontinue them until I heard from the NCAA on a method of restructuring the sessions to minimize the risk. It's too bad because the kids benefited from the orientation sessions. They are the ones that will suffer, not me. For me, it's just one less responsibility.

I keep an eye on offers from well-intended alumni and make sure my assistants do too. I recently turned down an offer from a professional fishing guide to take me and a player on a fishing trip. Furthermore, I closely watch the distribution of complimentary tickets and have written high school coaches informing them of NCAA restrictions on comp tickets.

For several years, along with other members of the athletic department, I have sent letters to alumni reminding them of various NCAA rules. Boosters present the greatest chance for a major rules infraction, particularly alumni groups that form without notifying our staff. Our staff needs to be included in their planning to ensure compliance with NCAA rules.

One year, a booster offered a hot fried chicken dinner to the team after a game. I had to tell him that this well-intentioned gesture was against NCAA regulations.

The distribution of athletic apparel is tightly controlled by Kit Lisauskas, a member of the university equipment staff. Athletic apparel must be checked out from the equipment room and later checked in. Only three keys exist to this room, all in the possession of the equipment staff. No one from the coaching staff has a key to the room.

I have insisted that any incidental charges appearing on hotel bills be paid by players before checking out. I've made it our trainer's responsibility to review each bill. Even after taking these measures, I admitted some violations were not detected. I am dedicated to improving the monitoring where it is needed.

But the way the report reads, it sounds like I was operating separately from the athletic department. Some people within the university may have felt this way. There have been several athletic directors and several administrations at Missouri over the 24 years I've been at the school. Sometimes a new administrator isn't satisfied with a coach who just does a good job. Maybe an ego gets in the way and he wants something more. How do you supply that? Is it up to me to politic to keep my job?

I have always had the feeling that I was working for the school and the people of the state of Missouri. I have the attitude, "What would you like me to do?" On the other hand, very seldom does anyone contact me. So I assume all they want me to do is continue doing my job.

Casino Night

"Illegal inducements" and "excessive entertainment" sound pretty serious, don't they? As a result of one "Casino Night" in October of 1987, we got hammered with violating these rules. What were the alleged inducements? One pair of tennis shoes that as far as we know don't exist. The excessive entertainment? Judge for yourself how extravagant our setup was.

Bob Sundvold arranged for Casino Night because we had two recruits — Anthony Peeler and P.J. Mays — visiting during homecoming weekend. Because it was homecoming, there was little chance of making a dinner reservation for a large group.

Bob, with the help of my secretary, Dawn, made the arrangements. It was held at a small meeting room at the Executive Center Hotel. It consisted of a modest buffet-style dinner and casino games. We "gambled" with play money.

According to the records, the buffet dinner consisted of roast beef, ham, rice, bean salad, rolls and butter, at a cost of $13.20. The games of chance were roulette, craps and blackjack.

Besides the two prospects, P.J.'s mother and her boyfriend were there, along with the coaching staff and their wives, members of the team and their dates, Tiger Hostesses and a student group of fans called "The Antlers."

The idea of a Casino Night is similar to what fraternities and sororities do when they rush someone. The recruits have a party and meet several people. A meal is served, which is perfectly legal. There are hosts and hostesses, who also get a free meal. Part of the trouble was that some of the athletes brought their girlfriends and they received a meal as well. It's a silly rule, but dates aren't supposed to get a free meal and it was a violation.

One of the recruits, P.J. Mays, would later have an ax to grind because we took away his scholarship for reasons you've already read about. He and his mother would be the source of other allegations concerning Casino Night.

Some of our people went to Cincinnati during our internal investigation of the P.J. Mays situation. During this trip they were told that Mrs. Mays had received a pair of tennis shoes sometime around P.J.'s official trip to Missouri.

But as it was reported to us, she told several stories. Once she said she got the shoes while she was here. The next time, she claimed that they were mailed to her. In the third version, it was a gift certificate she had to turn in so she could pick them up in Columbia. Every time one of the stories came back to us, we would check it out. Meanwhile, other participants were interviewed.

Doug Smith, then a student-athlete, said he remembers players and recruits were told not to participate in the auction at the end of the evening. Smith stated once he learned that, he began to intentionally lose his money.

Several people, including my secretary Dawn and part-time coach Anthony Smith, recalled someone saying before the auction that only certain girlfriends and Tiger hostesses were eligible, and that players and prospects could not participate.

No one, outside of P.J. Mays, his mother and her boyfriend, recalls P.J. or his mother winning the shoes.

Mrs. Mays said that right before the auction, other women gave her their winnings so she would have more money to bid. She claimed she tried unsuccessfully to bid on a gift certificate from one store. Then she said she turned her attention to a gift certificate for athletic shoes. Mrs. Mays unknowingly began bidding against P.J., with her son eventually winning. P.J. claimed he asked one of the coaches to mail his mother the shoes.

The NCAA interviewed Mrs. Mays. The university attorneys, Slive and Glazier, talked to her as well. None of them asked her a very simple question: Where are the shoes?

When my attorney, Steve Owens, came aboard, he inquired, "Where are the shoes? What kind are they? If we have the shoes, we can find out where they came from."

There were no shoes. You know what her comment was? She said she had the shoes during her first interview, but threw them away shortly before her second interview. This was a woman who had gone to the trouble of tape recording phone conversations in order to nail us. Why didn't she show the investigators the shoes during her first interview? Why would she throw away a key piece of evidence shortly before her second interview?

There was a record of a package that was sent from our department to the Mayses. The NCAA, without ever locating the tennis shoes or where they came from, assumed they were in that package. The university admitted the allegation.

Several people remember P.J. had left some of his belongings in Columbia when he went home after his recruiting trip. We think somebody wrapped up the stuff Mays had left and sent it to him. P.J. Mays' possessions may well have been the contents of this mysterious package.

Does the entertainment sound "excessive?" The rule on this matter reads, "A member institution may not arrange or permit excessive entertainment of a prospect on campus or elsewhere (e.g., hiring a band for a dance specifically for the entertainment of the prospect, a chauffeured limousine, a helicopter)." A Casino Night is not mentioned. But once again, the NCAA enforcement staff showed that it can interpret its rules to suit its own purposes, regardless of what members of the NCAA might think.

21
Nickels & Dimes

So many of the NCAA's charges were just about trivial things most sensible people wouldn't pay any attention to. The plan, I guess, was to make many small infractions into a pattern, to build a mountain from a bunch of molehills.

"Flawed Reimbursements"

The NCAA checked at least 1,500 financial reports over a five-year period. They came up with five "flawed reimbursements" to prospective student-athletes during their recruiting visits. Our records showed we reimbursed them for taxi rides, while the kids say they never took a taxi or received the money. The NCAA claimed this amounted to part of a major violation — a lack of control over recruiting expenses.

The total of all the five reimbursements was a staggering $206.

The process involving reimbursing recruits for their official visit has changed over the years. One in effect at one time allowed a coach to fill out an expense form before the official visit weekend. The coach would ask the player in advance whether he was going to take a cab and how many meals he would be on campus for. The recruiting coach or the student host would then receive the money.

We are allowed to give a recruit reimbursements for his expenses for a trip to this campus and his return home, which is practically the same arrangement the university uses for job candidate interviews. We can pay for the cost of his trip: air transportation at coach fare and taxi service to and from the airport near his hometown. We would ask a recruit what was the cost of the round trip taxi ride. He would say $30, $40, or $50 and we would reply that was fine.

However, the NCAA said that on five occasions over a five-year period, we had reimbursed visiting recruits for taxi fares they had not incurred.

Did the NCAA prove we had an unmonitored recruiting expense fund? Is this a clear example of a lack of institutional control? I certainly don't think so. The university's own attorneys concluded this wasn't the case. How many other schools could undergo this kind of scrutiny to find just five discrepancies in a five-year period?

As far as we're concerned, our handling of money in each of the questioned instances met all financial requirements. There was no requirement by the athletic department, by the university, or the NCAA to have a taxi receipt.

The NCAA asked these five players if they got reimbursed, and all of them said no. Well, my feeling is they were reimbursed. Not knowing the nature of the allegation, they may have thought they were helping the university by saying they did not receive any money at all. In some instances, you give a player taxi money, and what does he attempt to do? He tries to save it and get someone else to pick him up. The university cannot regulate that sort of activity.

Is it so surprising if the kid did pocket the $30 or $40 and have someone else pick him up? Don't many people do that? How many people behave this way when they interview for a job?

What the NCAA didn't write in its report was how the university attorneys changed positions on these allegations. First they said the individuals did not receive their money. So there was no rules violation, but where was the money if the kids didn't get it? Then, right before the hearing, they said they were going to accept the fact that the kids did receive the money but didn't use it for taxis. So we had located the money, but now there was a violation.

Because the kids got the money, they had to be declared ineligible. Shortly thereafter, by their own power, the NCAA immediately reinstated them. It got ridiculous. The university attorneys changed positions at will, and the NCAA did whatever they wanted.

Why did they do it? Was it a deal? Was someone negotiating? Who was negotiating? Could it have been Slive and Glazier?

The NCAA, I'm sure, was trying to find out if we had created a slush fund of some kind. But it's difficult to make a case for a slush fund with $200 over a five-year period.

It's impossible to keep track of every dollar and cent. Here's an example: We go on the road for an away game, and we give each player some money to go to the movies. We put three in a cab, giving each player two bucks to pay for the cab and five bucks for the movie. Well, most players won't go to the movie. They'll take the seven dollars and put it in their pocket.

You might suggest, "Well, make sure they give you a ticket stub."

All they'll do is send one guy by the movie house and he'll get 12 ticket stubs and hand them out. You aren't going to win that game with kids. Some of them will change their mind about seeing a movie and go to the arcade and play some games. How are you going to get a receipt for that?

Sometimes a coach asks a player the next day if he got his movie money, and the player says no. Maybe the player hopes the coach forgot so he will receive his movie money again. Or maybe the player just wasn't paying attention when the money was distributed.

Some might conclude the best idea is stop giving players any money. That is not the right solution either. There has to be some trust involved here.

Because the NCAA found these "flawed reimbursements," the athletic department has a new procedure for reimbursing athletes for their recruiting visits. They will be allowed to receive only $20 in cash for the expenses they incur including meals and ground transportation. Any expenses over $20 will be reimbursed by a check only after the athlete has supplied receipts and filled out a cash reimbursement form. This procedure is handled entirely through the Athletic Business Office.

Cost-Free Lodging

The NCAA said a Columbia hotel gave free lodging to the mother of one of our players on one occasion and reduced-cost lodging to the same woman on another occasion. The NCAA, in its Infractions Report, tied this to other violations in its effort to prove "these violations when considered together constituted a major violation."

The episode involved the mother of Nathan Buntin back in 1986. After Nathan decided to become a Missouri Tiger, Mrs. Buntin wanted to move here, without our encouragement. Not that we didn't like her, but we told her Nathan should be on his own. It's part of growing up. When you go to college, you cut the cord, you go on your own.

She apparently found it difficult to find work, taking a job at night that didn't pay very well. I think she was always near the end of her purse strings, and I would get calls from people who would say, "I would like to help."

I would have to reply, "You can't. You absolutely cannot help her. She has to find work on her own."

I think she began working two or three jobs to make ends meet. She.wanted to be here in Columbia with her son, right or wrong.

She stayed in this hotel when she first moved to Columbia. Then she went back home to get her belongings and returned to the hotel for another night.

She claims she paid for the hotel, and evidence on one of the bills confirms her statement. But there was also another bill where one of the rooms was marked "$20 comp." Neither I nor my coaches asked that she receive free lodging, and we don't know whether somebody just wrote it off as a bad debt or what.

As for reduced-cost lodging, the motel has a lower rate for people moving from one place to another. I don't understand why the NCAA made such an issue out of reduced-cost lodging. The total amount in question was $20, but more to the point, no one from the school made any arrangements for her to stay at the motel.

Since this infraction, the university has sent letters out to establishments reminding them about the rules, but it doesn't prevent them from doing what they want. I can see someone adversarial to the program giving a player or a relative something for free just to get us in trouble again.

Hotels and restaurants are naturally inclined to be gener-ous toward people associated with the athletic department be-cause we supply much of their business on game days. It is very hard to enforce a rule like this, which means watching over their shoulders all the time. We can't do that; all we can do is send them reminders about the rules.

This allegation was one the NCAA investigators found after re-opening their investigation. After months of searching for new violations, all the NCAA could produce was a $20 motel bill the university had absolutely nothing to do with.

The Highlight Tape

Division I and II schools may only provide certain materials to prospects, such as an annual press guide, a game program, a wallet-sized playing schedule and an athletic recruiting bro-chure. The rules even regulate how many colors of printed material can be inside the covers (only one color in the printing of the recruiting brochure). Any other tangible recruiting aid that's not specified in the *NCAA Manual* is considered an im-proper inducement.

Videotape highlights are not mentioned, therefore giving a tape to a recruit is an illegal inducement. You can use a highlight tape in recruiting, but if you show one to a recruit on a visit, you can't leave it with him.

I have a few stories about our use of videotapes, some funny, others not so entertaining.

Most basketball fans have heard of Derrick Coleman, who had a great career at Syracuse. Before he went to Syracuse, we visited his home in Detroit. Although Coleman was being recruited heavily throughout the country, we thought we had an outside chance. We brought videotape highlights of our team, extolling the virtues of the University of Missouri and its basket-ball program.

But as we pulled into his driveway, I got a feeling this wasn't going to be so easy. The first thing I notice is a Doberman Pinscher. I still have this image in my mind: a Doberman straining at the chain with a little froth dripping from his mouth. I told Rich, "You know, I really want to sign Derrick, however, I will feel real comfortable if we can just get out of here without that dog chewing off my leg."

We got out of the car and walked into Derrick's home, one eye on the Doberman. Safely inside, we could focus on the task at hand, convincing Coleman to come to Mizzou.

We brought in a device to attach to his television set so we could view the videotape. After some preliminaries, Rich began hooking up the video equipment, detaching some wires from the television and attaching other wires to it. As he did this, we heard a little pop. I realized then we weren't going to sign Derrick Coleman.

For all I know, we ruined the Coleman television set. Looking back on this incident, I have an interesting thought. If we did ruin the television, are we responsible for replacing it? This could be a great recruiting gimmick: Walk into a recruit's home, blow the TV set, buy him a brand new one. The family might feel pretty good about your school.

Needless to say, we were very embarrassed. It ruined our whole presentation. We talked a little bit, but we couldn't leave the tape. We left with the tape in hand, and one eye on the Doberman.

Daniel Lyton, who went on television to announce to the world that he hoped Missouri would go on probation so he could transfer to another school and not lose his eligibility, accused us of leaving a highlight videotape with him. Lyton originally said we recruited him cleanly, but then his high school coach, Ben Kelso (who was angry at us because he thought one of our coaches reported him to the NCAA) told him he was making a mistake by coming to Missouri, and Lyton's story changed.

It was the fall of 1988, when Coach Daly and I visited Lyton's home in Detroit. We took a VHS tape with us, but it wasn't the official university highlight tape; it was one called "Motown Tigers," containing highlights of past and present athletes from the Detroit area who had played at Missouri. Lynn Hardy, Lee Coward, Nathan Buntin, Bradd Sutton, John McIntyre and Doug Smith were all featured on this tape. The tape is less than five minutes long, and the last 30 seconds were devoted to Lyton, introducing him as a future University of Missouri basketball star. The entire video was narrated against background music.

The videotape equipment at Lyton's house was not VHS, so we had to go to a neighbor's home.

During interviews with investigators, Lyton reportedly said the tape he viewed with us was about 35 to 40 minutes long. He recalled a section on players recruited from the Detroit area and a personalized segment about himself at the end.

Mrs. Lyton apparently told an investigator the tape ran about 20 to 25 minutes. She remembers that the final segment of it may have contained a piece about her son.

A neighbor, Tammy Burnett, who viewed the tape with the Lytons, stated she thought the tape played for about 20 minutes, recalling players featured from Detroit and concluding with the segment on Lyton.

All of this testimony tends to support the conclusion that they viewed the "Motown Tiger" tape, because the official Missouri highlight tape didn't have a personalized ending for Lyton or a section on the Detroit players. Furthermore, Lyton delivered the official highlight videotape, "The Beat Goes On — 1988 Mizzou Tigers Highlight Film" to a university investigator.

Lyton first stated that after we viewed the tape, we told him to return it when he came to Columbia for a visit. Then in a later interview, he radically changed his story, claiming Daly pulled him aside and said, "Don't tell anybody I gave this to you, but you can keep it."

Even if Rich did commit such a violation, this statement doesn't make sense since Daly knew the tape didn't fit Lyton's VCR. Why would we try to induce a guy to come to Mizzou by leaving him a videotape that doesn't fit his VCR?

Mrs. Lyton would not permit investigators to interview her and Daniel separately, a privilege that was not granted to us. Lyton's changing testimony, his mother's refusal to allow him to be interviewed alone and his obvious malice toward the university should have hurt the credibility of this allegation. But the NCAA still charged us with a violation, because somehow Lyton got hold of an official tape.

First of all, we didn't leave it. We brought the tape back, and kept it in our possession. The tape he claims we left was a tape he must have received some other way. He either got access to it the short time he was at Missouri or he picked it up somewhere else. Obviously, there was no way we could prove how he had obtained this tape.

According to the NCAA, the basketball coaching staff is responsible for maintaining control of all videotapes, although there is no rule to this effect. Even though we did not leave a tape with Lyton, we had to accept responsibility for a violation in this particular instance.

Yet, leaving a tape with a player shouldn't be a violation to begin with. It probably costs a school $2.50. In today's recruiting, you jump on an airplane, and $300 is spent to get there. One day someone is going to wake up and realize there is nothing wrong with giving a kid a $2.50 tape that introduces ourselves and the school to him.

The rules even prohibit a university supporter from showing a videotape, but I'm sure this happens a lot. It's just unenforceable. My coach's show is shown on ESPN two or three times a year. Somebody could tape that and take it over to an individual completely unbeknownst to me.

It probably has happened that a coach or a supporter of a program has taped the coach's show and given it to a prospect in California or Washington D.C., saying, "Here, watch this tape. Take a good look at the coach. He is someone you ought to see." This is illegal, but how can you police it?

Once I had two kids from Oregon show up for my basketball camp because they said they saw my show. Modern technology is providing all sorts of means for producing recruiting material beyond my control.

The purpose of the rule is to prevent a school from gaining an advantage, but I don't see how any advantage is achieved this way. In fact, a tape might work to our disadvantage. The player may not like the way I look on videotape; maybe he thinks I have a funny nose or maybe he has the misconception that I have a bald spot.

But I believe you should encourage the use of videotapes. Tapes are less expensive than a personal appearance. They are replacing that first meeting. It is a new technology any school can afford.

The Courtesy Car

One of the biggest mistakes I feel I ever made was to hire Dennis Beckett as a graduate assistant. When you employ someone as a graduate assistant, you want him to feel as important as the next person. He has duties to perform like everyone else, but when push comes to shove, he is low on the totem pole.

I think Beckett assumed that he was the associate coach for Norm Stewart. He did not accept any role other than that at the outset.

When I hired him, I told him his compensation included a scholarship, dining hall privileges if he paid for it, and the use of a car for university business.

At some point I allowed him to use a car so he could distribute information on my basketball camps and perform other business, like speaking with coaches in the St. Louis area.

Well, one time he didn't return the car. He was authorized to use it for a weekend trip to St. Louis to distribute information on my camp, but he kept the car. I went to the assistant athletic director, Jack Lengyel, and suggested to him that Beckett be informed that personal use of the car violated NCAA legislation. I really felt foolish that I couldn't get my own car back. I think Jack wrote a letter telling Beckett to turn the car in.

Later, Beckett claimed that we gave him permanent use of a car and free dining hall privileges.

According to the university response to the NCAA, he said he received the courtesy car from a car dealership in Lebanon, Missouri. The dealer, however, stated he never met Beckett.

Beckett's roommate, a former assistant coach, testified that Beckett didn't have the use of any of the courtesy cars. This former assistant coach testified under oath that Beckett was obsessed with his treatment and lack of assigned duties while at the university. In his opinion, Beckett appeared to have a vendetta against the school and wanted to get back at the coaches, too.

I had told Beckett that while he was driving the car on business, he should submit bills and I would pay him. One time he turned in bills for about a hundred dollars worth of gas. I just laughed at it. I figured he might have burned forty at the most on business travel.

We didn't have enough room in our crowded facility for all of our full-time coaches and our graduate and student assistants. I decided to move the graduate and student assistants into another locker room. I forgot to tell Beckett, and he became upset because he had to dress with the student assistants. I think he had a chip on his shoulder from then on.

One day I went down to practice where Beckett and Coach Daly had gotten into an argument that turned into a shoving match. It really irritated me. These things shouldn't happen. At first I was mad at Rich until I found out what had occurred.

Beckett had his duties severely restricted because of his poor performance. He eventually left the university in 1987.

I've had many graduate assistants who did the job correctly and went on to bigger and better things. George Scholtz is with Orlando in the NBA. Kim Anderson was an assistant at Baylor, and now my assistant at Missouri. They could handle being a graduate assistant.

Some people just don't like doing menial work because they feel it degrades them. Well, they see me sweep the floor; what do they think of that? If you want to be successful, you can't let your ego be in charge.

The Float Trip

One of the allegations we won that I still hear a lot about regards a float trip. From my attorney's investigation, it appears the NCAA made this charge before they interviewed Greg Church, a key witness.

It was alleged that Bob Sundvold and I arranged a float trip for the players on the Current River in the fall of 1988. The NCAA also said in the letter of inquiry that we arranged for the team to eat a free meal during this outing.

What may have touched this off were three phone calls the university claimed Sundvold made to a campground on the river the week before the float trip. Sundvold said he remembered calling once, not to arrange a steak cookout, but simply to check on the depth of the river.

When asked what I recalled, I said I remembered somebody told me the kids wanted to go on a float trip. I remarked, "That's great. Let them organize it and get it done."

The players took their own cars. The coaching staff drove a school van.

A float trip, if you've never been on one, is a rather austere program. The idea behind it is that of a survival outing. You've got two-man metal canoes, in a river. You can select the length of the trip; ours was about a four-hour float. You float for a couple of hours, then you stop on a bank and have lunch.

It was pretty, a lot of sand and scenery. Many players were

from urban areas and had never experienced a place like the Ozarks.

In a two-man canoe on the river, you and the other person are dependent on one another. It is just you and him for four hours going down river. You can do a little swimming, depending on the temperature of the water. Usually, the players haven't any experience doing this, so obviously, some boats get turned over; that's part of the program, too. I've done it before and still haven't learned how to do it very well. If the water becomes swift, I'm not very good.

A lot of other activities go on. You can hide behind bushes around a bend in the river, and when another canoe comes by, you jump out and turn it over. There are many things that can happen to make it an enjoyable experience. We'd laugh like crazy, but then again, some of our guys didn't swim very well; they might have five life preservers on.

At one point while we were paddling through some thick brush, it was raining like hell, just drowning us. That's when the players all started chanting, "Vietnam! Vietnam!" Except for snipers on the bank, that was what it felt like.

The players arranged for this trip. At the conclusion, we had a big steak dinner, which the kids paid for. I'd say the cost of the gas for each player was about two or three bucks, since they were packed inside their own cars. The total cost per man was probably around $15.

According to the university's investigation, two of the seniors were the organizers of the float trip. The purpose of the float trip was to show the city guys what the outdoors was all about. The university said the cook was paid for the steaks with money he collected from other players.

We left early in the morning and got back late at night. We were tired, wet, and cold but we had a hell of a lot of laughs.

The basic purpose of the trip was camaraderie. Coaching staffs do such ventures all the time. Our football coaching staff did this for years. They have fabulous stories about these trips.

This experience has been written about considerably, and at times we're still questioned about it. One of the interesting things concerning the float trip was the reaction of the Infractions Committee. I think even they were perturbed that it was listed in the letter of inquiry.

A committee member asked, "What is the violation?"

The enforcement staff said, "Some of them may have not paid their way."

The committee member said, "Well, most of them did. You mean there might be a freeloader in the bunch? From what I can tell, the coaches were the only freeloaders. So nothing's new in the world."

They threw it out.

When the enforcement staff lists something like this, they are simply trying to stick somebody.

The float trip got so much attention for a long period of time. I kept hearing stories about how extravagant it was. Anybody who's been on a float trip knows they are not extravagant.

Why didn't the NCAA verify all of the stories before including them in the letter of inquiry? Instead, you have to prove yourself innocent in their eyes, a time-consuming process. It was necessary to bring in a lot of attorneys and everyone was remunerated quite handsomely. The NCAA likes this, and so do the attorneys. The more allegations to investigate, the better off the lawyers are; after 20 months of investigation, there was a very large bill.

Besides the float trip, two other allegations come to mind that were eventually dismissed, but should never have been on the Official Inquiry to begin with. One concerned an accusation that Rich Daly reimbursed a high school coach $100 for the purchase of an airline ticket for a prospective student-athlete. There was no proof of a payment, Rich denied the payment, and according to the university response to the NCAA, there was possible friction between Rich and this high school coach. Rich beat out the coach in applying for the MU assistant coaching job.

Another accusation in the Official Inquiry was that Bob Sundvold provided three meals to "Bob Bohren, a friend and AAU coach for prospective student-athlete Jamal Coleman."

The university investigation found that there was no NCAA rule at the time that specifically prohibited the entertainment of a prospect's AAU coach, and no evidence to suggest Bohren was Coleman's friend.

I guess the NCAA thought it was time to spank the children as they saw fit. But of course, this was more than just a spanking. These allegations were hurting reputations.

22
Silly Rules

Another category of charges against us pertained to violations of what I would call "silly rules," things that common sense tells you should never have been on the books in the first place, or should now be revised to reflect the world as it exists today, not as it used to be when the rules were made. At the very least, the rules should be applied with a little common sense, and a little compassion. Some of them seem to go against the whole notion of college athletics, which, as I understand it, is supposed to be most concerned with getting these athletes an education.

Arranging a Tutor

The last thing you want to have happen to a student-athlete is for him to illegally enter the university. You don't want to tamper with his transcript, you don't want somebody else to take a test for him. You want him to legally pass the test and be admitted to your university.

That's exactly what happened with Anthony Peeler. Anthony, like a lot of students, needed some help to pass his ACT test. His father called the school for help and Rich Daly arranged for a tutor. The athletic department did not pay for it; Rich merely arranged it, and even then his role was minimal.

The NCAA criticized us for that. First, they suspected we may have paid for the tutoring. When they knew that wasn't the case, they just said our arranging it violated a rule.

Okay, Daly helped find a good tutor. How is the Peeler family going to know how to find a good tutor?

The tutor wasn't a full-time employee of the athletic department then, but the NCAA maintained she was a staff member. This was another mistake that somehow managed to slide into the NCAA report, one we've sought corrective action for.

The university investigation quoted Larry Peeler as saying he initially hired a tutor in Kansas City to assist his son with his ACT. But Larry became dissatisfied with Anthony's progress, so he called Rich Daly to inform him of the problem.

Daly recalled that after he received Peeler's call, he went to see Chris Sinatra-Ostlund of the Total Person Program to find out whether she knew of a program that could help Peeler prepare for the ACT. Daly remembers Sinatra-Ostlund recommending a tutor named Judy Wells, a part-time staff member.

Larry Peeler said he remembered Daly telling him that the university would not be able to pay for the tutoring. Anthony received 30 hours of tutoring at $10 an hour. Anthony's parents scheduled the sessions and paid for them.

He passed the requirements for scholarship after taking the tutoring sessions.

There were a lot of vicious rumors flying around that someone else took the test for him, or that he flew to Arkansas to pass the test. That wasn't the case at all; he took the test at the prescribed time and in the prescribed place. He had been only one point off in his test scores before. If he had been eight points short, you might understand the suspicion.

Still, there is the rule about arranging for a tutor. Now obviously you have to draw a line somewhere in helping a recruited athlete. You can't pay for his tutors. But when the parents call you and say, "Coach, my son has to have a tutor," wouldn't you want to go out and help them find one? Why would the NCAA crack down on this and call it a violation? Apparently it is a violation, but how serious is it?

Sometimes I think rules like that are made by other coaches who lose out in a recruiting effort and are in a position to go to the rules committee and say, "Let's make it so they can't provide anything in regard to tutoring."

While on the one hand, the NCAA wants the kids to do well, so they can graduate, they also tie your hands, making this difficult to accomplish. They won't let you do what a normal human being would do for a normal student. The rules send coaches confused messages about what we are supposed to do for a student-athlete.

Summer Orientation

The media have been critical of our graduation rates, as well as other schools'. Yet we're not allowed to go out and arrange certain programs that would enhance an athlete's ability to earn good grades. An example of what I'm talking about is encouraging incoming freshmen to attend summer orientation.

First, in defense of our graduation rates, I think we've done a good job. Less than 50 percent of all students graduate from the institution at which they begin; should we expect more from the athletes? We want each athlete to graduate and work hard toward that goal. But remember, the athlete is a special individual within the institution. He is spending many hours each day in practice or on the road, and his efforts benefit the university immeasurably.

The NCAA wrote in its Infractions Report that we brought "prospective student-athletes to campus in the summer [of 1988] prior to their enrollment, which triggered a variety of violations." The NCAA went on to say that I didn't properly monitor the situation, "almost assuring rules violations."

The NCAA alleged members of the university's basketball coaching staff provided free meals, local automobile transportation, summer camp employment and excessive entertainment at no cost to the prospects while they attended summer orientation.

As I have explained in our answer to the NCAA, the university and the individual athlete benefit greatly from these orientation sessions. The athlete becomes acquainted with the town, the campus, and college life in general. For some athletes, it is quite a culture shock to come to Columbia, and some are more prepared than others to begin college life. In order to give some student-athletes a good head start, and to provide them with a better opportunity to survive the academic rigors, we encouraged them to come to summer orientation.

History has shown that the first-year students have the

hardest time. Between a period from 1981 and 1989, 12 athletes left the basketball program, all either during or at the end of their first year at school.

During the summer, the athletes attended summer school, worked at part-time jobs, and played in pickup basketball games. In compliance with NCAA rules, I instructed coaches to take a hands-off approach while the student-athletes were in town.

When the school began its own investigation into the basketball program in the winter of 1989, assistant coach Bob Sundvold admitted that on one occasion in the summer of 1988, he picked up Jamal Coleman, Anthony Peeler, P.J. Mays and Mike Wawrzyniak, all freshmen-to-be, and took them to the Old Heidelberg Restaurant. The place was a hang-out for players because the meals are fairly priced and we can get some privacy. As a frequent customer, Sundvold said he was able to charge meals, and he admitted that on this occasion he charged the meal with the players, then later paid for it with his own money.

Sundvold said he did not think of the meal as a violation at the time. I first learned about this meal during the investigation, and the violation was self-reported. I imagine it was a hamburger and a Coke. I don't know what Bob's intention was in giving them a free meal. Maybe one of the guys was very homesick or having trouble making the transition. This may have been an opportunity to keep in touch with how they were progressing.

The NCAA tried to make the violation sound worse by saying the meal was provided by a booster. Well, just about every restaurant in town is a booster. If you were a restaurant owner in Columbia, wouldn't you want to have hungry fans know you were a booster? A $50 donation makes you an official booster. I'd want to contribute at least that much to show support for an institution that brings in so much business.

Some of the players, who left the school on bad terms, alleged they were permitted by restaurant employees to sign for meals. The owner of the restaurant, Dick Walls, denied having any knowledge of this practice and said if it had occurred, the players convinced the manager or the waitresses they could sign for the meals.

On another occasion, Sundvold admitted providing a meal at his home for these same four athletes. Sundvold explained part of the reason he had them over was to find out who could live with whom, whether they could get along, whether they were good guys. He said he wanted to be in the best position to help them in the fall, and having them over was one way of accomplishing this.

Again, I was not aware that this had occurred until after the investigation. Yes, it constitutes a violation, and I wish Bob hadn't done it, but it's not the kind of thing you lose your job over. If you're a good teacher, a good counselor or a good coach, those aren't incidents worth firing someone over. It would make more sense to dismiss you for not doing such gestures, which boil down to simple human decency. If you had guests in town for a month, and you never had them over to your house, what would they think? It wasn't something Bob did regularly. He probably thought, "Hey, these guys are human beings. I'll have them over for a hamburger."

The NCAA had a foolish rule at the time that prevented coaches from picking up the players when they arrived during summer orientation. But someone's got to pick up these kids. They're from out of state; many of them don't know how to get into town from the airport. It doesn't make sense to leave them on their own. You're the coach, you've just recruited this guy. Now he arrives at the airport or bus station and calls you. "Hey, Coach, I just made it in."

What are you going to say? "Hey, sorry. We can't pick you up. Find your own way to campus." That's just not the way you treat another human being. The NCAA finally saw the logic behind that, and it's legal now to pick the kid up, but it wasn't in the summer of 1988.

Sundvold told the university he didn't know of a rule prohibiting the coaches from picking up these freshmen-to-be. He recalled picking up Wawrzyniak from the Columbia Airport, about 15 miles from campus, and he also recalled picking up Coleman.

The university also self-reported that Sundvold and our other assistant, Rich Daly, on one occasion each, gave players a ride from their apartment to a bookstore where they worked during this summer session.

Daly's son was in the same apartment complex as some of the players. One day he wanted to trade cars with his son when two or three of the players waved him down. I don't know whether the weather was bad or what, but the ride was not pre-arranged. Daly reportedly told the university he knew providing the transportation was a violation, but the players were late for work. What was he supposed to do? Did the NCAA want him to say, "Sorry, I can't give you a ride?"

You would have to do that to strictly conform to the rules. Although these are instances where the NCAA should have said, "We're glad you self-reported this incident. You must correct it. We don't want to see this happen again."

This was the way such situations were handled for years at our institution. It is the way they are still handled at many other institutions. What made it any different this time? Who knows?

Another violation during the summer of 1988 was for allegedly providing summer camp employment to several incoming freshmen and some of our players. The NCAA said the coaching staff arranged for Coleman, Mays, Peeler, Wawrzyniak, Byron Irvin and Nate Buntin to officiate games during my summer basketball camp.

If these kids called any games — they may have called a game or two — it was not with my knowledge. I employed high school coaches, trainers, aerobic instructors, assistant coaches and graduate assistants, but never prospective or enrolled student-athletes.

I attend my camps — I'm one of the few coaches who actually does. I think it's a good attraction. At a recent camp in Mexico, Missouri, I conducted the camp and gave the lectures. I felt obligated to be there, even though other coaches may rely heavily on their assistants.

Since I am in my office for much of this camp, I can look out and watch many of the courts. It's easy for me to go from one facility to the other to observe. During those times, I never saw a player officiate, and there was never any record of my paying them to officiate.

A number of players said they officiated some games, but only one told investigators he was paid: P.J. Mays, who said he received $5 a game.

For the sake of argument, let's say I did pay them. The camp paid referees about $5 a game. So what's the most a guy's going to make if he officiates at a camp? Fifty bucks? That's a helluva summer employment, isn't it? But from the language the NCAA used when it released its Infractions Report, you'd think we slipped the players a couple of hundred bucks.

The final violation cited in connection with the summer of 1988 concerned a concert in Moberly at the ranch of Floyd Riley. I knew Riley was a big fan because he attended most of the home games. Riley lives about 35 miles from Columbia and has an annual cattle auction. In conjunction with that sale, he has a mammoth party, always with great entertainment. This particular summer he had the Miami Sound Machine. It was phenomenal.

Anyone putting on a party like this is going to invite clients and people involved in his business. I would say the guest list was about 5,000. I receive an invitation each year.

Coach Daly told investigators he and Riley had known each other since childhood. Daly said Riley was a basketball junkie and a close friend. According to Daly, this cattle auction was one of the biggest in the Midwest.

The testimony from several players was conflicting as to whether any of them received an invitation; they may have just crashed the gate. Nathan Buntin reported he attended the concert with Peeler, Coleman and Mays. Wawrzyniak claimed he went along, too. Their attending the event was a violation, because it was entertainment supplied by a representative of the school's athletic interests.

Buntin's driving the other players to the concert was another violation. Players are not allowed to provide transportation to recruits who have not started their freshman year. Here's another quirky rule. What would you do if you were going to be a teammate with a guy and he wanted a ride to the grocery store? According to NCAA rules, you'd have to tell him, "Sorry."

There were a lot of students at the university that summer who wanted to attend the Miami Sound Machine concert, and were looking to find someone with an invitation. How could the coaches prevent several players from getting a ticket or crashing the gate? Were we supposed to be watching their every move?

I've been told other coaches like to get their new kids to school in the summer before they enroll. I believe some of these arrangements are suspect, and we are looking into them. I saw a recruiting film about a school in our conference in which a player said how much he enjoyed playing basketball with his teammates all summer long on campus, and that this was helping him make the adjustment to college. What he did may well have been a violation, because you can't have any supervised practices. And what about the arrangements for this player to live and work on campus before entering school? Were any of his teammates-to-be giving him rides around the city? Or are the same kinds of minor infractions that got Missouri in trouble going on everywhere, without being investigated?

The NCAA investigators made it look like the summer of 1988 was a disaster at the University of Missouri. They wanted it to appear that way. It made their case stronger, giving them more power. I wonder how many other programs would have survived the examination we underwent.

Surrogate Father

Our coaching staff arranged for Greg Jones' meals and lodging during P.J. Mays' official paid visit in October of 1987. Jones was a long-time friend and companion of Yvonne Mays and "acting father" for P.J. Mays. While Jones isn't P.J.'s father, Yvonne and Jones both reportedly said Jones acted as a father for P.J. since he was 2.

University records show assistant coach Bob Sundvold reimbursed Mays $285 for mileage and per diem meal expenses for himself, his mother and Jones for both legs of their trip from Cincinnati, a round-trip distance of 960 miles. Our staff had informed Mays that if he flew, we could pay only for Mays' air fare, so they decided to rent a car.

The amount of the reimbursement was a violation, according to the NCAA, because it has no provision for a surrogate father. The payment would have been permitted had it been directly incurred by Mays or his mother.

We are allowed to pay for the transportation costs of a prospect coming to campus and any expenses incurred by the prospect's family. According to the university investigation, Jones and Yvonne Mays said they didn't live together but had maintained a close personal relationship since 1972.

Well, we didn't consider it a violation to reimburse them for his expenses. We felt he was a member of the family. It appeared some members on the Infractions Committee agreed with us.

One of the rules the NCAA cited against us stated, "A member institution should limit entertainment and lodging on the prospect's official visit to the prospect, the prospect's parents [or legal guardian(s)] or spouse.

In today's world, wouldn't a lot of people consider some-one who had a fifteen-year relationship with a woman as part of the family?

But this was one of those allegations that stuck and I cannot understand why. The NCAA shouldn't allow reimbursements for all boyfriends or girlfriends, but they should take these situations on a case-by-case basis.

In my opinion, this was just a tack-on violation, something for the NCAA to use to show a "wide range of violations." It was absurd.

23

"Bonked" by the NCAA

My reaction to the penalties handed down by the NCAA were voiced well by a columnist for the *Lawrence Journal World*, a Kansas paper. Chuck Woodling, in comparing Missouri's penalties to KU's penalties in 1988, wrote, "Kansas was hit; MU was bonked."

Yes, we got bonked all right. What's more, we spent at least $400,000 to get bonked.

We received two years' probation with the following terms:

1. No postseason play for the 1990-91 season.
2. No expense-paid recruiting visits to prospective student-athletes for men's basketball in 1991.
3. Only one member of the coaching staff may engage in off-campus recruiting in 1991.
4. Limit of one basketball scholarship for the 1991-92 school year.
5. Only two basketball scholarships for the 1992-93 season.

We did all right without any NCAA tournament action, because we had achieved our goal of winning the Big Eight Tournament.

It really hurt to have no expense-paid recruiting visits, which practically eliminates out-of-state recruiting. Who is going to pay for his own visit? Who is going to come to Missouri without making a visit?

It will be difficult to have just one member of the coaching staff engaged in off-campus recruiting, but we can live with that. As for limiting our scholarships, Kansas has done fine, so maybe we can, too.

The university had to pay considerable legal expenses. Also, I had to pay for my own attorneys, which I felt was unusual and unfair, but the university's legal fees, separate from my own, reportedly cost about $400,000. I understand they had two sets of fees, one listed as investigative fees, the other listed under compliance. These costs really arouse my curiosity because it's taxpayers' money.

Some people have asked, "Why spend $400,000 to investigate yourself and find yourself guilty?" Woodling suggested we made some mistakes, but perhaps the biggest error was hiring Slive and Glazier to defend the university.

Why hire attorneys? The NCAA has people. Let them investigate and find out what happened. Or someone could have been appointed to investigate the program without its costing $400,000.

We got bonked.

Another administrative oversight affected the penalties we received. The NCAA asked one of our business officers how many scholarships we'd be out if they limited us to one for the 1991-92 school year. He said we'd be minus just one because only Doug Smith was graduating. He was wrong: We had three scholarships available, so we'd be penalized two scholarships.

I think we should have had just one year of probation, no ban from postseason play, scholarships reduced for two years and all but one assistant coach suspended from going on the road to recruit.

When you self-report, when you turn yourself in, your penalties should reflect your cooperation. A clean institutional record apparently did not mean much to the NCAA, either.

The message this sends to other schools is, don't self-report. Conducting your own investigation won't help much. Implementing your own corrective actions and admitting to minor infractions may do little to curb the punishment.

The more I think about the fact that the NCAA and the university attorneys examined over five years of records and 1,500 documents, and only found five discrepancies involving taxi receipts, the more bewildered I am about the penalties. Under those circumstances, you should get a "nice going" or "great job" review. Not some stupid innuendo.

24

The Voice of the Coaches

When the best-looking girl from the best family comes to the teacher and says, "Johnny pulled my hair," before you thump Johnny on the head or kick him in the rear end, you should at least ask Johnny if he did it, and then why. You may find out that he did indeed do it, but only after she kicked him in the groin. The NCAA investigative process needs to look for causes, too, not just violations.

This investigative process is in drastic need of reform. Rather than just point out faults in the system, I took some time to survey college basketball coaches in eight major conferences about NCAA enforcement procedures and ideas for reform. Of the 72 coaches who received a questionnaire, 34 of them responded almost immediately. I'm sure I will continue to receive responses, but deadlines won't permit me to wait for all of them. What I've discovered from the responses is some persistent themes:

Clarify the standards for calling an investigation. Out of the 34 college basketball coaches who responded to my survey, 30 agreed that the NCAA standards for beginning an investigation needed to be more clearly defined.

I have the same gripe about the university process. What is the standard for calling a full-scale NCAA investigation? What is the standard for calling a full-scale university internal investigation?

The *NCAA Manual* says it's up to the enforcement staff to determine whether an allegation or complaint warrants an official inquiry. The enforcement staff also determines the scope of the investigation.

It's anybody's guess how the enforcement staff determines who to investigate these days. My guess is they investigated Missouri because of media pressure, and because we self-reported the P.J. Mays incident.

During the investigation of our basketball program, it was alleged that our football team may have induced two players to transfer from the University of Texas-El Paso. There was no full-scale investigation of the football program. How come? What's the standard? Who decides?

The University of Missouri needs a standard policy not only to determine when there should be a full-scale investigation, but what that investigation will include, and when it will involve an outside law firm, with the expense that entails. When the university conducts its investigation, it should take the side of the coaching staff until the evidence proves otherwise. The university and NCAA were more like prosecutors than investigators.

What university presidents may have realized is that if the institution wants to remove a coach, the easiest way to do it is to go to the NCAA.

I contacted some coaches who are being investigated, and they are completely unaware of what they're about to go through. I'll say, "I'm calling you as a friend. This is what will occur."

I talked to one coach, and in Stage 2 he is just beginning to recognize what is happening. Until you go through it, it is almost like dealing with cancer: You can't believe it's ever going to happen to you. If it does, you think it will be different. No, it won't be.

Other coaches have been judged by different standards. Recently it was reported Denny Crum, head coach at Louisville, took a parent out for dinner during a "dead period," when contact with recruits and their families is prohibited. If Louisville was judged by the standards Missouri was judged by, it would receive a full internal investigation and a penalty, but obviously

Denny forgot, or it was unintentional. Did he make a written report, and that was it? Well, fine, that's the way it should be. But at what point do you draw a line and decide upon an investigation? A standard must be set.

Another case comes to mind involving a staff member at Indiana who reportedly took a young player off a bus, brought him into a room, and talked to him about coming to Indiana. This was supposedly done during a "dead period," too. We heard this story because one of our players was the prospect's roommate at the tournament and was on the bus with him. What did Indiana do? Did it make a written report? Did its administration call for a full-scale investigation?

Everybody has a different definition of cheating. For most people, cheating means inducing an athlete to come to the school with money, cars or promises of something of monetary value. Trips home and clothes do constitute cheating in my opinion regardless of what others may think.

Decide on due process. We have to decide whether there is going to be due process in an investigation. By due process, I mean protecting the rights of the accused, presuming they are innocent until proven guilty, using procedures similar to a court of law. If we decide on due process, the system will need an overhaul.

Some state legislatures may force due process on the NCAA by passing their own laws. With the amount of public money that's being spent on NCAA investigations, I can see why legislatures are interested in reforming the NCAA. Nebraska has already passed a "due process" law. In Kansas, where the NCAA headquarters is located, Senate Bill 234, the "Athletic Association Procedures Act," passed 36-0, but the Kansas House may not get around to voting on it until 1992. This bill would force the NCAA to follow the legislature's guidelines for investigating and penalizing schools. Kansas legislators claim that if the bill passes, it would cover all institutions in the NCAA because Kansas is the state where the NCAA does its business.

In Illinois, their state legislature has passed by a vote of 101-3, House Bill 682, the "Collegiate Athletic Association Compliance Enforcement Procedures Act." This bill would require the NCAA to follow state requirements in enforcing rules upon an institution in Illinois. In Missouri, there's been talk about introducing a "due process" bill as well.

These are just some of the states involved. Congress, too, has scheduled hearings on "due process" in the NCAA. They reviewed the NCAA enforcement procedures back in 1978 and recommended the NCAA create a blue-ribbon committee to explore ways of improving its procedures. Finally, in 1991, faced with states passing their own laws on due process, the NCAA set up a panel for review. Now the NCAA is asking government to hold off on passing new laws restricting their powers until this review panel has done some work, but the panel primarily is made up of administrators with no athletic background. It will be interesting to see what reforms they can agree upon.

The NCAA enforcement arm is another group altogether, distanced from the NCAA itself. It has evolved into a mighty, untouchable entity, with the power to interpret rules the way it wants to, to prioritize its investigations, and to take some things out of an investigation or leave them in.

There is an NCAA Committee on Infractions that is supposed to act impartially. The material they receive is voluminous; there's no way they can read it all. They are not just looking at information handed to them by the school, they are studying material supplied to them by the investigators also. The members of the panel occasionally have to ask for assistance. Who do they ask? The enforcement staff. Their opinions are shaped by what the investigators say.

NCAA investigators would interview people at Missouri often writing their notes afterwards. This allowed them to reconstruct the testimony the way they wanted to tell it. Sometimes the notes were transcribed six months following an interview, then they were torn up.

In my coach's survey, I asked coaches whether they felt NCAA investigators should tape-record interviews. Thirty-one out of 34 said yes, and some said to take it a step further: Have the recording transcribed and have the person interviewed sign it. That way there would be no question about what was said. Since the survey, tape recording has begun on an experimental basis, and the NCAA has recommended to the membership to make it a permanent rule.

I also asked coaches if they or a legal representative should be allowed to cross-examine accusers. Thirty-two out of 34 said yes. I think if you asked people this question across the country, you'd get a similar response. You have to be able to ask your accusers, "Why did you accuse me of this?" Maybe they have a good reason, maybe there was a misunderstanding, or maybe they're just lying. But hardly anyone feels comfortable with a process where an accuser can't be cross-examined.

The process of picking a panel needs to be reformed, as well. The NCAA selects its own people to sit on the Infractions Committee, and the panel is spoon-fed information from the investigators. They presently receive biased views.

One of the complaints I heard from my assistants was, "Here are four people that are going to sit down with me one day and maybe determine if I should continue in this profession." The people who should make that decision are the people in your own community.

As it stands, the NCAA puts too much of a burden on the coaches to prove their innocence. If we are members of their group, shouldn't they be trying to find us innocent?

Give coaches and athletes more say about all matters regarding the NCAA. The NCAA should not be so autonomous. They argue that membership in their organization is voluntary, and technically it is, but a school has no other choice if it wants to compete on a national level and participate in the NCAA Tournament. The coaches have little say in the rules, the players even less. The annual NCAA convention is in the middle of basketball season, and the school presidents and administrators run the show.

In the survey, it was unanimous, 34-0, that coaches wanted more coaches and players to participate in the NCAA rules-making process.

Whether you're playing, coaching or managing a company, it comes down to people. "The system will prevail," educators and other institutional types like to say, but they're just hiding behind words and ignoring the meaning. What is the "system?" It's people. Maybe the system is good, but what about the people running it? To me, that is the crux of the problem of administering athletics in the NCAA and at the university level.

When someone like Art McAfee, an NCAA investigator, comes to the University of Missouri, he should know the name of the athletic director. Bub Sundvold told me that McAfee once wrote that our athletic director was Jesse Hall, the name of the university administrative building.

The NCAA is composed of people primarily from non-athletic backgrounds. If you look at the NCAA today, for the first time, we have a former coach as the executive director. Dick Schultz is someone who at least is familiar with all the procedures in what we call field training. I hope that he will make some constructive changes.

On the other hand, some will argue Schultz was an unsuccessful coach. It seems there are a lot of administrative people who were unsuccessful coaches or have no athletic background at all. Very few highly successful coaches enter the administrative level. The perception among some is that all the bad coaches are retired to administrative jobs.

At this writing, I think Schultz is in a strained position at the NCAA. He was the athletic director at the University of Virginia from 1981 to 1987. It just so happens that the University of Virginia discovered a number of small loans were made to student-athletes between a period from 1982 to 1990. According to a university press release, the loans ranged from $40 to $1,700. UV began an internal inquiry to see if any of the loans violated NCAA rules.

It is almost humorous to note what Dick was quoted as saying in a published report about the inquiry. He reportedly said, "I had no knowledge of that." It doesn't matter if you have knowledge of it, Dick. Your group of people say athletic directors are responsible for overseeing such things.

Also adding to the irony in this story: the faculty representative for the University of Virginia is D. Alan Williams, the chairman of the NCAA Infractions Committee. Williams was acting as a consultant to the University of Virginia inquiry group.

It sounds to me like a little conflict of interest. The chairman of the Infractions Committee, Williams, is not only a member of a university where loans to student athletes are being questioned, he helped his university prepare its own internal report. This report would not only determine if the loans violated any NCAA rules, it would be presented to the NCAA.

I was involved with an NCAA group about ten years ago that wanted to implement change. Bob James, the commissioner of the Atlantic Coast Conference and an extremely gifted individual, was the chairman of the group. The NCAA selected people from around the country—football and basketball coaches, faculty reps, administrators and NCAA members — to sit down and talk about sports from field levels to administrative levels.

We were trying to identify problem areas and determine what coaches could do to reverse these situations. We talked about what rules could be made and enforced realistically.

Then the media caught on to the big money event, the NCAA Final Four. All of a sudden, there were monsters lurking. According to the media, something was terribly wrong with college athletics.

We entered into a new period of "the dumb jock" — a perception the public had of college athletes. I had seen it during the '40s. When I was in school in the '50s, we had just ended a "dumb jock" era.

This time, people responded by saying, "Hey, the presidents of institutions are running the schools. Let them solve the issue." The pressure went to the executive director of the NCAA, and the Presidents Commission was born.

The presidents responded by assigning committees, and suddenly they were in charge of the entire show. It's been that way ever since, the presidents and the chancellors at the helm. While I don't fault their leadership, they often have ignored the people best qualified to help them to do a better job. The athletic directors, coaches, assistants and recruiters are left out of the decision-making process.

Reduce the number of administrators. I know many administrators, several of whom are very good. However, there are people who have taken these jobs, and built themselves a niche. You can't fault them for that, but what can happen is that they come to be self-serving instead of being part of a support staff.

At the university level, I know some people in these jobs that have nothing to do with the sports program and the student-athlete. They don't even take them into consideration. It's as though their job is the continual promotion of administrative duties: They aren't working to do a job, they are working to keep a job.

You could visit the University of Missouri Athletic Department — see the department that collects funds, for instance — and you'll find more people than I have on my coaching staff. And only one of them has an athletic background. That's not to say they aren't competent, but we have to worry about a pre-dominance of workers with non-athletic backgrounds. An administration lacking former athletes or coaches can be out of touch, or uncaring.

Right now the NCAA claims it's in the midst of "sweeping changes" — they have reduced the coaching staffs in football and basketball, and they cut scholarships. But you'll notice they didn't reduce administrative personnel. If you want to save money, cut down the number of administrators. We now have staffs of ten doing office work that used to be handled by two people. If we have fewer athletes and coaches, why do we need so many administrators?

I didn't put this particular issue on the survey, although a half-dozen coaches volunteered comments that they were disgruntled about reductions in staff and scholarships.

There should be a review of rules pertaining to the media. Does the media accurately and fairly cover investigations? The response in the survey was a resounding 34-0 "no" vote.

The media have a tremendous influence. One member of the Infractions Committee went up to Rich Daly at the beginning of a meeting and said, "We know all about you because we read the newspapers." This was a person who would be judging our program on the basis of evidence presented by the NCAA and the university. It sounded like this person already had come to a conclusion or formed some ideas based on the news coverage, much of which was derived from hearsay. Someone who makes a prejudiced comment like that should be excused from the proceedings in the same manner a juror would be eliminated during a jury selection.

When the media finds out that the NCAA is looking at a program, the story is played as if "They got Al Capone." The NCAA seemed to use this publicity to its advantage in our case, initially coming up with 30 allegations, knowing full well just a handful of them could be proven. The media, subsequently learned the number of allegations, and without having the details, interpreted this as, "Oh-oh, something is really wrong here."

The media are immediately led to believe that it was a serious problem, and they convey that perception along to the public. If you are caught speeding, you should get a ticket. If you hit a bus and kill someone, you may be charged with manslaughter. The media more often than not plays the speeding ticket just like hitting the bus.

Review the process for issuing penalties. Of the coaches in the survey who indicated their programs had been under investigation and received penalties, none agreed the punishment was appropriate to the violations. All felt the penalties were too severe. Many also believe the system isn't equitable, that some schools enjoy a different status and receive special treatment.

Take UNLV, for example. The NCAA has what's been reported as a billion dollar television contract. If you have this type of contract for your national tournament, your big show, and you discover your lead actor in the show, UNLV, can't participate, you've got to come up with a way to get that star back in the show. You must make the television people happy, so the star, UNLV, suddenly can participate in the show. Now a supporting actor, one that the show does not depend upon — a Missouri, for example — you can still leave that actor out of the show.

I think the NCAA was hiding behind the curtains on this decision. UNLV had the opportunity to repeat as national champions, a great story line for the tournament. The NCAA reinstated UNLV despite its initial ruling that the school be put on probation and banned from playing in the 1991 tournament.

In the case of the highlight tape that we allegedly gave Daniel Lyton or the shoes that were allegedly given to P.J. Mays' mother, if these items could not be produced, they should not have been called a violation. And unless you have evidence of a real pattern, minor recruiting violations should be handled as isolated incidents, not grouped together as a major violation.

When P.J. Mays was admitted to school while ineligible, the hammer shouldn't come down on us, because 800 other students were admitted on the same basis at Mizzou. When we found out his final semester transcript was missing, we removed him from practice. After 25 years of coaching at Missouri, one ineligible player slipped through the cracks, and I then became guilty of a "lack of institutional control." I believe my overall record indicates pretty good institutional control.

The NCAA should not distort every allegation it receives. Of the coaches in the survey who were investigated, the majority said they and their programs weren't treated fairly by the NCAA.

"I felt I was treated like a criminal," one coach wrote. "The treatment did not fit the crime. Hounded like a criminal!"

"All concerned felt that they were grilled unfairly and felt helpless," wrote another. "The NCAA was here for nine days and totally disrupted our players and staff on an anonymous tip that proved inaccurate. The players were threatened repeatedly by the investigator with eligibility status. The NCAA should never investigate anonymous tips. You have a right to face your accuser in a free society."

I thought there was a time when if I stubbed my toe, I could go in and say, "Look, here's what I did. I inadvertently committed an infraction." Some coaches still enjoy this privilege. If they make a mistake, they can go to the NCAA and have it written up as an isolated incident. But the same standards aren't applied to everyone.

One time we out-recruited Kansas for a guy from St. Louis. You're supposed to sign kids in your state, but Kansas was the dominant team in the Midwest. As this young man was about to make a decision, we had him go to a movie to keep people away from him and to keep him off the phone.

The movie ended around 11 p.m. The next morning at 8:01 a.m., we signed him. As we left his apartment, we ran into the Kansas coaching staff. When you win in recruiting, it's almost more satisfying than winning a game. We didn't want to gloat, but we walked a little straighter. We were very pleased.

The next thing I know, somebody tells me Kansas has reported us to the NCAA, saying we kept the recruit out and signed him before 8 a.m. This was tommyrot.

I went to Art Nebel, the faculty representative at Mizzou. I was furious; here I am in my own state being accused of improper recruiting. Now if I was in Kansas recruiting, I would expect some rough treatment. The allegation was around for three or four months before it was dropped.

I sent in a response and never heard from the NCAA again. I attribute this to the credibility of Nebel, Dan Devine and Don Faurot. The credibility of our people back then must have had some influence on the NCAA. Today, there's no Nebel, no Devine, no Faurot at the University of Missouri. But there's still a Norm Stewart. I wonder how the NCAA would have ruled on our case if Faurot and Devine had been around? I wonder if we would have ever been investigated?

I remember one time when a crazy allegation was made after I went to watch a high school game in Waco, Texas. One of the assistants had given me a ticket and after practice I flew to Dallas, got into a rent-a-car and drove to Waco. On the way to Waco, I got stopped for speeding. The officer asked me what I was doing, and I told him I was on a recruiting trip.

"Are any of them worth driving this fast?" he asked.

"No, not a one," I answered.

"Not even the best one?"

"Not a one."

He didn't give me a ticket, just a warning.

I went to the game and met two friends, Don Edwards, and Aileen Faurot Edwards. When the game was over, I walked up to a coach because I wanted him to tell a certain player I was there. As I was ready to leave, he said, "Would you come to the dressing room to talk to my players?"

"Well, I'd be happy to," I replied, "but it's against the rules."

Then he asked me, "If I brought them to the dressing room door, would you wave to them?"

I said, "I'm embarrassed, but if that's what you'd like them to do, I will stand outside the doorway and I will wave to them."

He lined them up so they could all see out the door, and I waved to the ballclub. I was flattered, but a little embarrassed. I understood what the coach wanted to do: He wanted to motivate them by showing that a major college coach was interested in seeing them play.

Shortly afterward, we received a complaint from the NCAA. Someone turned us in, alleging I went into the dressing room and talked to the players. We had to go through a question-and-answer session with faculty representative Henry Lowe and Athletic Director Mel Sheehan.

"Where did you see the game?" I was asked.

"Waco."

"What high school?"

I said, "I don't know."

They said, "You don't know?"

"Don't know."

They asked me where I sat.

"That's ridiculous. That has nothing to do with anything. Look at the allegation. I met two friends at the game, Dr. Don Edwards and Aileen Faurot. I was with them the entire time and went to eat with them afterwards. If you would ask them about that evening, you would find out I was never inside the dressing room."

This was a situation that had gone too far. A couple of phone calls could have straightened things out right away. It didn't matter where I was sitting. There was nothing to this allegation.

"I assume you have something more important to do than this," I told them. "I certainly do."

It appeared they were trying to build a case about whether I was forthcoming in my answers. I didn't know the name of the high school, and I couldn't tell them where I sat. If I said I sat in a certain place in the gym, maybe I moved and didn't think anything about it. The investigators can build a case on the smallest details.

Too many rules. I asked coaches to name some NCAA rules they felt were unnecessary. The majority of those who responded to this question said there were too many rules to even name.

"It would take several days and many pages," one coach wrote.

Another coach: "Start over."

"Common courtesy is a no-no with some rules," wrote a third.

Maybe we should insist every school be audited and investigated on a regular basis. It's been suggested. But if the NCAA continues to interpret its rules the same way as it does today, every school would be put on probation. The *NCAA Manual* is thick and ambiguous. No one could withstand the type of investigation we went through and not be penalized. Every coach has his own list of rules he thinks are unnecessary.

As a result of all these rules, the athlete's needs are rarely considered, especially the athlete from a poor background.

When I first came to the University of Missouri, I had three pair of jeans, two shirts and one suit, and I worked the whole summer for the suit. I knew when the basketball team traveled, they wore suits. I worked hard for $29 a week so I would not be embarrassed and not embarrass anyone else.

We have players who come to the university today who do not have a sport coat. When we go on certain trips, I'd like the University of Missouri to be well-represented on an airline or in a hotel. We want the players to wear a jacket. Some kids don't see this as being very important and they don't see it as their responsibility. As a player, I did. Most of the kids in my era did.

I watch teams such as Duke and other teams in the ACC get off an airline or a bus when they are in the NCAA Tournament. They are really decked out, and look great. I think, man, this is tremendous. But soon a second thought occurs to me. How can they recruit athletes who have all these good clothes? Then a third thought hits me. How come I recruit athletes who don't have good clothes?

It's a fact that teen-age blacks have one of the highest unemployment rates in the nation. When players come from the inner city, they usually come to school with no money and little job experience. Schools need to do more to provide these players with jobs. The NCAA rules need to reflect an understanding of the needs of athletes from poor backgrounds.

The rules don't end once a player graduates. A rule insiders named after a famous football coach and a famous basketball coach states that you can't provide anything for a former student-athlete, even 20 years after he graduates. Let's say a player graduated from Missouri, and a few years later, he moves back to Columbia. He goes out to a car dealer, and the dealer wants to offer him a discount. The NCAA would construe this as an inducement. Supposedly the reason for this rule is that some players used to receive a car and $10,000 at the end of their eligibility. Well, it's not hard to recognize the difference between giving a guy a car and $10,000 and giving him a discount on a car. This rule could use a little revising.

Lengthen the scholarship period. I didn't put this suggestion on the survey, but maybe it belonged there. There's been a proposal the last few years at NCAA conventions to give a student-athlete a scholarship that begins during the first summer after high school graduation. Everyone recognizes some students need to be in summer school before their freshman year. The administrators don't want this rule: Anytime athletes cost them more money, it makes them unhappy.

I believe you need to help an athlete who performs at your institution and makes a concerted effort to go to class and study hall, but is unable to graduate in four years. He deserves the opportunity to return to the school and finish. How do you finance it? The NCAA has a billion dollar television contract. The player should have access to some of that money. Each institution can decide for itself how much money it can provide for this extra schooling.

For years, this sort of opportunity was available at Missouri. The first call I received when I was released from the St. Louis Hawks was from Don Faurot and Sparky Stalcup. "Why don't you come back, get your master's and help us a bit?" they asked. This was the humanitarian thing to do. When Nathan Buntin and Gary Leonard were released from ballclubs, I wrote to them, saying that they should keep in mind that with just a little more work they could complete their degrees. I don't think the university would pay for them today, but in the past, during the administrations of Faurot, Devine and Stalcup, yes, they would have paid for it.

Athletic departments spend a lot of money unnecessarily. Every football game, we feed the press lavishly and hold parties for them the night before. I would like to know how many reporters' expense accounts reflect this free food and entertainment.

The bottom line is, the athletes are producing much of the revenue because they are the key attraction. They deserve more of a reward, and lengthening the scholarship period would be an appropriate reward.

The NCAA must provide quicker and more accurate rules interpretations. We are still under a microscope. I went to a high school game to watch Steve Horton, a young man who had signed an early letter of intent in the fall of 1990. I had watched him since he was a freshman, a player with good size whose team had done very well. Horton had an injury and was not playing well his junior year, but he came back in the summer and showed good quickness, good hands, and played above the rim. We gave him a scholarship. He earned it. After his signing, when his team played at Columbia Rock Bridge, I went out to watch him. In the early minutes of the game, he hurt his knee and had to undergo surgery. I received word later that he might be out 9 to 12 months, and I wanted to see Horton in the hospital to show him some support.

I had to ask the NCAA if it was all right for me to visit Horton. By the time I received an answer, he was already out of the hospital. The NCAA finally said I could have visited him, but my assistants couldn't.

In another instance, we lost a player, Todd Satalowich, due to a career-ending back injury. We asked whether he still could get complimentary tickets because he was at one point on scholarship. The NCAA's written response from a member of its legislative staff was "No." Then a little later, they sent us another letter reversing themselves: Satalowich could receive the tickets.

One coach who responded to my survey recalled a similar experience. The NCAA first reported he could talk with players he had signed and their parents at postseason all-star games. But then the NCAA subsequently ruled the coach couldn't talk to anyone from the time he got to the site of the all-star game to the time he left it.

If the NCAA legislative staff can't come up with decisive rules interpretations, some changes are in order.

This is why the NCAA can't have an 800 number for rules interpretations. The rules are so ambiguous that you would get a ruling from one person, then call back 10 minutes later and somebody else would give you a different answer. The NCAA used to allow coaches to call. However, after they found out so many conflicting rules interpretations were being issued from their office, they prohibited coaches from calling. Now only certain people from your athletic department can call. The irony of this situation is that any fan or reporter can call them and get information — but not the coach.

The response to the coaches survey was 34-0 in favor of an 800 number providing quick and accurate rules interpretations. I think what many of the coaches were saying was that the NCAA's rules shouldn't be so complex that you can't get a correct interpretation during a phone call. Furthermore, an 800 number would be a nice way of investing some of the several hundred million dollars the NCAA receives every year. It is more important to have an 800 number than a private jet. Plus, it's less expensive.

More about the survey —

Twenty-six out of 34 coaches said schools should pay the coach's legal fees during an NCAA investigation. Of the 11 coaches who had been investigated, 10 said schools should pay.

Some "stupid" rules cited by coaches:

— A new rule that limits the number to two coaches recruiting on the road at any given time. One coach says this will cost his school more money because it will force one coach to immediately fly back when another one prepares to leave for a recruiting trip. Allowing a third coach to stay on the road could reduce the amount of total air travel.

—Restrictions on complimentary tickets. The *NCAA Manual* says a prospective student-athlete gets a maximum of three comps during an unofficial visit. If the player signs, he cannot receive any more complimentary tickets until he is enrolled, and then tickets can only be in the sport in which the player participates.

— Not being able to give kids meals on weekends when the dining hall is closed and they have no money.

— Not being able to transport parents to the NCAA Tournament. Football is allowed to do this for bowl games.

— Not being able to watch kids practice before October 15.

25

The Fun Profession

Abe Lemons once said, "We used to have fun doing this, but we didn't make any money. Now we don't have any fun, but we make some money."

Coaching used to be known as a fun profession. You would put some pressure on yourself, but not to the extent you do today. You used to work seven months or so; the rest of the year, you might have another job or just do nothing.

When I went into coaching, I had to take other jobs to make ends meet. Today, this is a big controversy — outside income for coaches. But show me an educator who doesn't have outside income. I took a head coaching job at the State College of Iowa with a salary of $7,000. I worked another job in the summer to make $1,400, for a total of $8,400. As small as that sounds, Missouri head coach Sparky Stalcup was making $9,700 after 25 years.

We didn't care very much about the money then because we liked to play and loved the competition. I have some great memories as a result of my association with other coaches during those prior years when it was a more fun profession.

I remember in the '60s going to the Old Coliseum in Lincoln, Nebraska, to take on Joe Cipriano's Cornhuskers. It was a tumultuous period on college campuses across the nation —

bomb threats, riots, protests were all part of the scene. One day our team was practicing when all of the sudden, there was a terrific explosion.

"My gosh!" I thought. "What do we do?"

It really rocked the place, scaring the hell out of us. And then I heard this cackle. I recognized the voice: It was Cipriano. He had thrown a cherry bomb under the bleachers.

Another time, when he had us beat at the Coliseum, Cipriano thought it would be a good idea to add salt to the wound. He called on a popcorn vendor who happened to be handicapped. The popcorn man had a great sense of humor. Joe said, "You know, Norm might want to buy some popcorn."

It's nearing the end of the game and I'm not in the best mood, mind you. While I'm sitting at the bench this handicapped popcorn guy comes up to me and tries to sell me a bag. A smile came over my face right away because I knew who had sent him. If I had been somewhere else, I would have thought it was an insult, but I knew Cipriano was pulling my leg. The vendor and I had a special relationship for years after that episode.

Joe was full of shenanigans. He had a set of false teeth, the ones with fangs. Sometimes he'd be complaining to a referee about a call, then he'd stop and slip his hand into his pocket for the false teeth. The next thing you know, you're looking at a guy with fangs. What could you do but laugh?

Then there was the time Cipriano shot the referee. His team was getting beat at Oklahoma and he was looking for a way to stop the clock without using up any of his timeouts. You can stop the clock if you point out a correctable error, but if you're wrong, it's a technical foul. Cipriano started yelling about an error, but he stopped himself because he couldn't come up with any real reason to halt the game. So he devised another plan.

Joe saw the starter's pistol near the bench, the one they used to signal the end of the half and the end of the game. As referee Boomer Bain ran by, Joe grabbed the gun and fired it like he was shooting Boomer in the rear end, then quickly put the gun back and returned to the bench.

Everyone in the building fell silent because a gun had gone off. Many didn't know what happened. John MacLeod, coaching Oklahoma at the time, saw Joe's stunt and ran to Boomer. With all of the confusion, MacLeod demanded that a technical foul be called on Cipriano. Joe, meanwhile, sitting on the bench like a choirboy, wouldn't even look over at MacLeod and Boomer.

It took several minutes to calm everyone and figure out what had really happened, and by then Joe had gotten what he wanted. His team was getting smashed by Oklahoma, but he was able to get the clock stopped without calling a timeout.

And talk about the guts of a burglar. Cipriano walked over to Bain and asked, "What the crock is going on? Let's get the game restarted."

"I caught your act before," Bain said. "You go back and sit down."

MacLeod asked Bain, "Are you going to call a technical?"

Boomer, who had a quick sense of humor himself, replied, "If you show me a place in the rule book where it says a man who shoots a gun gets a technical, I'll call a technical."

MacLeod just laughed and sat down again.

Joe called me the following morning with some advice: "Don't shoot a gun during a game."

"Well, I never really considered it."

"Well, don't," Joe said. "You'll hear from people you didn't hear from before."

"Like who?"

"The chancellor, the governor, the Big Eight commissioner, and the police."

"Okay," I said, "I'll remember not to shoot a gun during a game."

Coaches' clinics can keep the fun in the profession, too. I asked Indiana coach Bobby Knight to come to a clinic in Columbia once. The next morning, we were supposed to have someone wake him early so he could catch a plane to St. Louis. But it was after one of those nights when a lot of coaches stayed up late sharing stories. Our guy apparently forgot to pick up Knight and take him to the airport.

I barely had fallen asleep when I received a phone call. It was Bobby.

"Where's that no good bleeping assistant who was supposed to pick me up?"

"Don't worry about it, I'll pick you up," I said.

I drove him to the airport and went back for another day of work at the clinic. While I was introducing a program to the coaches, my secretary approached me quite flustered.

"Coach Knight just called and he's madder than hell," she

said. When he arrived in St. Louis, he'd missed his connecting flight.

When Bobby calls back he tells me a long story. He missed his flight to Cleveland, so he was going to fly to Pittsburgh and drive to Cleveland. But Pittsburgh was fogged in, so he had to fly to Philadelphia. Now he wanted us to pay for a private jet so he could fly to Ohio in time to meet his next obligation.

"I don't care," I said. "Go ahead and rent a jet and send me a bill. And don't call me anymore."

A week goes by and we receive a bill for $1,200 for a jet from Philadelphia to Akron. Fortunately, we made enough money from the clinic to pay it. They wanted us to make the check out to the Indiana Booster Club. A few more days go by and I get a letter from the vice president of the Indiana Scholarship Fund. Now I realize I've been had.

The letter thanked me for my special gift to the athletic department. Since I had given the money, I was entitled to a Big Red license plate, a plasticized Big Red identification card, and other Indiana boosters benefits.

At the bottom of the letter, the guy wrote, "I hope you continue to be a booster and support us financially. And one more thing. I want to let you know I lost a bet with Bobby Knight. He bet me two weeks ago that he could get someone from another university to donate a thousand dollars to Indiana. I lost a hundred dollars."

Well, I wasn't going to sit back and let Knight get away with that.

I had a lawyer write a letter saying he needed some information about a check written to Indiana University. He claimed my wife Virginia had filed for divorce, and one of the reasons was because I wasn't good with finances. The lawyer wrote that the information about the check was important in an upcoming hearing.

Knight smelled something because he didn't answer the letter.

At about the same time, CBS was preparing to do a story on Bobby. Dan Rather called Knight's office asking to speak with him. His secretary walked into his office and said, "Coach Knight, Dan Rather is on the phone for you."

"Yeah, Dan Rather, my ass," Knight replied. "It's that darned Stewart. You tell him I'll call him back later."

When Knight went home, his wife said, "Bobby, Dan Rather called here." Knight still thought I was up to some game.

Mrs. Knight eventually persuaded Bobby to pick up the phone and call the number she'd written on a note pad. When a very recognizable voice on the other end answered, "This is Dan Rather," Knight had to go into a long explanation why he hadn't returned the call earlier.

It helps to have a good imagination in coaching to keep things zipping along. I used to brag that I was a founding member of the S.W.D.A.C. — the Shelbyville Whiskey Drinking Athletic Club.

The S.W.D.A.C. was a spoof, of course. It was our way of poking fun at the exclusivity of athletic clubs. We could include anybody who ever played in the gym. Because I was a player, I was a charter member. Even though Shelbyville didn't have many blacks, our club had a black member, Bum Woods, 75 years old. Since many people assume all blacks can jump well, we called Bum the S.W.D.A.C.'s first skywalker. In reality, Bum couldn't jump over a newspaper.

Eventually, we would expand our mythical membership to include anyone who did something that got our attention. Maybe the night before, someone overindulged and made a real scene. Instant membership.

Quincy used to be a favorite spot for people from Shelbyville to visit for entertainment. This town was about a 45-mile drive across the state line into Illinois. One night, someone didn't negotiate a curve and rolled his car into a ditch. We saw the story in the newspaper and granted this man instant membership into the S.W.D.A.C., then solemnly announced, "It's a great tragedy that one of the members of the S.W.D.A.C. couldn't make Sunday's game because of an auto accident."

When I was at the University of Missouri, out on a date or at an event, people would ask me, "Norm, do you belong to a fraternity?"

"No," I would answer. "I belong to a secret organization that doesn't allow my association with a fraternity."

"Oh, really? What is it?"

"It's the S.W.D.A.C."

In most cases, that would stop the conversation. They would rarely ask what it meant. I am sure many people walked away mystified.

Later on as a coach, I would revive the S.W.D.A.C. every now and then. I would participate in coaches' camps all over the state and tell people about the club and the exploits of one member named Poo-Poo Ralls.

"Ralls invented the double-reverse hook shot," I told them.

Many coaches naturally thought I was just making up a silly story, so one day at camp in Mexico, Missouri, I introduced the real Leon "Poo-Poo" Ralls. It brought the house down.

Leon Ralls, in truth, ran the service station in Shelbyville. A faithful S.W.D.A.C. member, he put together a scrapbook about the club. It had a picture of himself and several other members, but the best photo was of his dog, Sport. Sport's distinguishing characteristic was that he couldn't stand it when someone ran over the hose that rang the bell at the service station. In this particular photograph, Sport was howling because a person was standing on the hose. But the caption read, "Here's the S.W.D.A.C. mascot, Sport, howling for his team."

Stories about the S.W.D.A.C. were imaginative ways of passing time that only folks from small towns like Shelbyville can understand. It's kids. It's fun.

Despite my recent trouble, I've had some great associations with people in the media. You don't run into guys like Dick Wade, Bob Broeg, Bob Burnes, Charlie Paulsel, Russ Smith and Maury White very much any more. It's a different situation now, a different breed of cat. These were people who loved the sport, the players, and the game itself. When you met with them and talked about a loss or some difficulty a player was having, they shared your feelings, rather than examining whose fault it was. In those days, the writers sometimes tried to help.

I got to know Dick Wade, a columnist with the *Kansas City Star*, through Dan Devine. I guess he was probably intrigued with Dan's success. Our basketball program, meanwhile, was just starting to win a game every once in a while. But Wade became interested in what we were trying to accomplish, and he'd stop by or call to do a story on the team. It grew into a good friendship.

One of my main recollections of Dick is a party we had after a football game in the '60s. About 400 of our dearest friends from all over the state associated with the University of Missouri, attended. After the party was over, Dick and I were sitting at the bar, talking late into the night.

At 2 o'clock in the morning, he says, "What do you do now?"

"Well, I clean up the mess."

"Really?" "Yeah. I'll pick up all of the things, put things that need to be thrown away in a sack. Then Virginia and I will get all the dishes and wash them. The last thing I do is vacuum."

Dick asked, "Why don't you do that when you get up?"

"That's the way I was trained, you know. That's what we do. And Virginia and I get a lot of enjoyment out of it, because we can talk about who was there and how their children are doing, the whole bit."

He said, "By golly, I'll help."

So he and I began the process. Then Virginia and I started washing the dishes, with Dick lending a hand. I didn't get done vacuuming until around 4 a.m. That's when Dick took off.

I can virtually remember what stretch of road I was on as I drove to a speaking engagement at the Lake of the Ozarks when I heard over the radio that Dick Wade had died of a heart attack. I was so surprised I nearly ran off the road. I just stopped the car and sat there for some time recalling fond memories of Dick and his wife Betty. Now she is gone, too.

Today there are writers who cover your games, and you don't even know their names. They don't introduce themselves, neither do they follow any business procedures. You don't get the impression of professional responsibility or respect. I think this sort of attitude has helped lower the credibility of the press.

One thing no one should have to put up with is a personal vendetta a reporter may have towards you. I'm reminded of a story former Mizzou football coach Warrren Powers told me not long ago. A reporter had gone to Powers soliciting information about me. The newspaper the reporter worked for had been bashing us pretty good.

Warren told the reporter that he had known me for a long time as a friend and a coaching colleague. Warren explained that he and I spent a great deal of time together at the Lake of the Ozarks and at other social occasions. Warren said that if I was ever worried about our program, or if I knew there was something wrong, I would have told him about it. The reporter then said something to the effect, "It doesn't matter. We know Norm is dirty."

There's an example of a person I feel is taking advantage of their position in the media. The reporter had a pre-determined position, and apparently was going to stick to it.

Nowadays, if an 18- or 19-year-old kid quits the squad, the writers will take advantage of him. They'll get him to say something negative about the school or the team, which he may regret for a long time afterwards.

There's a different mentality today. But that's like a lot of things in sports right now. We are in an era where if you are a coach, you are expected to play a tough schedule, win your games, fill the stadium or arena, make a lot of money, and go to the national tournament. The kids are expected to attend every class, make good grades, and graduate on time. Everything has to be near-perfect, and if it's not, it's a media story.

Because of the reputation of Missouri's journalism school, we have people at the university-run media who want others to be aware of their work. They have used the basketball program as their launching pad to better jobs. Unfortunately, most of them have no sense of history. These aspiring writers from out of state slam the program then leave for other jobs. There have been some good people who have gone through journalism school, but like anything else, there is a bell curve. I am particularly bothered that one of these youngsters can write something about our school and the wire services will pick it up all over the nation. These kids are still learning their trade, but their stories may be carried by the Associated Press, United Press International, and the *New York Times*.

Money especially has changed the heart and soul of the coaching profession. The money is so great now that it attracts all sorts of people. People think, "If I can coach, I can make a lot of money." Yes, the remuneration is much greater than I ever anticipated, but that's not the reason I do it. I used to coach for $7,000 a year.

Now everything revolves around television exposure. It's show business, and you have to play to your audience. Whoever thought there would be a screaming color analyst on television yelling, "OOoohhh . . . Baby!!!"

Many of the new coaches do not follow what I consider the old basic code. They don't adhere to a certain set of understood principles. I see many coaches today that when the excrement hits the whirling blades, suddenly are hard to find. The older guys, the ones with good fiber, don't change or sway.

I had chances to leave coaching and do other things, but I chose to stay because I like it and because the rewards are worth the long hours and the extra pressure. Moreover, I'm talking about rewards you can't pay the rent with.

In the 1974-75 season, our team won 18 games and went to a postseason tournament, the National Commissioner's Intercollegiate Tournament in Louisville, an off-shoot of the NIT. Then in 1975-76 we really came on and were within an eyelash of going to the NCAA Final Four. This ballclub was a favorite of mine, it had something special. We won the Big Eight championship, the first time the school had won it outright in 46 years. My reward for that victory was a $1,000 raise, putting my salary at $23,000. I came to the league making $14,000, coached nine years to make $22,000, won a league championship and was rewarded with a $23,000 contract.

I didn't think much about this at the time. I hope this says something for my love of the game; I was doing exactly what I wanted to do and enjoying the work. But thinking back on it now, the raise was an insult. The person in charge might as well not have given me a raise; you should realize what's appropriate and what isn't in a situation like that.

If I accomplished today what I did then, I would have 10 job offers, and today we're talking about a minimum of $250,000 for a head coaching job.

I still had to fight for benefits such as an extended contract. I told the administration the basketball coach needed an extended contract to help our recruiting. It makes the situation easier when the players know you are going to be around awhile. Other schools know when a coach's contract is up and they can use that against you. We needed to tell our players that Norm Stewart was going to be their coach. If they are coming to the University of Missouri, I would like to think they are coming because of the university and because of the coach.

I never had an agent, so I never had an agent deal, but I was always able to find something to supplement my income. All of the extra sources of income I have at Missouri, my wife and I worked for. No one packaged it together and said, "We want you to have this." We didn't keep up with the times — I didn't keep up. I guess I've been a little naive.

In 1986 I found out I was one of the lowest-paid coaches in the Big Eight. I had been coaching more than 20 years, and I believe I had won more games than any other coach ever had in the conference. Yet here I was, the sixth-highest-paid out of eight coaches in the league. I was receiving around $50,000 a year when other coaches in my league were getting around $70,000 or $80,000.

There was excitement surrounding our program, people were talking about us. When I first came to Missouri, if I spoke 50 miles away from Columbia, people might have known who the starters were. After a couple years, they knew the top substitutes. Now, if I have a walk-on quit the team, the people in the Bootheel want to know what happened to him.

Some of the school's reluctance to give me a higher salary may have been because of my outside income. Whenever someone's outside income grows, people stop and say, "Hey, why should he make that?"

There are always people asking, "Why? How come? Is it right? Should we take this away from him? Should we limit him?"

In America, why are we trying to limit people?

When I found out my salary was sixth in the league, I told school officials, "You know that's not right. That's going to make me look like I'm not aware of what's going on. I want my salary commensurate with the type of job I'm doing, and something that is comparable to what's being offered around the league."

It appears the only way you're going to get a raise is to threaten to leave, or get offered a job by another school. That's a procedure that definitely needs to be corrected.

I did look elsewhere one time. Several years ago, someone from Iowa contacted me so I went there for an interview. It was done professionally. I told the Mizzou people I had been contacted and that I wanted to talk to the people at Iowa, then the Missouri administration began to scurry around a little. I may have taken the Iowa job, however, their interest enabled me to receive a salary increase at Missouri. I got a raise and an extension, but nothing wild. Today my salary is commensurate with what is being paid in the Big Eight.

My record after 30 years was sixth among the nation's active coaches, which brings me to the next point. One of the perks about being a head basketball coach is getting to drive a car supplied by the university on a lease basis. There's an Oldsmobile-Cadillac dealer who for years kept giving me an Olds. One year

I said, "Why don't you give me a Cadillac? Hell, I'm a Cadillac coach." Actually, I was considering my wife more than myself. I knew she would really enjoy driving a Cadillac. I actually didn't need it.

He said, "Well, if you win a championship."

"That's the problem," I said. "You guys always want something more. Geez, I've won championships before."

"Well, if you win another one, I'll give you a Cadillac," he said.

The next year, we won the league championship. I didn't see my Cadillac, so I called the dealer and asked, "Hey, what happened to my Cadillac?"

He replied, "You know, I could have gotten away with making that promise with just about anybody else. But not you. I'm sending you a Cadillac." I received a Cadillac for one month.

There is a commitment to big-time football in the university. I have no problem with that. While our fans each year want to see Missouri in the Orange Bowl, they can find more things to talk about in a season with just seven wins. Don Faurot did great things for the program. It was Missouri kids, playing a good schedule, and Faurot taking them to a few bowl games. Dan Devine came along and won more games, beating a lot of good teams, and went to several Orange Bowls. When they fired Al Onofrio, the situation seemed to change. Warren Powers' teams won seven or eight games a season and went to a few bowl games, but he was fired after one bad year.

Folks keep talking about this football tradition. But some people lately have said it's been like a U.F.O. But I think Bob Stull has a good chance of putting the football program back on track. Currently, we just aren't excelling nationally. In contrast, the basketball program garners a lot of respect outside our regional borders. I can walk into many recruits' homes and they will recognize me; previously I had to explain where we were located.

Even with the apparent emphasis on football, the basketball fans have been great, and the loyal ones will help make my job more enjoyable in the future. One thing I can never put my finger on is the reaction I get from kids and young adults who see me in public somewhere. They'll come up to me and say, "Hi, Norm."

It's unusual that they would view me as "Norm," not "Coach" or "Mr. Stewart." I guess it's because they consider there is some common ground between us. I hope that's what it is, anyway. My small-town upbringing helped me in this regard. When I return to Shelbyville and go to the pool hall, I'll get the old quiet treatment. Finally, someone will speak.

"You still coaching at Mizzou?" they'll ask. I get a real kick out of that.

The next day, I'll hear that the same guys who gave me the silent treatment in the pool hall had fought some outsider who said something derogatory about my coaching.

I am not completely comfortable with the name "Stormin' Norman." It's one thing the image maker did. I am an instinct person. I can be very open in a crowd of 15,000 people. Others may become inhibited, but not me. However, I think I am in control now. When you see one of your players get knocked in the back, or shoved out of bounds, and a foul isn't called, it's difficult to remain calm. I always want to protect my players from being treated unfairly. Then sometimes I'll try to motivate a player by yelling to get his emotional level up. Occasionally the silent treatment works better. You have to try different avenues. Once you get the proper reaction, it's something a player can remember forever.

The people I most admire were my high school coach and the coaches who appear satisfied with themselves and are in control. Coaches like Henry Iba.

There will always be detractors, and they'll always find something wrong: If you win a championship, you were lucky. I don't know where they get their satisfaction; I think they must be frustrated people.

Life is about making adjustments. You have to deal with media criticism, as well as the undue praise. It all balances out eventually.

The future of the Missouri basketball program looks sound. There's no reason why a player shouldn't want to come to Missouri. His chances might be enhanced now that we are down scholarships for the next two years. He may get more playing time.

I am not looking forward to sitting here and not winning as many games as we used to. I have worked hard and long, like when you build your own company, so I could make a profit, and turn the corner. We got out of the red a long time ago. I don't want to see us falling back there once more.

I don't know exactly how I would react if I ran into a losing situation again. It will just have to be overcome; we've had lulls before.

Will I treat my assistants differently now? I was criticized for not overseeing my staff closely enough, but I think given the rules that were broken, there's no way that could have been prevented. They were aware of the rules; I played my role in keeping them informed of the rules. Taking a kid out for a sandwich or picking him up after he hails you are humanitarian gestures, not the type of violation a person should be fired over. But if another assistant comes in and does the same thing, he would probably be dismissed immediately. There's too much at stake now.

I get less work done presently, since I have to spend considerable time writing memos and letters to comply with new policies. But I think we're over the worst of it.

I have an assigned duty, working for the university. I will get along with the administration just fine. The fact that anything else may exist between us won't keep me from doing my job. I don't harbor any resentment against the chancellor, although I do disagree with him at times. But it's America. I will cooperate as I have in the past.

I hope the University of Missouri administration feels the same way. I would have appreciated more support in the past. Since I am an alum, a former player and now a coach for 25 years at Missouri, I think I deserve something in return, as any faculty member would with this much experience. In many ways I am a teacher, only my classroom is the basketball court. I don't know what areas the administration wants to control, but I will control the team, what offense we run, what defense we run, who plays, and who sits.

I'm going to do everything I'm told to do. I'm going to go the extra mile. That's what you do if you are a competitor.

26

Stormin' Back

As Gilda Radner used to say, "It's always something." The 1990-91 season was like that. One problem after another popped up to distract the team. With the NCAA investigation behind us, you'd think our troubles were over. They weren't. But it was great that we persevered and finished on a triumphant note despite the many setbacks. We were able to storm back.

It didn't look altogether promising from the start, but we had to play with the hand we were dealt.

Anthony Peeler, Big Eight Newcomer of the Year his freshman season and a first-team All Big Eight selection his sophomore year, was ruled academically ineligible for the fall of 1990.

Another returning starter, Travis Ford, asked for his release before the season began. Ford, a standout high school guard at Madisonville, Kentucky, wanted to transfer to the University of Kentucky.

Kentucky wanted him, but they couldn't openly express it. Still, they could convey that desire to other people interested in their program — writers and alums, for example. One Kentucky writer wrote in July of 1990 that Ford is one of those Kentucky kids "who would be 10-12 points better wearing a jersey with 'Kentucky' across the front."

This writer reported that LSU coach Dale Brown, who coached Ford in the Olympic Festival, told Ford he would be welcome at LSU if he wanted to transfer. That comment created a little controversy in itself, but after talking with Coach Brown, I was assured his comments were tongue-in-cheek.

The rumor of a possible transfer wouldn't die. Ford reportedly told *USA Today* that if he did transfer, it would be to Kentucky because he had a lot of friends there.

Finally, his dad called me to ask for the release and said he would be in Columbia the following day. I told him, "No, you don't have to come up. I'll just fax it to you."

"No," he said. "I will come up."

We certainly didn't want him to leave. He had a nice future here. We liked him as a player and a student. I thought his scenario at Missouri was better than at Kentucky. He could have stepped in his sophomore year and run the ballclub.

"Well, why are you making this decision?" I asked.

They said it was because of the things they were reading in the newspaper about the NCAA investigation and all the speculation about what the penalties would be.

I told them I couldn't sign the release, that they needed to go to the athletic director. Then we said our good-byes. I think Travis was a little embarrassed.

In Kentucky, Adolph Rupp really established a big basketball tradition, a mainstay in the state. But Travis Ford wasn't initially recruited by Kentucky. I think Duke would have been Ford's second choice, but Duke took Bobby Hurley. Ford came to Missouri because it was the next natural choice. It was a good fit.

With our program facing probation, the Fords thought it was the right time to transfer to Kentucky, and I can't find fault with him. If he can find a niche there and produce, it will be a good decision. Kentucky was certainly glad to have him back. One thing still disappoints me about the transfer, however. We sent him a championship ring, and we haven't heard from him. It surprises me because he's a nice guy, and I thought we would have heard from him by now.

Another setback in the 1990-91 season came the same day the NCAA handed the school its penalties. Three of our freshmen were injured during an exercise in an ROTC class. Melvin Booker, Lamont Frazier and Jevon Crudup were doing a one-rope bridge exercise. Booker was less than a third of the way across the span when the rope broke. He fell a short distance and the rope smacked him in the face, knocking out some teeth. Crudup and Frazier, who had been holding the rope, fell. Crudup suffered a sprained wrist while Frazier sprained his back and neck and received a concussion.

When I came back from meeting with reporters about the NCAA penalties, somebody told me what had happened. Melvin was still in the dentist's chair. I got into the car and drove to see him as fast as I could. He'd had a lot of work done in his mouth, but the dentist said Melvin was a tough son of a gun.

Lamont was in the hospital for a short period of time. Jevon was the only one of the three to practice the next day, with a taped wrist.

These injuries really affected our practice. They were a lot to contend with. When something like this arises, you simply try to reassure the players of the basics.

"You came here to go to school, play basketball and grow up," I told them. "You're getting some real character builders. Just hang in there and it will be all right. Everybody will be okay."

Finally, there was the matter of explaining to the team that assistant coaches Bob Sundvold and Rich Daly were resigning at the end of the year. It was a very emotional moment for me. You don't spend thirteen years with someone, eight years with another, and not feel a great attachment. I know I was visibly shaken when I explained the situation to the players because afterwards, Doug Smith came to me and said, "Coach Stewart, it will be okay."

Our first regular-season game was with Rutgers in New Brunswick, New Jersey. Without any postseason play in our picture, this was the only big trip of the year for the team. We wanted to make it a special trip for the new players. We flew in to New York a day or two early, hoping to cement the team together and give us some time to relax. We also saved the school hundreds of dollars per player on air fare by having them stay an extra day.

The first game was still a struggle, a 68-60 loss. In fact, the first seven games were a struggle. Everyone tried so hard, Doug Smith especially. It appeared at times that he was trying to carry the team.

We lost to a good Creighton team on the road, 74-68.

We were 2-2 going into the Hearnes Center to host the Arkansas Razorbacks and Nolan Richardson's "Forty Minutes of Hell." They were ranked second or third, and our record 34-game home winning streak was on the line. The score was even in the first 20 minutes. But during the second half, the Razorbacks began to wear us down. The final score was: Arkansas 95, Missouri 82.

Then after a win over Bradley, it was time for the annual showdown with Illinois in St. Louis. Lou Henson's team was going through some of the same problems we were having because of NCAA probation. Yet it appeared both teams really picked up their game. We came out on a losing end, 84-81, but the experience really prepared us for a seven-game home stand.

With all of this happening, I was very pleased with how freshman Jevon Crudup played. He was stepping in and performing some plays we didn't know he could do. We never really know about a young player's defense or his ability to perform in a game situation. Crudup was a big boost for us. Then Peeler proved he could concentrate on his schoolwork over a long period of time. He became eligible after the first semester and rejoined the team just in time for the seven-game home stand.

It was a quirk in our schedule, getting to play seven games in a row at home. Looking back, we would have been better off playing three games at home, one on the road, then another two or three at home. There are too many chances to lose concentration when you play that many consecutive games at home. But we won all seven, including victories over highly regarded Oklahoma State and Oklahoma. The Sooners were in the top 15 at the time.

One of those wins was the result of a last-second shot from Jeff Warren. We were tied with Kansas State 60-60 with only seconds to go. Peeler took the shot and missed, but Warren grabbed the rebound and put up an awkward one-hander that gave us a 62-60 victory. It was a great moment for Jeff, who had missed the two previous games because of a swollen hand. Jeff is a very tough-minded individual and a good student, whose grade point average is above 3.0. He is well-mannered off the court, but put him on the hardwood and he is a great competitor.

Unfortunately, just as Jeff was getting over his injury, the team was hit with other injuries.

Crudup's play started to fall off a little. I compare it to the first time you go out and play golf after being away from it for a while. You hit the ball real well at first, but then you start thinking about what you are doing, and you begin to play poorly. I think Crudup was entering that period when freshmen begin thinking about how well they are playing. Then he was knocked down in the Kansas game and got hurt. He took a shot and somebody took his feet out from under him. We thought he could try to play a little later in the game, but he couldn't do anything. After the game, we had his wrist X-rayed and found a break. I think he would have really come on strong during the last part of the season.

Now just as we were getting settled with Peeler in the lineup, Anthony got injured. I believe he was taking the last shot during a practice. He was about to stuff it, and he landed the wrong way. I don't even think he knew he was hurt at the time, but something was wrong above his right knee. When he warmed up for the next game, we discovered that he couldn't play.

Everything seemed to work against us right when we hit the toughest part of our schedule, the conference road games.

With a 12-5 record, we lost on the road to Nebraska and Oklahoma back-to-back. We picked up a win at Colorado, then lost to Kansas at home and Oklahoma State on the road. Two games later, we lost at Iowa State.

Jamal Coleman and Doug Smith received some negative publicity in the *Columbia Missourian* after the victory over Colorado in Boulder. According to the newspaper, a woman had left her purse at the Hearnes Center. The paper reported the purse was returned by Coleman, but when the woman received her telephone credit card bill several weeks later, it was discovered as much as $145 worth of calls had been made to relatives or friends of Smith and Coleman.

We conducted our own investigation into this matter. There were discrepancies not mentioned in the paper. Sports information director Bob Brendel and assistant athletic director Joe Castiglione asked to see the *Missourian's* records before the story was printed. But the paper wouldn't release the records until after publication. How were we supposed to make a comment beforehand?

We discovered that two players and two student assistants gave a different story from what the paper printed. It was our understanding that another person gave the players permission to use the credit cards. The woman never filed charges.

I was proud of the way my team contended for the league title despite all of these distractions and injuries. We were still in the hunt.

Peeler began playing with some discomfort, although he'll deny he was in any pain. He learned to adjust his play and was still phenomenal.

Chris Heller came on strong at the end. In the preseason, he had played well, but then he leveled off. Chris is not a practice player. However, late in the season, after we tried so many different lineups, I said to him, "You are going to play."

I gave Heller the basic instructions. "Play through your mistakes. If you make a mistake, you run faster. You keep your head up. If I take you out of the game, you're going back in."

At first Heller made a lot of fouls. But the team responded to his presence in the lineup and to his speed. We started to take on a certain character then.

Jamal Coleman was becoming what we had hoped for all along. A lot can be said about Jamal's contribution. Here's a talented player who had been prevented from playing much the previous year because of players like Doug Smith, Anthony Peeler, Byron Irvin, Greg Church, Mike Sandbothe, Gary Leonard, Nathan Buntin, Lee Coward, John McIntyre and Travis Ford.

But Jamal stayed in there. At times, we didn't think he worked hard enough, but it was difficult for him. He didn't think we had confidence in him. Finally we let him play 30 to 35 minutes a game to show our faith in him.

I pulled him aside one day and said, "I know you are not going to believe this, but we do have confidence in you. There are still one or two things you need to work on to be a better player."

Then it started happening. Jamal showed more confidence in himself. His relationships with the coaching staff and the players changed. I think Jamal is just beginning to be the type of player and individual that he wants to be. It's very rewarding to watch this transpire. During the final stretch, it became commonplace to see Jamal score in double figures and achieve double-figure rebounds.

At this writing, Jamal is involved in a legal problem, having been charged with theft at a bookstore on campus. The university has suspended him for a semester, a decision that troubles me. Here we have a kid being judged and punished before going on trial. Meanwhile, a football player who is charged with another crime is not suspended. The reason? The football player's alleged crime was not committed on campus. The university's decision to suspend Jamal at this stage has attracted the attention of the Justice Department, which is looking at the equity of it. This unfortunate development leaves his basketball status up in the air for now. But it's important to support him when he needs it, and provide help. He may have to be disciplined, but I'm sure Jamal will know how to handle it.

The freshman guards, Reggie Smith and Melvin Booker, started making good contributions also. We were getting fine assistance from anyone we put into the ball game.

After the loss to Iowa State, we ended the regular season with wins over Kansas State, Colorado and Notre Dame.

In the last month of play, I don't think there was a better person in the United States than Doug Smith. Before Doug's final game in Columbia, Governor John Ashcroft declared it Doug Smith Day. Doug played another great game. Although he didn't score his usual 20 or 30 points because he was double- and triple-teamed by Notre Dame, he almost had a triple-double.

We had a comfortable lead against the Irish, and Doug wanted to come out of the game early. But I wanted to leave him in until the last part of the game.

"Stay in," I told him. "Don't you want to shoot another three-pointer? You shot one and missed it."

"Yeah, one more," Doug said.

I left him in. Doug came dribbling across the top of the key. Up went the three-pointer.

He nailed it.

If nothing else happened, if we didn't do well in the Big Eight Tournament, this still would have been the most fitting end for his career. Doug can shoot the threes. I'm sure he'll shoot them in the pros.

After the game, we had a special ceremony to retire Doug's jersey and raise it to the rafters. As I saw his number go up in the air, I thought how quickly it's over. I always tell players the four years will go by in a hurry, so work hard, but enjoy it.

We entered the Big Eight Tournament with a record of 17-10. Some teams were angry that we were allowed to play in the tournament while on probation. If we won the tournament, they argued, it might prevent one of the conference teams from gaining an automatic bid to the NCAA Tournament.

Oklahoma coach Billy Tubbs went on a sports show and said there's no doubt Missouri shouldn't be in the tournament.

"If they played us in the finals," Tubbs said, "we'd kick their butts."

That's a favorite saying of Billy's: "We'll kick some butt."

Our team just ignored it. I enjoy competing against Billy, because he is a genuine guy, he doesn't change. He gets angry every now and then, but he's the same guy. I appreciate that.

Conrad Dobler, who's on the radio in Kansas City, asked me about Tubbs' comment.

"First of all," I said, "Billy is not going to be in the finals, so we won't have to worry about playing him. But if we do, he knows he's not going to win that game either."

In the Big Eight Tournament, it was a showcase of Doug's talents: 92 points, 30 rebounds, assists, steals, and blocked shots. Whatever had to be done, he did it.

The players accepted the fact that there would be no NCAA Tournament. They responded so well, first with a 97-81 win over Iowa State, then with a big double-overtime win over Oklahoma State in the semifinals. The 90-82 victory over Nebraska in the championship game was even more exhilarating.

While I'm sure our players were still disappointed that there could not be an NCAA Tournament in store for them, we were ranked 12th in the power ratings. The players knew they were an NCAA team; I guess that's what counted. They showed maturity beyond their years.

Someone wrote that Billy Tubbs' comment before the tournament won it for us. I want to assure this writer that what another coach says does not motivate my players. We had our own game plan.

I joked in the post-game news conference that we'd be one of only four or five teams to finish the season with a win. We had a 20-10 record for the year, not a bad way to start out a new decade after all the turmoil our team had been through.

As the reality of what we accomplished began to sink in, I couldn't help but recall what someone had written two years before. A writer described some of the great moments we had experienced in our program throughout the last few decades, but then proclaimed, "the best days of Mizzou basketball were over."

Since this statement was made, we've had two 20-win seasons, sold out the Hearnes Center before the season began for two years in a row, won a Big Eight regular-season championship, been ranked No. 1 in the country and won a Big Eight post-season championship. Not bad for a team that had seen its best days.

27

Lo and Behold, We Beat 'Em

Prior to our experience with the NCAA, making an appeal to the NCAA was considered useless. If you were found guilty of a violation, you had little, if any, chance in getting a reversal.

After a rehearing in June of 1991, the NCAA rescinded its previous finding of unethical conduct for Coach Rich Daly. I have never heard of this happening before. It is unprecedented.

The NCAA was originally concerned about Daly's recollection of a flight from Columbia to Detroit on an Easter Sunday in 1985. As I had pointed out in an earlier chapter, Daly said he may have been on the flight, but he didn't recall for sure.

The allegation was brought up by a former recruit who had an ax to grind. The recruit claimed Daly and I flew with him to Detroit, that Vic Adams met us at the airport and gave us a ride to the recruit's house, and with the assistance of Adams, we encouraged the recruit to come to Mizzou.

The NCAA reported that "new information" was presented at Daly's rehearing. In its Infractions Report, the NCAA said "this new information derived from the plane log, which placed the head coach in the private airplane on the day in question, together with the assistant coach's further elaboration of his travel procedures, while not completely satisfactory, presented an explanation of why the coach may have been unable to recall these event with more certainty."

Many of the newspapers have continually reported that the "new information" was my name on this flight log. If they would just look at their own file on the Mizzou case, they would have seen this information was presented to the NCAA long ago. It was ancient history. I had already addressed the issue in a July, 1990, news conference, and we all discussed it with the NCAA for about an hour during the September, 1990, hearing. The pilot of the flight, as well as another local pilot, said that the entry "Norm Stewart" on the flight log was a generic term for anyone associated with the basketball program, just as "Governor Ashcroft" may be a generic entry for a member of the Governor's staff. I also produced sworn affidavits and business records showing I was in Columbia the day of the flight.

I am not aware of any new information brought before the NCAA. I feel the real key to Rich's victory was what was on eight hours of tapes. The NCAA taped the first Infractions Committee hearing in September of 1990. After the hearing, the NCAA wrote in its Infractions Report that Daly said during the hearing he "could not recall spending an Easter Sunday afternoon on a private airplane with a recruit while returning to Detroit, Michigan; could not recall being in Detroit; could not recall riding from the airport with a representative of the university's athletic interests, and in fact, would not remember anything connected with this or other highly visible recruits in the Detroit area."

I think what probably caused the reversal was the NCAA listening to the tapes and discovering it screwed up. I feel if the NCAA had reviewed these tapes earlier, they never would have made the unethical conduct finding against Rich in the first place. I think the NCAA reviewed these tapes and heard a much different set of answers than what it wrote in its Infractions Report. As far as I know, from Rich's review of the tapes of the hearing, Rich said, "I can't recall for sure," just one time in regard to the trip in question, and that was when he was asked if he was on the private plane. He categorically denied ever riding with a representative of the university's athletic interests from the airport. He did remember being in Detroit, he just wasn't exactly sure how he got there. After all, the trip had occurred four-and-a-half years prior to the hearing.

The press had asked me months earlier what I would do if Daly won his rehearing. I made the statement that I didn't see any reason why I wouldn't rehire him.

When Daly won his rehearing, Chancellor Monroe said he would do what he had done in all other hiring procedures and listen to the recommendation of the coach and the athletic director. That placed it in Dick Tamburo's court, because I already stated my position.

It took about a week to go through this procedure and Rich was rehired.

Because of an unfortunate set of circumstances, Rich could not be reinstated at the same salary as before. After Rich and Bob Sundvold resigned, Dwight Evans and I were holding down the fort. We moved Dwight up in salary, though not the salary of a full-time coach. Dwight and I tried to carry on, but were getting buried.

At this time, we were going through the process of finding a replacement for Bob. That's when we hired Kim Anderson.

I was ecstatic about getting Kim because I watched him since he was a freshman in high school. Kim was a great player for Mizzou, and a model student-athlete. He was an assistant on my staff at Mizzou for three years. Then Kim went to work as a coach for Gene Iba at Baylor for six years. Chancellor Monroe and Dick Tamburo were also elated about Kim joining the staff. People across the state went out of their way to comment that it was an outstanding move.

Our salaries at Missouri are not very high, about the middle of the Big Eight in salary scale. In order to hire Kim, we could only pay him what he was making at Baylor. In doing that, it left us short in our budget for assistant coaches.

When Daly won his rehearing, we could not give him what he was making before, plus he lost a country club membership that he previously received for being a member of the coaching staff. On top of that, the administration suspended him from recruiting activities for the duration of the probation.

I feel once again, it's the same old story of Mizzou going out of its way to penalize itself. On the other hand, I am very happy Rich is back. The players, who have endured a lot, are also pleased Rich is back. It stabilizes the staff. I also feel the fans have been very supportive, even more so, now that the investigation is behind us.

Looking back over what has transpired, these things keep coming to my mind. After an intensive two-year investigation, the university spent about a half million dollars, we had one coach lose his job after admitting his mistake, lives have been altered, and reputations — including my own — have been smeared.

And what for?

The only thing they told me was that I had to supervise my assistants better. Rich is back on the staff. Two of the three coaches are still employed. Bob Sundvold lost his job for a violation he had self-reported two years earlier, and for which he had already been disciplined. As far as I know, what's left of Rich's charges is he helped arrange for a tutor, which he was asked to do by the player's father, and Rich picked up one player and gave him a ride to campus, which was not pre-arranged.

Our program was the subject of a media carnival. There were many different accusations brought forth in newspapers, television, radio, and the book *Raw Recruits,* especially about our recruiting in Detroit. But when it was all over, the only infractions regarding Detroit were that Vic Adams may have given a player a ride from an airport in 1985 (which we don't think happened), and one recruit obtained a videotape. That's it. That's all. They investigated five years worth of recruiting in Detroit and found one car ride and a videotape.

Obviously someone over-reacted when Bob's self-report became public.

From my viewpoint, there shouldn't have been an investigation from our side. The NCAA should have looked at the original self-report and the other charges, and should have given us some sort of reprimand. It would have been done in much less time, for much less cost, and with a constructive result — we would be more careful in the future. Instead, it took almost two years, cost a great deal, and achieved a very disruptive result. Reputations were ruined, careers damaged, and the images of the university and the NCAA were tarnished. It didn't have to be this way.

I hope this type of thing doesn't happen again, at Missouri or anywhere else.

I think universities should come up with a set of standards for starting their own investigations. I question a policy that allows a university administration to hire attorneys and conduct an investigation, when the duties of the administration are also in question.

It's also time the NCAA not only revamp its enforcement procedures, but discourage the mentality that a school and its coaches are guilty of an alleged violation, regardless of the credibility of the accuser or his evidence, unless the school or coaches prove their own innocence, at their own expense, without the assistance of the enforcement staff. It doesn't matter what rules they have. If they don't change the mentality, nothing will change. Without a change in attitudes, I don't think any number of reforms will help.

Appendix A

Comments of Coach Norm Stewart
July 18, 1990

I called this news conference today to discuss the NCAA's allegation that was published last week. As most of you know, the NCAA issued a Supplemental Letter of Inquiry. The Supplemental Letter alleges that I provided false or misleading information to the NCAA and University investigators. The purpose of this news conference is to confirm to you that that allegation is false. I also wanted to provide the people of Missouri an opportunity to hear my response to the allegation. I feel that the people would like to hear both sides of the story and deserve the opportunity.

I want to put the NCAA's latest allegation in perspective. I have been coaching college basketball for 33 years. For 29 of those years, I have been the head coach of a college program and, as you know, during the last 23 years I have served as the head coach at the University of Missouri. During that time I have enjoyed a reputation for running a "squeaky clean" program. During my 33 years of coaching, I have never been involved in, or connected with, an NCAA rules infractions case—until this one.

As most of you know in late 1988, one of my assistant coaches reported to me that he had lent $135 to P.J. Mays. At the time, I was stunned. I told the assistant coach to immediately self-report the violation. The University, with my concurrence, investigated the events surrounding the self-reported violation. I feel that at that time, I acted as one would hope a head coach would act: Before the violation, I had already instructed my staff to follow the rules; when the violation was discovered, I ordered it self-reported; and after it was self-reported, I supported an examination of it.

In February of 1989, Chancellor Haskell Monroe and Athletic Director Dick Tamburo broadened the scope of the inquiry beyond the Mays incident. They ordered a program-wide investigation of the basketball program. Chancellor Monroe and Athletic Director Tamburo hired attorneys Mike Slive and Mike Glazier to represent them and conduct an investigation jointly with the NCAA. During the ensuing 18-month joint investigation, the University and the NCAA interviewed 135 individuals in 21 states.

The 135 individuals interviewed during the investigation include past and present players and assistant coaches, former recruits, high school coaches, opposing college coaches, and boosters. Many, if not most, of the individuals interviewed, had reasons to be biased against either me or the University. Certain past or present players probably felt that they had not received enough playing time. Some former assistant coaches probably felt that I did not appreciate their efforts enough. Some recruits who went to different schools obviously did not feel overly favorable towards me or the University. During the recruiting process, they had been either rejected by the University or they chose to go elsewhere because they did not care for the University in the first place. Some high school coaches often complained because we did not give one of their players enough attention or did not give them a job when they had a blue chip recruit. The potential bias of opposing college coaches is obvious.

The investigation resulted in the issuance of a Letter of Official Inquiry in May of this year. Of the 135 individuals interviewed who could have made allegations against the University or its coaches, virtually all of the allegations are attributable to 4 individuals and their families or friends. Each one of these 4 individuals has publicly expressed a bias against the University or one of its coaches. And each one of these individuals has a motive to fabricate, or at least embellish, the facts.

I am prepared to acknowledge that some of the allegations contained in the original Letter of Inquiry are correct and that some violations have occurred. For several of the allegations, however, the evidence boils down to a conflict in testimony between disgruntled individuals who have a motive to lie, on the one hand, and the coaching staff, on the other hand. My coaching staff has been in good standing with the NCAA for over 7 decades, collectively. For those allegations where the evidence boils down to us versus them, I feel the question should be resolved in favor of the coaching staff.

But, apparently, the NCAA does not see it that way. They have now issued a Supplemental Letter of Inquiry. In this Supplemental Letter they allege that I provided them with false and misleading information. They make this allegation because my testimony conflicts with the testimony of certain individuals. In some cases these individuals have stated publicly that they hope the University goes on probation. In some cases these individuals have stated that they don't like me or my assistant coaches. In some cases these individuals have changed their story two or three times. And one of the individuals has a criminal conviction.

The new allegation arises out of an interview I held with the investigators in November of 1989. During that interview, I told the truth and I was straightforward. During the interview, I admitted that the school had mistakenly allowed P.J. Mays to practice when he was ineligible (part of Allegation No. 1). Obviously I also admitted that we had loaned money to P.J. Mays (Allegation No. 2). I admitted that we had entertained players and recruits at a Casino Night (part of Allegation No. 3). I was the first person, or one of the first, to say that we had conducted an auction during Casino Night (part of Allegation No. 3). I acknowledged that we may have made a mistake when we entertained a man who was the surrogate father, rather than the natural father, of a recruit (Allegation No. 4). I admitted that my staff had provided meals and local transportation for students during summer orientation (parts of Allegation No. 5). I was the first individual to provide the investigators with the name of the cook and the resort at which the players ate a meal after a float trip (Allegation No. 6). I admitted that an assistant coach or I may have inadvertently left a videotape with a prospective student-athlete (Allegation No. 11). I admitted that I was aware that one of my assistant coaches had provided meals for an assistant AAU coach (Allegation No. 12). I admitted that I had dined with Vic Adams. I also admitted that I had employed my graduate assistant coaches to work at my summer camps—which could have been a violation if my camps had been designated "institutional" camps under NCAA rules.

Whether infractions are found as a result of these admissions, only time will tell. But, during my November interview, I was not trying to mislead the investigators in order to avoid a rules infraction. I made several admissions that I knew could result in a finding of an infraction. My admissions in these various regards were consistent with my early instructions to my staff to tell the truth and to fully cooperate. It was also in keeping with my personal rule of thumb that if we have committed an infraction, we will admit it; but if we have not committed an infraction, we will contest it.

The NCAA has now issued its Supplemental Letter of Inquiry alleging that I have provided false and misleading information during the November 1989 interview. It recently made this allegation, despite all of the things I admitted to during the interview and despite the fact that it did not make the allegation in the original Letter of Inquiry issued in May. The new allegation relates to two issues.

The first issue involves a recruit's return flight to Detroit. The flight allegedly took place on a non-commercial airplane on Easter Sunday over 5 years ago. During the November, 1989 interview, the investigators told me that they felt I may have returned to Detroit with the recruit on Easter Sunday, remained in the Detroit area for the following two days, and then made a visit to the recruit's home.

During the interview, I told the investigators that I did not recall this return trip. I did not deny being on the flight; I simply told them I could not recall it. At that time I was, and I continue to be, reluctant to concede that I was on the flight because I have absolutely no recollection of it. Now, 8 months after the interview, the NCAA alleges that I misled them when I said I could not recall this particular flight.

The flight occurred more than five years ago, and I frequently fly on non-commercial airplanes. In fact, over the past five years, I estimate that I have flown on over 200 non-commercial flights. Therefore, there was no reason for me to specifically recall this particular flight. Also, the flight occurred on Easter Sunday. In attempting to recall the flight, I have had a difficult time believing that I would have flown to Detroit on Easter Sunday. Additionally, I tended not to believe the accusation because it was based on information provided by a former recruit, who has a motive to fabricate the story, or at least embellish the facts. This individual knows that Missouri coaches reported him to the NCAA and I am sure he has resented it ever since. Additionally, his credibility is questionable. He was convicted for forgery and theft in 1987. At any rate, during my November, 1989 interview, I told the investigators that while I was not denying being on the flight, I had no recollection of this flight—a flight that occurred more than five years, and 200 flights, ago.

After the issue of the flight arose during my November, 1989 interview, I asked my attorney, Steve Owens, to attempt to ascertain whether or not I was on the flight. If he discovered information indicating I was on the flight, I was prepared to admit it. However, the information uncovered by my attorney tended to indicate that I was not on the flight.

Among other things, my attorney found documentation indicating that I was in Columbia on the days in question. As I mentioned before, at one time investigators theorized that I was on the Easter Sunday flight, remained in Detroit for the following two days, and then made a home visit. However, various documents confirmed that I was in Columbia for at least a portion of Easter Sunday and all of the next two days. We presented this information to the University and NCAA investigators on January 8, 1990.

Additionally, I remained suspicious of the source of the accusation. I felt the recruit had reasons to fabricate such a story. He was coached by an individual who admits he hates the University and its coaches. This coach and the former recruit know that that Missouri coaches filed a complaint with the NCAA regarding the manner in which other schools recruited the prospective student-athlete. Their names surfaced as a result of this complaint and they have resented it ever since. The complaint is still on file with the NCAA. This coach told me that Missouri was responsible for him spending a "miserable summer" after we made the report to the NCAA. Regardless of motive to lie, the recruit's general truthfulness is questionable. As I said, he has been convicted of forgery and theft.

Up until June of this year, I believed that I was not on the Easter Sunday flight of five years ago because: (1) I could not recall the flight;

(2) I found it hard to believe I would travel to Detroit on Easter Sunday; (3) the documentation which my attorney obtained indicated that I was in Columbia for at least part of Easter Sunday and all of the following two days; and (4) the accusation was based on information from an unreliable source, a source who had a motive to lie and who has been convicted of forgery and theft. For these reasons, and consistent with my attorney's advice, I was naturally reluctant to concede that I was on the flight.

In June of this year, the pilot of the Easter Sunday flight was interviewed. That pilot has supplied an affidavit in which he swears under oath that he does not recall who was on the flight. Quite frankly, I would hope that if I had been on the flight I would have enough notoriety that the pilot would remember whether I was on it. But he does not. The pilot has also provided copies of flight logs that list "Norm Stewart" as the entry under the category entitled "Passengers-Title-Company or Customers and Company Visited". With regard to this entry, the pilot has provided a sworn affidavit explaining that the notation "Norm Stewart" under this column is a generic term and does not mean I was actually a passenger on the flight.

What is significant to me, however, is that the flight logs indicate that a flight from Columbia to Detroit did occur on the date in question. The information obtained from the flight logs, while certainly not conclusive, tends to shift the evidence to the point where I do not intend to contest the accuracy of the allegation that such a flight occurred, even though I still have no recollection of the flight and find it difficult to believe I would have flown to Detroit on Easter Sunday.

On June 18th of this year, I informed University investigators that I still could not recall the flight, but that I intended to admit that such a flight occurred. In my mind, whether it was actually me on the flight or not was irrelevant because I informed the investigators that I was willing to accept responsibility for the alleged violation either directly, if I was on the flight, or indirectly, because I am the head coach. For some unknown reason, the University did not communicate this information to the NCAA. I had to present it directly to the NCAA in a hurry-up fashion on July 8. 48 hours later, the Supplemental Letter was issued.

I intend to vigorously contest the NCAA's allegation that I provided them with false or misleading information when I said I could not recall a particular plane flight which occurred more than five years, and over 200 flights, ago. When I told them I could not recall that particular flight, I was telling them the truth. I still do not recall that particular flight. But I am willing, based on other evidence, to admit that a violation probably occurred. I think the fact that I am willing to make such an admission (and was willing to do so before the Supplemental Letter was issued), should indicate to people that I was telling the truth in November.

I think that those of you who are 55 years old, like me, will understand my inability to recall this particular flight. I would challenge any of you, of any age, to recall where you were or what you were doing on a specific date five years ago, especially if it involved doing something you've done over 200 times. Seriously, I want each one of you to stop and think: where were you and what were you doing on Easter Sunday five years ago?

As I said, I intend to vigorously contest the allegation that I provided false or misleading information. Assuming I can get a fair hearing, I anticipate that the charges will be either dropped, or that the Committee on Infractions will find in my favor. If I cannot get a fair hearing from the NCAA, I will have to take my case somewhere where I can get a fair hearing. Be assured, however, that I am not going to stand still and be called a liar because I can't recall whether I was on a particular plane flight five years ago.

The second issue alleges that I provided false and misleading information when I told the investigators that I had not instructed Vic Adams to obtain an already signed letter of intent from a recruit's home. The source of this accusation is the recruit's family and his high school coach, who is the same coach that we reported to the NCAA several years ago. Each one of the individuals involved in this allegation refuses to be interviewed separately: they insisted on being interviewed in the same room while the others were present so they could hear each other's testimony. This is contrary to NCAA customary procedure and, to my knowledge, no one else was allowed this privilege. Each one of these individuals has a motive to fabricate or embellish the facts. The recruit stated in a live television interview with KOMU-TV in Columbia that even though the University had recruited him fairly, he hoped the University basketball program would go on probation so he could be released from his commitment under his letter of intent. His former high school coach admits he passionately dislikes Missouri because he thinks we reported him to the NCAA and because he thinks we "went behind his back" to recruit one of his players after he had advised that player to "avoid" the University of Missouri. These individuals clearly have a motive to lie.

Despite the fact that these individuals were interviewed together, their testimonies are significantly inconsistent with one another, and inconsistent with documentary evidence and the testimony of Coach Daly and me. For example, these individuals claim that I telephoned them on two, and perhaps three, occasions on a certain evening to arrange for the letter to be picked up; but telephone records indicate I made only one telephone call. That call was in keeping with my customary practice of calling a recruit to congratulate him once he has signed a letter of intent. On some occasions, the recruit claims that Vic Adams picked up the letter of intent; but on other occasions he claims

Adams <u>delivered</u> the letter of intent. Initially, the recruit's mother claimed she knew it was Vic Adams who supposedly picked up the letter; but later had to admit she had never met Vic Adams before. She then changed her story and said she had met Vic Adams before—when a coach from another school was leaving her house; but the coach that she identified has provided an affidavit where he swears under oath that he never saw Adams at or near the recruit's residence. The recruit and his mother claimed that they signed the letter of intent in the <u>evening</u> shortly before it was allegedly picked up; but the letter itself shows it was signed in the <u>afternoon</u> at 2:00 p.m. When asked about this discrepancy, they had no explanation. In sum, these people, who have publicly expressed a hope that Missouri goes on probation, have changed their story repeatedly. And even though they were interviewed together, they cannot come up with a story that hangs together.

More importantly, there is absolutely no evidence to support the allegation that I telephoned Vic Adams and instructed him to obtain the letter of intent. There is <u>no</u> statement by <u>any</u> witness that a telephone conversation took place where I instructed Adams or anyone else to obtain the signed letter of intent. Additionally, all available documentary evidence supports my position. I have talked to Vic Adams over the years, but my telephone records show <u>no</u> telephone calls from me to Adams during the evening in question. More importantly, my telephone records show no calls from me to Adams during the <u>entire</u> relevant academic year. Simply put, there is no evidence to support the allegation that I instructed Vic Adams to pick up the letter of intent; and my response to the NCAA in this regard was <u>not</u> false or misleading.

This allegation points out a fundamental flaw in the NCAA's process. During an investigation, the NCAA interviews numerous witnesses. NCAA rules prohibit these interviews from being tape recorded. Many of the witnesses interviewed have an axe to grind with me or my coaches. Keep in mind that people who make accusations against the program do not testify under oath, so they are not subject to perjury. Nor are they subject to any disciplinary action from the NCAA if they are not part of a member institution. In essence, people who have an axe to grind have nothing to lose by lying because they cannot be punished by the NCAA. If a witness makes an accusation, regardless of whether it was truthful, it then became incumbent on the coaches to refute it. If the coaches successfully refute it, the NCAA then goes back to the witness and reinterviews that person. The witness has nothing to lose so he can change his story, and it is then incumbent upon the coaches to refute the new story. If the coach successfully refutes the new story, the NCAA goes back to the witness and the witness may change his story again. This process continues until the witness finally comes up with a story that coaches are not able to refute—other than simply deny it. The NCAA Enforcement Staff then makes the allegation in a letter of inquiry. The school which receives the letter of inquiry feels an obligation to publish the allegations. At no time during the process is anyone allowed to confront or cross-examine their accusers. Nor are they allowed to review the Enforcement Staff's interview memos before they have to file their responses to the letter of inquiry.

A good example is in the new Allegation No. 21, alleging I instructed an individual to pay a hotel bill for a player's parent. That allegation is based on an accusation made by an individual whom I fired. People have told me that this individual has said he is out to get me. This individual's accusation regarding my involvement has been refuted by me and Coach Sundvold. It has also been refuted by sworn affidavit testimony of an independent third-party. This third-party has no motive to lie. In fact, he is best friends with the person making the accusation and he was in his wedding. Nonetheless, the NCAA has ignored my testimony, Bob Sundvold's testimony, and the sworn testimony of this individual's best friend, and made the allegation against me based solely on the accusation of one person—a person who has told others he is out to get me because I fired him. It illustrates the unfair process: a person makes an accusation; the NCAA puts it in a Letter of Inquiry; the school releases the allegation; the allegation is published in the media; and here I am.

It boils down to this: to support its allegation that I provided false and misleading information, the NCAA is relying on people who have motives to lie; who have openly expressed ill will against me or my coaches; who have not testified under oath; who refuse to be interviewed unless they are in the same room as other witnesses so they can hear one another's testimony; whose stories are inconsistent and frequently changed; whose testimony is contrary to documentary evidence; and who refuse to talk to us. In a least one instance, the NCAA is relying on a person with a criminal conviction. In refuting the allegation, I intend to rely on people who have no motive to lie; who are willing to testify under oath; whose stories are consistent and remain the same; whose testimony is consistent with documentation and records; and who have decades of clean track records. Assuming I can get a fair hearing, I expect to defeat the NCAA's latest allegations.

But the question remains, why did the NCAA bring this charge at this time? It did not bring the charge when it issued the original letter of inquiry in May. The only new evidence is the flight log, which is unrelated to whether I recall the flight. The flight log only relates to whether the flight actually occurred—an issue I informed the NCAA I would admit. Moreover, the flight log is totally unrelated to whether Vic Adams picked up a recruit's letter of intent. Perhaps the enforcement staff made the allegation because it has been receiving pressure to bring more charges in the aftermath of some recent cases. Perhaps it felt that it did not have enough allegations to show for itself after an eighteen month, several hundred thousand dollar investigation.

The NCAA's investigative process is unfair, and I feel certain that changes will be made in the future. I don't mind being a part of those changes, but I won't be a scapegoat. In 1976, in the closing minutes of an NCAA game, a technical foul was called on Kim Anderson when he hung on the rim in order to protect himself from getting hurt. That technical foul may have cost us a chance to go to the Final Four that year. The next year, the rule was changed so that a player could hang on the rim if he needed to protect himself. That rule is still in effect today. When rules and procedures result in unfairness, they should be changed. It is my belief, and hope, that the NCAA's procedure in making allegations, that they know will become public, will be changed so that more discretion is used before an allegation is made.

In conclusion let me say this: I have not provided false or misleading information to the investigators. I told the truth during my November, 1989 interview when I said I could not recall a particular plane flight that occurred over five years ago. I also told the truth when I said I did not instruct Vic Adams to pick up a recruit's letter of intent. Truly reliable witnesses and documentation support me on these issues. I intend to contest the NCAA's recent allegation at every stage of the proceeding. I am willing to assume at this point that the NCAA process will provide me with a fair opportunity to be heard. If the NCAA gives me a fair hearing, I am confident I will prevail against the allegation. But, if the NCAA process does not provide me with a fair hearing, I intend to go beyond that process to be heard.

Appendix B

Official Inquiry
to the Chief Executive Officer
of the University of Missouri, Columbia

1. [NCAA Constitution 2.1 and Bylaw 14.3.1]
    It is alleged that during the first semester of the 1988-89 academic year, the university violated the provisions of institutional control and certification of eligibility for student-athletes by awarding institutional financial aid to student-athlete Robert "P.J." Mays while the young man was a 2.000 nonqualifier. Specifically, Mays was awarded athletically related aid in the amount of $7,467 for the 1988-89 academic year and received approximately half that amount for the first semester in addition to a Supplemental Education Opportunity Grant (SEOG) in the amount of $300; further, on one occasion while ineligible, Mays was permitted to practice with the university's men's basketball team.

2. [NCAA Bylaws 16.12.2.3-(a) and 16.12.2.3-(d)]
    It is alleged that during the period October 22-24, 1988, men's assistant basketball coach Bob Sundvold arranged for student-athlete Robert "P.J." Mays to receive round-trip commercial airline transportation between Columbia, Missouri, and Cincinnati, Ohio, at no cost to Mays in order for the young man to return home to obtain information concerning his high school academic records. Specifically, on October 22, Sundvold gave Mays $135 cash near the Hearnes Center to purchase an airline ticket and, on October 24, Sundvold arranged for Mays to obtain a prepaid airline ticket through the Canterbury Travel Agency (Columbia, Missouri) in order to return to the university, and finally, the $248 cost of the ticket remains unpaid at the travel agency.

3. [NCAA Bylaws 13.2.2.2-(b) and 13.4.2]
    It is alleged that on or about October 10, 1987, during the official paid visit of prospective student-athletes Anthony Peeler (Kansas City, Missouri) and Robert "P.J." Mays (Cincinnati, Ohio), men's assistant basketball coach Bob Sundvold arranged excessive entertainment that included a casino night banquet; further, following the casino night activities, participants were allowed to

purchase items at an auction by using their earnings from the evening. Consequently, Mays received a certificate for a pair of athletics shoes at no cost to him and, on October 28, 1987, Sundvold exchanged the certificate for a pair of Reebok athletics shoes from the university's athletics equipment room that were mailed (via United Parcel Service) to Yvonne Mays (the young man's mother) in Cincinnati, Ohio.

4. [NCAA Bylaws 13.2.2-(e), 13.2.2-(h), 13.5.2.2.2 and 13.6.6]
    It is alleged that on or about October 10,1987, during the official paid visit of prospective student-athlete Robert "P.J." Mays (Cincinnati, Ohio), assistant basketball coach Bob Sundvold arranged entertainment, meals and lodging for Greg Jones, a friend of the young man's mother, at no cost to him, and Sundvold also provided $325 cash to the prospect for round-trip automobile transportation between Cincinnati, Ohio, and Columbia, Missouri (a round-trip distance of approximately 960 miles), even though this amount was excessive and Jones would not have been entitled to such funds; further, Sundvold arranged discounted hotel accommodations for Jones during the summer of 1988 after Jones transported Mays to the university for the purpose of enrolling in the university's summer orientation program.

5. [NCAA Bylaws 13.2.1, 13.2.3.2, 13.5.4, 13.12.1.3, 13.12.2.1.2.1, 13.2.2-(g) and 16.12.2.1]
    It is alleged that on several occasions during the period June and July 1988, members of the university's basketball coaching staff provided meals, local automobile transportation, summer camp employment and excessive entertainment for several prospective student-athletes at no cost to the prospects while the young men were attending the university's summer orientation program.

6. [NCAA Bylaw 16.12.1.4]
    It is alleged that on one occasion during the fall semester of 1989, men's head basketball coach Norm Stewart and men's assistant basketball coach Bob Sundvold arranged for the men's basketball team to receive a meal prepared by a chef at the Bunkerhill Resort located in Mountain View, Missouri, at no cost to the young men.

7. [NCAA Bylaw 13.5.2.1]
    It is alleged that on several occasions during the period 1985 to 1989, men's assistant basketball coaches Richard Daly and Bob Sundvold provided cash exceeding the actual cost of transporta-

tion to several prospective student-athletes during the young men's official paid visits to the university's campus.

8. [NCAA Bylaw 13.2.1]
It is alleged that in the fall of 1985, while recruiting a prospective student-athlete, men's assistant basketball coach Richard Daly reimbursed the boy's head basketball coach $100 cash for the purchase of an airline ticket in order for the young man to enroll at the university.

9. [NCAA Bylaws 13.2.1, 13.2.2 and 13.15.1]
It is alleged that on July 1, 1988, while recruiting prospective student-athlete Anthony Peeler (Kansas City, Missouri), men's assistant basketball coach Richard Daly arranged for Judy Wells, a university athletics department staff member, to provide private tutorial services to assist Peeler in improving his American College Test (ACT) score in order to be eligible at the institution upon enrollment; further, both the arrangement and provision of tutoring would be improper under NCAA rules; further, Daly provided an envelope containing $300 cash to athletics department staff member Chris Sinatra and instructed her to give it to Wells as payment for her tutorial services.

10. [NCAA Bylaws 13.01.5, 13.02.10-(c) and 13.02.10-(e) and 13.1.2.1]
It is alleged that on some occasions during the period 1985 through 1989, Vic Adams, a representative of the university's athletics interests from Detroit, Michigan, was involved in recruiting contacts with the parents of prospective student-athletes Curtis Kidd (Detroit, Michigan) and Daniel Lyton (Detroit, Michigan); further, men's head basketball coach Norm Stewart and men's assistant basketball coach Richard Daly were aware of these contacts. Specifically:

A. On or about April 7, 1985, following Kidd's official paid visit to the university's campus, Stewart and Daly accompanied the young man on a chartered airline flight from Columbia, Missouri, to Detroit, Michigan, and upon arrival at a Detroit airport, Stewart, Daly and Kidd were met by Adams, who transported them to Kidd's father's residence where Adams, Stewart and Daly encouraged Kidd to attend the university.

B. On or about April 7, 1985, Adams drove Daly to Kidd's mother's home and went to the door where he talked with Mrs. Kidd and learned the young man was not home.

C.   During several telephone conversations in the fall of 1989, Stewart and Daly instructed Adams to obtain the National Letter of Intent from Lyton at the young man's home and then to mail the letter to the university.

11.   [NCAA Bylaw 13.3.1]
It is alleged that in the fall of 1988, during a visit to the home of prospective student-athlete Daniel Lyton (Detroit, Michigan), men's head basketball coach Norm Stewart and men's assistant basketball coach Richard Daly gave Lyton a videotape, which featured the university's student-athletes from the Detroit, Michigan, area at no cost to the young man; further, after the young man failed to return this tape on his official paid visit, the coaching staff made no further effort to obtain the return of this tape.

12.   [NCAA Bylaws 13.2.1 and 13.8.2]
It is alleged that on several occasions during the period 1986 to 1988, men's assistant basketball coach Bob Sundvold entertained Bob Bohren, a friend and an AAU coach of prospective student-athlete Jamal Coleman (Denver, Colorado).   Specifically, on December 12, 1986; September 29, 1987, and February 19, 1988, while recruiting in the Denver, Colorado, area, Sundvold entertained Bohren for meals at costs of approximately $31.40, $56 and $29.46, respectively.

13.   [NCAA Bylaws 10.01.1, 10.1-(c) and 10.1-(d)]
It is alleged that men's assistant basketball coach Bob Sundvold acted contrary to the principles of ethical conduct inasmuch as he did not, on all occasions, deport himself in accordance with the generally recognized high standards normally associated with the conduct and administration of intercollegiate athletics.

14.   [NCAA Bylaws 10.1-(b) and 10.1-(d)]
It is alleged that men's assistant basketball coach Richard Daly acted contrary to the principles of ethical conduct inasmuch as he did not, on all occasions, deport himself in accordance with the generally recognized high standards normally associated with the conduct and administration of intercollegiate athletics.

15.   [NCAA Constitution 2.1]
It is alleged that the scope and nature of the allegations in this official inquiry demonstrate a lack of appropriate control and monitoring in the administration of the institution's intercollegiate men's basketball program by the institution and men's head basketball coach Norm Stewart.

Appendix C

Supplemental Official Inquiry
to the Chief Executive Officer
of the University of Missouri, Columbia

20. [NCAA Bylaw 10.1-(d)]
It is alleged that men's head basketball coach Norm Stewart acted contrary to the principles of ethical conduct inasmuch as he did not, on all occasions, deport himself in accordance with the generally recognized high standards normally associated with the conduct and administration of intercollegiate athletics in that Stewart provided false and misleading information during a November 16, 1989, interview with NCAA Director of Enforcement Robert J. Minnix, NCAA Enforcement Representative Arthur J. McAfee III, and university legal counsel Michael S. Glazier and Michael L. Slive concerning his involvement in and knowledge of Allegation Nos. 10-A and 10-C of this inquiry.

21. [NCAA Bylaws 16.02.3, 16.12.2.1 and 16.12.2.3]
It is alleged that on two occasions, Evelyn Buntin, mother of then student-athlete Nathan Buntin, received cost-free lodging from the Holiday Inn West hotel, Columbia, Missouri, which is considered a representative of the university's athletics interests; further, she also received local automobile transportation from members of the institution's men's basketball coaching staff during this visit.

Appendix D

<hr>

Infractions Report No. 52
by the NCAA Committee on Infractions
November 5, 1990

Case No. M30 - University of Missouri, Columbia

I. Introduction

This case began with the publication of a newspaper article in December 1988 concerning possible improper recruiting assistance in the Detroit, Michigan, area by a representative of the university's athletics interests. In February 1989, newspaper reports appeared concerning an improper airline ticket for an enrolled student-athlete from a men's assistant basketball coach. On February 20, 1989, the university reported to the enforcement staff that the assistant coach had lent money to the student-athlete for an airplane ticket. On March 7, 1989, a preliminary letter of inquiry was issued to the university, and an official letter of inquiry was sent on May 1, 1990, followed by a supplemental letter of official inquiry on July 10, 1990. The university and members of the men's basketball staff responded separately in writing in June, July and August 1990, and separate prehearing conferences were held with the parties in Overland Park, Kansas. The hearing before the NCAA Committee on Infractions took place on September 28, 1990.

This is a case in which a highly successful men's basketball program came to operate over time without direct accountable control by the university through the director of athletics. Over the past decade, the university has had four directors of athletics, a circumstance that permitted the men's head basketball coach to insulate his program from direct control. The committee found no evidence of regular education, compliance or monitoring procedures within the men's basketball program. The head coach delegated many of his responsibilities to his assistants, and neither the assistants nor the head coach maintained records, checks and balances, or identifiable processes for institutional control, which could have been used to reconstruct their actions.

In such a setting, a program that had had no previous history of violations became involved in a series of violations, some major and others secondary in nature, but in such abundance that they cannot be called isolated or inadvertent and, in fact, are symptomatic of a failure to follow basic Association recruiting rules involving prospective student-athletes or to seek advice on what those rules require. Each member of the men's basketball coaching staff operated without consulting each other or the head coach. Prudent management controls should have provided much closer day-to-day supervision of the program, especially the recruiting activities of the assistant coaches.

The most serious violations involved the admission of and awarding of athletically related aid to a partial qualifier whom the university's admissions process failed to discern was ineligible. Not until well into his first semester was this error discovered. Even then, upon being notified by letter that he was ineligible by university rules, the men's basketball staff ignored the letter and permitted him to practice until once again being directly confronted with his ineligibility. At this point, the assistant coach who was responsible for recruiting the young man became involved in a series of major violations.

In hopes that by sending the young man to his high school in another state, the young man could clear up some uncertainties on his transcript, the assistant coach lent money to the young man for the airline trip home. The assistant coach later arranged for the young man to receive a prepaid airline ticket to return to the university. No errors were found in the transcript, and the young man remained ineligible for athletically related financial aid and practice. Over the next several weeks, discussions between the young man, his mother and the assistant coach took place about the loan and the plane ticket, with the mother stating her understanding that the costs were to be borne by the coach. These activities came to light when the mother, in a discussion with the director of the university's Total Person Program, mentioned the airline tickets. The director immediately recognized that a violation had taken place, confronted the assistant coach with the violation, and extracted from him a promise to report the violation to the head coach and the director of athletics. The assistant coach claimed that he was unaware that his actions in giving cash to an enrolled student-athlete and in arranging for a prepaid airline ticket were violations of NCAA rules. Weeks went by before the assistant coach finally reported the matters to the head coach and then to the director of athletics, who in turn notified the enforcement staff.

In another instance, a different assistant coach could not recall spending an Easter Sunday afternoon on a private airplane with a recruit while returning to Detroit, Michigan; could not recall being in Detroit; could not recall riding from the airport with a representative of the university's athletics interests, and, in fact, would not remember anything connected with most of his recruiting contact with this or other highly visible recruits in the Detroit area. The committee determined that this individual's failure to recall the circumstances of his involvement in many of these situations was implausible. The committee found that this assistant coach had violated the principles of ethical conduct by providing misleading information to the committee at its hearing when other evidence before the committee led the committee to conclude that he was not forthcoming about his involvement in or knowledge of matters relevant to violations of NCAA regulations.

Other violations included: an unmonitored recruiting expense fund approved by the university that was used in violation of university, state and NCAA rules for payments to recruits on their official expense-paid visits; a "casino party" for recruits, which provided prizes to a recruit and his mother; bringing prospective student-athletes to campus in the summer prior to their enrollment, which triggered a variety of violations; arranging for a member of the athletics department staff to tutor a prospective student-athlete for his American College Test (ACT), and providing a graduate assistant basketball coach with dining hall privileges and a courtesy car for his own use. The wide range of these violations, mostly involving recruiting, confirmed to the committee the absence of institutional control and, more specifically, the ignorance of well-understood rules and the failure to comply with others. Therefore, the committee concluded that these violations when considered together constituted a major violation.

For a first-time major violator, the minimum penalties prescribed by the Association are: a two-year probationary period; elimination of expense-paid recruiting visits in the sport for at least one year; elimination of off-campus recruiting in the sport for at least one year; loss of postseason competition and television appearances in the sport for at least one year, and possible termination of the employment of staff members involved in the violations. The committee may impose lesser penalties if it finds that the case is "unique."

The committee did not find that this was a unique case. However, it did find that there were some mitigating circumstances, which it took into consideration in imposing the penalties. These included a history of no prior major violations and the university's acceptance of responsibility for violations that had occurred, but for which no member of the men's basketball staff would affirm responsibility.

While the committee did find that the involvement of two assistant coaches constituted violations of the principles of ethical conduct, the committee did not believe that their actions, as distasteful and as transparent as they were, warranted imposing individual restrictions on their coaching activities. Rather, the committee imposed certain

restrictions on the university and the men's basketball program generally, and leaves to the university the decision on how these restrictions
will be imposed individually.

In summary, the committee imposed the following penalties: a
two-year probationary period with required monitoring and compliance reports, including a specific plan to gain operational control of the
men's basketball program; elimination of all expense-paid visits in
men's basketball for one year; limitation of off-campus recruiting
activities in men's basketball to only one designated coach for one year;
no postseason competition for the 1990-91 season; a limit of one initial
grant in men's basketball for the 1991-92 season and two for the 1992-
93 season, and the disassociation of one representative of the university's
athletics interests. Further, the university's athletics program is subject
to the five-year "repeat major violator" provisions of Bylaw 19.4.2.3.

II. Violations of NCAA legislation, as determined by committee.

A. [NCAA Constitution 2.1 and Bylaws 14.01.4 and 14.3.1]
    During the first semester of the 1988-89 academic year, the
    university violated the provisions of institutional control and
    certification of eligibility for student-athletes by awarding insti-
    tutional financial aid to a student-athlete while the young man
    was a 2.000 nonqualifier. Specifically, the student-athlete was
    awarded athletically related aid in the amount of $7,467 for the
    1988-89 academic year and received approximately half that
    amount for the first semester; further, on one occasion, the young
    man was permitted to practice with the university's men's bas-
    ketball team while ineligible under the university's academic
    rules and regulations.

B. [NCAA Bylaws 16.12.2.3-(a) and 16.12.2.3-(d)]
    On or about October 22, 1988, a men's assistant basketball coach
    lent $135 cash to a student-athlete to purchase an airline ticket for
    travel from Columbia, Missouri, to the young man's home town
    in order for the young man to review his high school academic
    records; further, on October 24, 1988, the assistant coach arranged
    for the student-athlete to obtain a prepaid airline ticket through
    a travel agency in order to return to the university, and finally, the
    loan and the $248 cost of the return ticket remains unpaid.

C. [NCAA Bylaw 13.5.2.1]
    On several occasions during the period 1985 to 1987, two men's
    assistant basketball coaches provided cash exceeding the actual
    cost of transportation to several prospective student-athletes

during the young men's official paid visits to the university's campus. Specifically:

1.   During the fall of 1985, following the official paid visit of a prospective student-athlete, the young man received $40 cash as reimbursement for taxicab transportation between his home and the airport in his home town (a one-way distance of approximately 20 miles), even though the young man's mother provided this transportation.

2.   During the fall of 1987, following the official paid visit of a prospective student-athlete, the young man received $28 cash as reimbursement for taxicab transportation between his home and the airport in his home town (a one-way distance of approximately 30 miles), even though the young man's parents provided automobile transportation to the airport and the young man took a bus from the airport to his home after the return flight.

3.   During the fall of 1985, following the official paid visit of a prospective student-athlete, the young man received $40 cash for round-trip taxicab transportation between his home and the airport in his home town (a one-way distance of approximately 20 miles), even though the initial airport transportation was provided by another young man's mother and the return airport transportation was provided by a friend.

4.   During the fall of 1986, following the official paid visit of a prospective student-athlete, the young man received $50 cash for round-trip taxicab transportation between his residence and the airport in his home town (a one-way distance of approximately 20 miles), even though the young man's parents provided this transportation.

5.   During the fall of 1987, following the official paid visit of a prospective student-athlete, the young man received $36 cash for round-trip taxicab transportation between his residence and a local airport (a one-way distance of approximately 12 miles), even though the young man's parents provided this transportation.

D.   [NCAA Bylaws 13.01.5, 13.02.10-(c), 13.02.10-(e) and 13.1.2.1]
A representative of the university's athletics interests from Detroit, Michigan, was involved in recruiting contact with the parents of a prospective student-athlete; further, at least one

member of the men's basketball coaching staff was aware of the contact. Specifically, on April 7, 1985, following the prospect's official paid visit to the university's campus, at least one member of the men's basketball coaching staff accompanied the young man on a private aircraft from Columbia, Missouri, to Detroit, Michigan, where, upon arrival at the Detroit airport, they were met by the representative, who transported them to the young man's father's residence where the coach and the representative encouraged the young man to attend the university.

E.   [NCAA Bylaws 13.2.1, and 13.2.2]
On July 1, 1988, while recruiting a prospective student-athlete, a men's assistant basketball coach arranged for a university athletics department staff member to provide private tutorial services to assist the young man in improving his American College Test (ACT) score in order to be eligible at the institution upon enrollment; further, both the arrangement and provision of tutoring are improper under NCAA rules.

F.   [NCAA Bylaws 10.01.1 and 10.1-(c)]
A men's assistant basketball coach involved in this case acted contrary to the principles of ethical conduct inasmuch as he did not, on all occasions, deport himself in accordance with the generally recognized high standards normally associated with the conduct and administration of intercollegiate athletics. Specifically, the assistant coach demonstrated a knowing and willful effort on his part to operate the university's intercollegiate men's basketball program contrary to the requirements and provisions of NCAA legislation by his involvement in this case.

G.   [NCAA Bylaw 10.1-(d)]
A men's assistant basketball coach involved in this case acted contrary to the principles of ethical conduct inasmuch as he did not, on all occasions, deport himself in accordance with the generally recognized high standards normally associated with the conduct and administration of intercollegiate athletics. Specifically, the assistant coach knowingly provided misleading information by failing to be forthcoming concerning his involvement in or knowledge of matters relevant to violations of NCAA regulations during his appearance before the Committee on Infractions. Moreover, persistent references to lapses of memory and the repeated use of the phrases, "I do not recall," and "it may have happened, but I do not remember," were not credible.

H. [NCAA Constitution 2.1]
The scope and nature of the allegations in this official inquiry demonstrate a lack of appropriate control and monitoring in the administration of the institution's intercollegiate men's basketball program by the institution and by the men's head basketball coach. Specifically:

1. The university failed to adequately supervise the basketball program; failed to monitor it in terms of rules education and compliance programs; failed to provide routine and timely audit checks for the use of recruiting funds within the department; failed to have an admissions and financial aid system in place to determine whether prospective and enrolled student-athletes qualified for athletically related aid and practice, and, in general, permitted the men's basketball program to operate in a semiautonomous state within the athletics department.

2. The men's head basketball coach failed to adequately supervise his assistant coaches; did not maintain a regular rules-education and compliance program; did not properly monitor prospective student-athletes who were present in the university community during the summer prior to their first year of enrollment, thus almost assuring rules violations; did not monitor the use of recruiting monies under his control, and, in general, operated a program separate from that of the rest of the athletics department without providing the necessary checks and balances to assure that his administrative responsibilities were carried out according to NCAA rules and regulations by his assistant coaches.

I. [NCAA Bylaws 13.2.2-(b), 13.4.2 and 13.6.5.4.1]
On or about October 10, 1987, during a casino night banquet arranged by members of the university's men's basketball coaching staff or the official paid visit of two prospective student-athletes, one of the young men [Mays] received a certificate for a pair of athletics shoes at no cost to him that was exchanged for a pair of athletics shoes that were mailed on October 28, 1987, from the university's athletics equipment room to the young man's mother; further, during this banquet, basketball student-athletes other than the student hosts of the two prospective student-athletes were entertained for dinner at no cost as were the dates of some of the student-athletes.

J.　[NCAA Bylaws 13.2.2-(e), 13.2.2-(h), 13.5.2.2.2, 13.6.5.1 and 13.6.6]
On or about October 10, 1987, during the official paid visit of a prospective student-athlete, a men's assistant basketball coach arranged entertainment, meals and lodging for a close friend of the young man's mother at no cost to him; further, the assistant coach also provided cash to the prospect for expenses incurred by the friend of the young man's mother for round-trip automobile transportation between the prospect's home town and Columbia, Missouri (a round-trip distance of approximately 960 miles), for himself, the young man and the young man's mother, a payment that would have been permitted if they had been incurred directly by the young man or his mother.

K.　[NCAA Bylaws 13.2.1, 13.2.3.2, 13.5.4, 13.12.1.3, 13.12.2.1.2.1, 13.2.2-(g) and 16.12.2.1]
On several occasions during the period June and July 1988, members of the university's basketball coaching staff provided meals, local automobile transportation, summer camp employment and excessive entertainment for several prospective student-athletes at no cost to the prospects while the young men were attending the university's summer orientation program. Specifically:

1.　On one occasion, a men's assistant basketball coach provided local automobile transportation and a meal for four prospective student-athletes at a restaurant owned by a representative of the university's athletics interests; further, on several subsequent occasions, one or more of the young men were permitted by restaurant employees to sign for meals and receive additional meals at the restaurant, and neither the institution nor the young men have been billed for these meals.

2.　On one occasion, the assistant coach provided a meal at his residence for the prospective student-athletes.

3.　On one occasion, the assistant coach transported two of the prospects from the Columbia, Missouri, airport to the university's campus (a one-way distance of approximately 10 miles) for participation in the university's summer orientation program.

4.　On one occasion each, two men's assistant basketball coaches transported the prospects from their residence to a bookstore (a one-way distance of approximately 1.2 miles) where the young men were employed.

5.   On several occasions during the men's head basketball coach's summer basketball camp, members of the men's basketball staff allowed several prospective student-athletes and two student-athletes to officiate summer camp basketball games.

6.   On one occasion, members of the university's men's basketball coaching staff provided a written invitation to a then student-athlete to attended a rock concert in Moberly, Missouri (a one-way distance of approximately 30 miles), at the home of a representative of the university's athletics interests; further, the young man transported three prospective student-athletes to this concert at no cost to the young men.

L.   [NCAA Bylaw 13.3.1]
In the fall of 1988, a prospective student-athlete obtained a university-produced basketball highlight videotape at no cost to the young man.

M.   [NCAA Bylaw 11.02.4]
During the 1985-86 and 1986-87 academic years, a then graduate assistant basketball coach received dining hall privileges and use of university courtesy car benefits that exceeded the monthly tuition fees and room costs.

N.   [NCAA Bylaws 16.02.3, 16.12.2.1 and 16.12.2.3]
On October 31 through November 1, 1986, the mother of a then basketball student-athlete received cost-free lodging from a hotel, which is considered a representative of the university's athletics interests; further, on December 6-11, 1986, the young man's mother received reduced-cost lodging from the same establishment, and finally, the student-athlete also received local automobile transportation from members of the institution's men's basketball coaching staff at the conclusion of the December visit.

III. Committee on Infractions penalties.

For the reasons set forth in Part I of this report, the Committee on Infractions found that this case involved several major violations of NCAA legislation that occurred after September 1, 1985. NCAA Bylaw 19.4.2.2, as adopted by the Association's membership, requires prescribed minimum penalties, "subject to exceptions authorized by the Committee on Infractions in unique cases on the basis of specifically stated reasons." These minimum penalties include: (a) a two-year probationary period (including a periodic, in-person monitoring system and written institutional reports); (b) the elimination of all expense-paid recruiting visits to the institution in the involved sport for one year; (c) a requirement that all coaching staff members be prohibited from engaging in any off-campus recruiting activities in the sport for one year; (d) a requirement that all institutional staff members determined by the Committee on Infractions knowingly to have engaged in or condoned a major violation be subject either to termination of employment, suspension without pay for at least one year or reassignment of duties within the institution to a position that does not include contact with prospective or enrolled student-athletes or representatives of the institution's athletics interests for at least one year; (e) one year of sanctions precluding postseason competition in the sport; (f) one year of sanctions precluding television appearances in the sport, and (g) institutional recertification that the current athletics policies and practices conform to all requirements of NCAA regulations.

However, due to the mitigating factors in this case as described in Part I of this report, the committee hereby reduces the prescribed penalties and shall impose the following penalties.

A.   The University of Missouri, Columbia, shall be publicly reprimanded and censured, and placed on probation for a period of two years from the date these penalties are imposed, which shall be the date the 15-day appeal period expires or the date the institution notifies the executive director that it will not appeal, whichever is earlier, or the date established by NCAA Council subcommittee action as a result of an appeal by the university to the Council, it being understood that should any portion of any penalty in this case be set aside for any reason other than by appropriate action of the Association, the penalties shall be reconsidered by the Committee on Infractions. Further, the University of Missouri, Columbia, shall be subject to the provisions of NCAA Bylaw 19.4.2.3 concerning repeat violators for a five-year period beginning on the effective date of the penalties in this case.

B.   During this period of probation, the institution shall: develop and implement a system for administrative control and monitoring to ensure compliance with NCAA legislation; design and implement a comprehensive educational program (e.g., seminars and testing) to instruct coaches and athletics department personnel on NCAA legislation; submit a preliminary report by July 1, 1991, setting forth a schedule for establishing this compliance and educational program, and file annual progress reports with the NCAA enforcement staff by July 1 of each year thereafter during the probationary period with a particular emphasis on the degree to which the men's basketball program has been placed firmly under the control of the director of athletics' program for total structure and operations.

C. The institution shall be prohibited during the 1991 calendar year (January 1, 1991, to December 31, 1991) from providing any expense-paid recruiting visit to a prospective student-athlete in the sport of men's basketball. If this penalty becomes effective after January 1, 1991, as a result of an appeal or other action in this case, the one-year period shall begin on the date the penalty becomes effective.

D. All members of the university's coaching staff in the sport of men's basketball are prohibited from engaging in any off-campus recruiting activities (in-person contacts and evaluation) concurrent with the one-year period applicable to Part III-C above. [NOTE: For reasons set forth in Part I of this report, this penalty is suspended and only one designated member of the men's basketball coaching staff may engage in off-campus recruiting and evaluation activities during the one-year period applicable to this prohibition.]

E. The institution's men's basketball team shall end its 1990-91 season with the playing of its last regularly scheduled, in-season contest and shall not be eligible to participate in any postseason competition, including a foreign tour, following that season. In addition, during 1991, the men's basketball team may not take any advantage of the exceptions to the number of contests allowed in Bylaws 17.3.3.1, 17.3.5.1, 17.3.5.3 and 17.3.5.4

F. The institution's men's basketball team shall not be eligible to appear on any "live" telecast (as defined by Bylaw 19.4.2.5.2) during the 1991-92 regular season. [NOTE: For reasons set forth in Part I of this report, this penalty is immediately and completely suspended.]

G. During the 1991-92 academic year, the institution shall award no more than one initial grant in the sport of men's basketball; further, no person may be added to the 1990-91 squad as an initial recipient of athletically related financial aid who was not included on the NCAA squad list on October 15, 1990, as a recipient of financial aid; further, during the 1992-93 academic year, the institution shall award no more than two initial grants in the sport of men's basketball.

H.   During the period of probation, no member of the university's athletics program and its men's basketball program explicitly may have any contact with the representative of the university's athletics interests who refused to cooperate with the university and the NCAA enforcement staff in this investigation.

NOTE: Should the University of Missouri, Columbia, appeal either the findings of violations or proposed penalties in this case to the NCAA Council subcommittee of Division I members, the Committee on Infractions will submit an expanded infractions report to the members of the Council who will consider the appeal. This expanded report will include additional information in accordance with Bylaw 32.8.5. A copy of the committee's report would be provided to the institution prior to the institution's appearance before the Council subcommittee and, as required by Bylaw 32.8.6, would be released to the public.

Also, the Committee on Infractions wishes to advise the institution that when the penalties in this case become effective, the institution should take every precaution to ensure that their terms are observed; further, the committee intends to monitor the penalties during their effective periods, and any action contrary to the terms of any of the penalties shall be considered grounds for extending the institution's probationary period, as well as to consider imposing more severe sanctions in this case.

Finally, should any action by NCAA Conventions directly or indirectly modify any provision of these penalties or the effect of the penalties, the committee reserves the right to review and reconsider the penalties.

NCAA Committee on Infractions

Roy F. Kramer
Beverly E. Ledbetter
Thomas J. Niland Jr.
D. Alan Williams (chair)

Appendix E

NCAA Infractions Report
(regarding Rich Daly's rehearing)

Case No. M30
[University of Missouri, Columbia, Missouri]

On September 28, 1990, the NCAA Committee on Infractions held a hearing concerning alleged violations in the men's basketball program at the University of Missouri, Columbia. On November 5, 1990, the committee issued Infractions Report No. 52 setting forth its findings. Included among the findings were violations of NCAA legislation committed by a certain men's assistant basketball coach [Richard Daly] and the determination by the committee that this coach had "acted contrary to the principles of ethical conduct inasmuch as he did not, on all occasions, deport himself in accordance with the generally recognized high standards normally associated with the conduct and administration of intercollegiate athletics." Specifically, the committee found that the assistant coach knowingly provided misleading information by failing to be forthcoming during his appearance before the Committee on Infractions concerning his involvement in or knowledge of matters relevant to violations of NCAA regulations. The committee found his frequent lapses of memory and inability to recall specific matters not to be credible.

On November 15, 1990, the assistant coach filed a notice of appeal to the Division I Steering Committee and on February 21, 1991, submitted his expanded appeal. Included in that appeal was new information that had not been presented to the committee in the previous hearing. Under the provisions of NCAA Bylaw 19.4.2.8.1, when newly discovered evidence is presented, the committee may grant a review of the matter. The assistant coach agreed to withdraw his appeal without prejudice pending consideration of the new information by the committee.

At a hearing on June 29, 1991, attended by the coach and his legal counsel, university representative, and members of the NCAA enforcement staff, the committee reviewed the new information, which principally related to the utilization of private airplanes in the recruiting process by the men's basketball staff and the logs of those flights, particularly a flight form Columbia to Detroit on Easter Sunday. At the original hearing, the committee had been especially concerned about the coach's inability to account for how he managed to be present in Detroit that day if he were not on the airplane in question or why he could not recall events surrounding his activities in Detroit. The private airplane logs contain the names of the coaches on the airplane for most trips. For the flight in question, the name of the men's head basketball coach [Norm Stewart] was recorded in the log, but the name of this assistant coach was not.

Following the second hearing, the members of the committee who considered the original case deliberated on this new information. The committee remained concerned that this assistant coach was unable to recall with greater certainty events that most people would be able to recall. The committee remained concerned that neither this coach nor the members of the men's basketball staff collectively have been able to reconstruct events more clearly. The committee remained concerned, as it noted in the original infractions report, that "each member of the men's basketball coaching staff operated without consulting each other or the head coach." Prudent management controls should have provided much closer day-to-day supervision of the program by the head coach, especially the recruiting activities of the assistant coaches.

In that same report, the committee noted that the actions of this assistant coach were "distasteful and transparent" and violative of the principles of ethical conduct. The committee remained concerned about the transparency of this coach's explanations after the second hearing; however, the committee believed that the new information derived from the airplane's log, which placed the head coach not the assistant coach in the private airplane on the day in question, together with the assistant coach's further elaboration of his travel procedures, while not completely satisfactory, presented an explanation of why the coach may have been unable to recall these events with more certainty.

It was his inability to recall or to reconstruct the events of this particular recruiting trip that gave rise to the committee's concerns at the first hearing and which were instrumental in the committee finding that he had violated the principles of ethical conduct by failing to be forthcoming during the hearing. Therefore, in light of this new information, the committee has voted unanimously to rescind its finding of violation in regard to the principles of ethical conduct concerning this men's assistant basketball coach [Richard Daly] and to delete Paragraph II-G relating to the ethical conduct finding from the committee's Infractions Report No. 52 regarding the University of Missouri, Columbia.

The other findings in Infractions Report No. 52 relating to this assistant coach were not appealable and remain in place. With this action, the basis for further appeal is moot. No other issues remain in this case, and the actions of the committee with respect to the University of Missouri, Columbia, infractions case are now final.